AMERICA IN LITERATURE AND FILM

This book is dedicated to the Egyptian men and women who were murdered by Mr. Mubarak's regime with the dream of a free Egypt glowing in their eyes

America in Literature and Film
Modernist Perceptions, Postmodernist Representations

AHMED ELBESHLAWY

Routledge
Taylor & Francis Group

LONDON AND NEW YORK

First published 2011 by Ashgate Publishing

Published 2016 by Routledge
2 Park Square, Milton Park, Abingdon, Oxfordshire OX14 4RN
711 Third Avenue, New York, NY 10017, USA

First issued in paperback 2016

Routledge is an imprint of the Taylor & Francis Group, an informa business

British Library Cataloguing in Publication Data
Elbeshlawy, Ahmed.
  America in literature and film : modernist perceptions,
  postmodernist representations.
  1. United States–In literature. 2. United States–In
  motion pictures. 3. National characteristics, American, in
  literature. 4. National characteristics, American, in
  motion pictures. 5. Modernism (Literature) 6. Postmodernism
  (Literature) 7. United States–Foreign public opinion.
  I. Title
  809.9'335873-dc22

Library of Congress Cataloging-in-Publication Data
Elbeshlawy, Ahmed.
America in literature and film : modernist perceptions, postmodernist representations /
Ahmed Elbeshlawy.
    p. cm.
  Includes bibliographical references and index.
  Includes filmography.
  ISBN 978-1-4094-2525-0 (hardback)
1. United States–In literature. 2. National characteristics, American, in literature. 3.
Literature, Modern–20th century–History and criticism. 4. United States–In motion pictures.
5. United States–Civilization. 6. United States–Foreign public opinion. I. Title.
  PN56.3.U5E53 2011
  809'.9335873–dc22
                                                                              2010052525

ISBN 13: 978-1-138-27718-2 (pbk)
ISBN 13: 978-1-4094-2525-0 (hbk)

Contents

Acknowledgments

The occasion of having this volume between your hands requires not insipid and formulaic but specific and unequivocal acknowledgments. Many made this book possible, and a few, directly or indirectly, battled its eventual appearance or the appearance of certain parts of it – unsuccessfully. The former cannot possibly be identified and mentioned individually, so, a selection has to be made. The latter will certainly remain unacknowledged.

Therefore, I would like to thank my editor, Whitney Feininger, first, for her attention and commitment to this project throughout and, secondly, for the insightful opinions that she has generously given on several occasions. Hers was a reassuring presence all along. I would also like to thank the Ashgate reader – evidently a Lacanian theorist whose identity unfortunately has to remain unknown to me – for the close reading given to the manuscript and the perceptive comments made on it. The meticulous work done by Helen Fairlie and Pam Bertram cannot be given enough acknowledgment.

My warmest thanks go to Jeremy Tambling, that great mentor, for his unremitting support for my work; for lifting up my spirits in moments of skepticism as well as reigning in my impulsiveness in moments of self-satisfaction. My thanks also go to Ackbar Abbas for the few but invaluable conversations that we had about this work at its very first stages.

I am grateful to Gina Marchetti, Gordon Slethaug, and Christina Klein for the intellectual discussions that they gave to the thesis-form version of this book. Some sections of this book have appeared, in different form, in *The Comparatist*, *Scope*, and *fe/male bodies*. I would like to thank the editors of these journals for their interest in my work.

Last but not least, I would like to thank my dear wife for her constant encouragement and for providing me with a comfortable space to write while looking after Malak, Maryem and Omar.

Introduction: Approaching America

America has always been an object of Europe's imagination. Many writers perceived America in multifarious ways from the viewpoint of Europe. Alexis de Tocqueville, as one classic example, tried to make sense out of America's success as a democratic model as well as to explicate the extraordinary American mixture of down-to-earth practicality and Christian spirituality. In his classic work *Democracy In America*, the 19th century French statesman writes: "America is still the place where the Christian religion has kept the greatest real power over men's souls; and nothing better demonstrates how useful and natural it is to man, since the country where it now has widest sway is both the most enlightened and the freest" (291). Tocqueville's observation, even if debatable, does point to the uniqueness of America's character as a country whose quest for enlightenment, power, democracy and modernization, is mixed with an avowedly religious spirit.

Charles Dickens's literature about America reveals how it posed a problem for him as a novelist. He could not write a novel in America or about American society matching his English society-based novels arguably because of what he could feel as the absence of society in the European sense of the word then. Outside civil society, the American natural landscape seems to have been no less challenging. In his book *Imagining America*, Peter Conrad shows how Dickens, being a Victorian novelist with an "uproarious urban art which cannot comprehend the placidity of nature" (13), anxiously describes the Niagara Falls in such a rhetorically overstated way that cannot help but stress the fact that he felt absolutely nothing in front of the Falls. In fact, one is tempted to propose that being in front of such an extraordinary natural scene with an acute feeling of nothingness and incomprehension could have been almost a traumatic experience for a writer like Dickens, and not just a source of anxiety. Since his being could not actually respond to the scene, the more this apathy imposed itself the more the writer in him urged that something must be written. And so, Conrad observes, he "sets the rhetoric to do the work of responding for him" (13).

Out of Americans' patriotic assertiveness, Rudyard Kipling draws a picture of an American subject who seems to be insecure with regard to his relation to America: "It must be an awful thing to live in a country where you have to explain that you really belong there" (P. Conrad 95–6). It is as if what is commonly perceived as an absence of history in America produces an American subject who needs to explain all the time his presence on the land. On the other hand, Conrad shows how "Kipling understands this defensiveness because he shares it. He writes not as an Englishman but as an ersatz Indian, having elected to assume an identity other than the one assigned to him by birth" (95–6). The restless anxiety that the writer thus perceives in the American other with regard to his American identity could be symptomatic of his own restlessness with regard to his own identity.

D.H. Lawrence tried to articulate America through its literature. His critical work *Studies in Classic American Literature* is one of the richest texts ever written on an America which increasingly became an object of Europe's imagination. In spite of what seems to be its highly personal onslaught on America, and precisely because of that, Lawrence's collection of essays powerfully puts in sharp relief a symbolic America that is made up out of his unusual imaginative powers. At the highest point of his sense of it, America, being the self-imposed historical heiress of Europe as well as the radical other of Europe, is thought of as a deviant child as well as a cunning, hypocritical, and ultimately sinful woman.[1] Yet *Studies in Classic American Literature* does not only show, in accordance with Lawrence's desire, that Europe is the symptom of America; it also shows, arguably against the writer's desire, that America is the symptom of the European Self. The more the European writer knows America the more it feeds on his being.

Even though some of his best plays were written in America, Bertolt Brecht's ideology made his life there an unhappy one. America to Brecht, according to one of the authority writers on him, James K. Lyon, "represented the most advanced form of capitalism and consequently the most uncivilized, inhumane form of human existence" (341). His experience in America as a German socialist and anti-fascist who had to flee Europe's Nazi threat turned out to be no less than death disguised in a form of a life that seemed to be entirely meaningless to him. This unhappy experience of exile reached its climax in 1947 when he was investigated by the House Committee on Un-American Activities, among other personalities that America considered unfriendly to the American way of life.

Living in the United States for more than twelve years, Theodor W. Adorno, it is commonly believed, could not adapt to American society and returned to Germany after the end of World War II. By looking at works like *Dialectic of Enlightenment*, *The Culture Industry*, *The Authoritarian Personality*, *Minima Moralia*, *The Stars Down to Earth* and *Prisms*, it seems that what Adorno saw as social mutational vicissitudes of mass culture may be related one way or another to America. For example, it is in America, the place where motion pictures were invented, that "the elimination of the distinction between image and reality has already advanced to the point of a collective sickness" (*Culture Industry* 64). Adorno's point seems to be that the real major achievement of American cinematic production is producing America itself. Americans to him carry "faces of which one no longer knows whether the film has alienated them from reality or reality has alienated them from the film, as they wrench open a great formless mouth with shining teeth in a voracious smile" (47). It cannot be a coincidence that Jean Baudrillard writes

---

[1]   This is particularly evident in Lawrence's reading of Nathaniel Hawthorne's *The Scarlet Letter* in "Nathaniel Hawthorne and *The Scarlet Letter*" and James Fenimore Cooper's character Eve Effingham in "Fenimore Cooper's White Novels", *Studies in Classic American Literature*, Penguin Books, 1977, pp. 49, and 94–5.

about the same American "toothpaste effect" (34) in his book *America*. Between the 1940s and the 1980s the Marxist approach to America changed considerably, but how it sees the American smile seems to be a fixed idea. Adorno's attack on jazz goes beyond his attack on cinema. If cinema converts subjects into what seem to be heterogeneous social functions, jazz to Adorno does nothing less than a castrating homogenization (*Prisms* 12–9).[2]

Franz Kafka, who never went to America, seems to have expressed his desire for going there in the form of writing *Der Verschollene* (*The Unheard Of*, or, *The Man who Disappeared*), later entitled *Amerika*. In his preface to Kafka's *Amerika*, Klaus Mann demonstrates how Kafka, as a Jew living in Prague, in an era of European intimidation of Jews, saw America as a beautiful dream of freedom and a hope for the future. Kafka, according to Mann, "yearned for other landscapes, for a lighter and brighter beauty [… away from] the gloomy streets of Prague" (vi). Although the atmosphere of solitude prevails in *Amerika* like its predecessors *The Castle* and *The Trial*, *Amerika*, in Mann's words, "is the only one of Kafka's fragmentary novels on the last pages of which a confident mood prevails" (x). Yet a closer look at Kafka's *Amerika* can show that it is probably the gloomiest of Kafka's works. For if the other works of Kafka focus on the question of the law, *Amerika* is the one that creates a fantasy by which that question is repressed. The amazement of the subject in front of his symbolic mandate, which he cannot even begin to understand, in *The Castle* or *The Trial* for example, is replaced by a kind of an unquestioning submission to what is perceived as the castrating power of America.

The present book, therefore, is based on certain premises which maintain that America is more than a country in the imagination of the world. It has always been so. This world is not exclusive of America but inclusive of it. So, even America imagines itself. This is an established discourse as it will be shown by the texts analyzed, referred to, or just mentioned in the present book. All of these texts belong to America as master signifier, a trope in literature, and a philosophical concept. In this discourse, the distinction between America, symbolic America, cinematic America, and so on, is not clear cut in any sense. The reader is required to keep this in mind as he or she reads the text – not to say that this is trouble-free or effortless, as discussing the issue of representing America in literature and film with more than a few peers for the past eight years has revealed the difficulty this apparently painless distinction poses for both writers and readers.

Based on Jacques Lacan's psychoanalytic theory and Slavoj Žižek's philosophical adaptation of it, this book explores the idea of symbolic America – or that philosophical concept and literary trope created out of perceiving/representing America – and traces it in certain chosen texts. Part I deals with modernist perceptions of America. Chapter 1 explores the idea of symbolic America and

---

[2]   Another well-known essay by Adorno in which jazz comes under attack is "On the Fetish Character in Music and the Regression of Listening", *The Culture Industry*, edited by J.M. Bernstein, London and New York: Routledge, 2001, pp. 29–60.

establishes it as something that has been created even before America became aware of itself as a country. It discusses how America and the American Self are idealized in Ralph Waldo Emerson's "The Young American" and in Seymour Martin Lipset's "American Exceptionalism: A Double-Edged Sword".[3] It finally seeks to show how the ideological discourse of this idealized epical American self helps to explain the psychotic phenomenon by referring to Lacan's seminar on the psychosis. Chapter 2 gives an analysis of D.H. Lawrence's *Studies in Classic American Literature* as an instance of radical criticism of America with two main questions in the background. First, how much of America did Lawrence really know out of his analysis of classic American literature? Secondly, how deep did America reach in the writer's unconscious?

Chapter 3 discusses the fiction of the castrating power of America. The ambiguity in the title refers to both the fictional writing on America and to the fact that the castrating power of America is a fiction. The chapter argues that at the core of America's invented images lies the fiction of its castrating power. It deals with a text which was written as pure fiction, and which more or less explicitly perceives America as a castrating power: Kafka's *Amerika*. The chapter's argument is that it is this most innocent and unassuming of Kafka's works that gets to the core of the fictitious discourse of America's castrating power. Its conclusion is that the discourse of the fictitious castrating power of America is empowered by the very resistance to it.

Chapter 4 discusses the radicalized fascist image of America in some of Adorno's works, such as *Dialectic of Enlightenment, The Culture Industry, Minima Moralia, Prisms, The Stars Down to Earth* and *The Authoritarian Personality*. Adorno has been chosen out of the Jewish Diaspora created by Nazism in the middle of the 20th century because he is seen as one of the most eminent figures who expatriated themselves from America after living there for a long time. In the preface to the Italian Edition of their major work *Dialectic of Enlightenment*, Adorno and Horkheimer state that their book has been written "on the basis of social phenomena of the 1930s and 1940s in America" (xiii). Adorno's negative dialectics theory could be the most melancholic intellectual work of all time. To state that it has been based on social phenomena in America necessitates tracing the shadow of symbolic America in it as well as in other works by Adorno in order to see what America actually meant to him.

With the increasing interest in the writings of Adorno over the past two decades, it became important to reassess Adorno's relationship to America. The image of the unapproachable, pessimistic elitist who detached himself from American society even while living in the midst of it has been effectively altered by a whole new movement in the Adorno scholarship which seems to have been started by Martin Jay's influential essay "Adorno in America" published in *New German Critique* in the winter of 1984. The problem, however, seems to be that

---

[3]   Both essays of Emerson and Lipset can be found in *American Social and Political Thought*, edited by Andreas Hess, Edinburgh: Edinburgh University Press, 2002.

the new historical analysis of Adorno's American experience presumes at its very point of premise that America, in Adorno's mind, names something that is clearly distinguishable from Europe. It does not consider the possibility that Adorno's creation of a symbolic America that is as authoritarian as fascist Europe can, in effect, confuse the two. The argument of the final chapter in Part I is that Adorno's American experience is intrinsically tied with Walter Benjamin's virtual experience of America. Through a comparison between Adorno's and Benjamin's positions with regard to the materialist theory of culture, it argues that points which are thought to be markers of difference between the two thinkers are vitally tied together. Its conclusion is that Adorno's America comes out of an imagination which preconditions all experience of the present by the fascist moment of history, and that this idea itself is a Benjaminian idea.

Part II examines various postmodernist representations of America. Its title suggests that the postmodernist tradition leans towards representing without necessarily going through ordeals of interpreting what is perceived. This idea, however, gains strength as Part II progresses towards its end. It is not immediately obvious in the first three chapters which, more or less, fall between incomplete perceptions and unreliable representations. Chapter 5 examines two texts by two contemporary American writers: Charles W. Brooks and David Shambaugh. The two writers seem to have more or less the same concern: Mainly to reveal how non-Americans perceive America, how certain texts about America invent their own "America" and, therefore, communicate to their readers an unreliable message. One of the arguments of this book, however, is that those particular texts which try to reveal misconceptions about America themselves fall into other misconceptions.

This is not a film studies text; however, it does come across, and in certain instances indulgingly analyze, various cinematic productions, therefore, its approach to film must be made clear to eliminate any possible confusion. Readers will notice that the discussion of film often fluctuates between discussing their narrative and their stylistic traits with no commitment to either. Critically, choosing between discussing content and discussing form or style is to a certain extent irrelevant here. In the present work, certain films are chosen and approached at specific points where this writer thinks they relate to America, whether this happens to come under the film's narrative or under its cinematic stylistics. Similarly, in the bigger picture, a departure into film in the first place is necessary only insofar as cinematic America is concerned – and cinematic America cannot be ignored in a work such as this. On the other hand, since the topic of America as master signifier is a huge one, discussion of films had to be narrowed down to the main points that need to be illuminated either about America or about its readers or writers at certain moments of the writing.

In light of this, Chapter 6 designates D.W. Griffith's *Birth of a Nation* as marking the birth of an ideological cinematic America – an impenetrable symbolic being assuming a life of its own while representing an invincible civilization that is immune to the idea of historical decline or disintegration. Linking this to the surreality of America in non-American films, the chapter also discusses the notion of America as the Promised Land and how this idea is tainted by America's primal guilt of annihilating the Native Americans as well as given substance by America's image as a place where immigrants re-invent themselves. Chapter 6 finally discusses the idea of America as woman using Susan Sontag's fictional work *In America* and Lacanian psychoanalysis to problematize the existence of symbolic America as well as the idea of feminine writing itself.

Chapter 7 examines the image that Lars Von Trier's film *Dogville* invents out of America and the homage it pays to Brecht and Brechtian cinema. *Dogville* is chosen as a contemporary cinematic example of the living discourse of symbolic America. The argument of the chapter is that what *Dogville* as a cynical as well as a Brechtian cinematic work says about America reflects a vision that tries to render America a desexualized mutant of Europe. Put another way, *Dogville* as a European text seeking to read America is in one way capable of doing so by arguing how America, seen as an inheritor of European civilization, desexualized itself to be different and non-European. In the course of this, the structural and conscious processes by which *Dogville* invents a desexualized America and relates this desexualization to the idea of murder will be revealed. The conclusive point of the chapter, however, is that this anti-American European take on America, in spite of its outspoken aggressivity, seems to mark a certain unconscious erotic love affair between the inventing European subject and the invented image of America.

Chapter 8 discusses the changeful image of America in Said's writings – chief among them, *Orientalism*, *Culture and Imperialism* and *Out of Place*. It argues that Said's criticism of America paradoxically marks identification with it. In spite of its many representations in his works, there seems to be a clear allusion that Said's main feeling about America was that he was being devoured, consumed, and made utterly exhausted every day, by an insatiable, sadistic, highly authoritative and powerful feminine figure – a feminine figure which acted, in his imagination, as a tyrannical lover, as a rival, as an evil counterpart, and as a replacement for the mother all at once. The chapter argues that Said's subtle insinuations about America's "feminine power" seem to be interconnected with a tendency to act as a love object of an overpowering female, something which he implicitly – and sometimes explicitly – suggests through recounting various episodes of his life where he seems to have *enjoyed* this role. The conclusion is that Said's ultimate identification, in spite of his ideological stance with the Palestinians, and which always seemed to be fundamentally against America as Israel's biggest benefactor, was his symbolic identification with the gazing power of America itself and its symbolic role as the high-handed broker trying to process peace from afar, however unsuccessfully, in the Middle East.

Chapter 9 discusses the sublimated image of America in Ihab Hassan's writings, which include *Radical Innocence: Studies in the Contemporary American Novel*, *The Right Promethean Fire: Imagination, Science, and Cultural Change*, *Paracriticisms: Seven Speculations of the Times*, *Out of Egypt: Scenes and Arguments of an Autobiography*, *The Postmodern Turn: Essays in Postmodern*

Theory and Culture, and *Between the Eagle and the Sun: Traces of Japan*. It argues that at the root of Hassan's sublimation of America lies his radical turn away from Egypt. As a result, America comes to one of its most romanticized epical images in Hassan's writings. Sublimating the American Self seems to inspire most of them. In spite of the image that Hassan draws of himself as an apolitical thinker, the argument in this chapter risks tracing the political element in his thought. By doing this it will eventually be revealed that the way Hassan dealt with his version of America is particularly and startlingly political. Unlike both Adorno and Said, Hassan's writing seems to denote in an almost Kafkaesque way that he is constantly aware that America *is* his own version of America. His unwavering radical identification with America, however, seems to paradoxically suggest that America was always already sealed to him. It is precisely in the sense generated by this paradox that this final chapter concludes that Hassan's radical act of sublimating America and the American Self is in its essence a political act.

Hassan and Said have been chosen as American writers, from non-European origins, who went to America at a certain stage in their lives. There are many reasons for comparing the two thinkers – a subject about which it is clearly well worth writing a whole book in its own right, and therefore to which it is not possible to do justice here. However, a few points in this regard should be pointed out as they seem to be useful in the present context. Both writers, coming from an underdeveloped part of the world, made it to the ultimate West and were able to firmly establish their names in the registers of Western thought – in different circumstances and with different intellectual positions. Both were educated in Egypt in their youth, went to America to continue their education within the same decade and made literature, criticism and the study of culture their lives' axis. Both of their names became synonymous with two major theories in the field of cultural studies: Orientalism and Postmodernism. Yet, while Said's and Hassan's biographical similarities are remarkable, the differences between them as writers and critics are so deep-seated to the point of an acute non-reconciliation, even antagonism. In the course of tracing America in their writings, a minor comparative study of the two thinkers will draw itself.

This book thus is based upon a certain view which maintains that America is a master signifier in language the way terms like "democracy", "communism", "love", "ideology", "liberty" or "death" are master signifiers. None of these terms are clearly defined and they always remain as topics for philosophical discussions. America, from the viewpoint of the present work, belongs to the world, and not just to any specific people. The topic of America therefore cannot, and should not, be a monopoly of the field of American Studies. In fact, America in particular belongs as much to the field of Comparative Literature and Cultural Studies as it belongs to American Studies. Since this book argues that inventing America is tied with inventing subjectivity, the articulation of America always remains in the future, meaning that it cannot be realized. Though its conclusion may appear deconstructionist by stating that America is inarticulable, the argument of the book builds up very much within structuralist boundaries.

Because it maintains that the unconscious is at the heart of articulating America, the argument and the methodology of this book reciprocally shape each other; in other words, it is a psychoanalytic story. The preliminary reason why Jacques Lacan in particular was chosen is simply because neither the unconscious nor the effects of a master signifier in language can possibly be talked about without Lacan. And, because one of the greatest contemporary purveyors of Lacanian theory, Slavoj Žižek, has become inseparable from Lacan, Žižek is also a central figure in the present work. The choice of the psychoanalytic approach is significant, as this book talks about America within the very specific context of creating subjectivity. It is obvious that the subject of America is so huge and complex that the list of writers is endless. So, in order for any book to talk about America it has to be humble; in other words, it has to set certain limits for itself so as to deal with the subject of America from a specific angle.

In the present work, therefore, the reader will come across diverse *imagos* of America. The word 'imago' is used instead of 'image' to indicate that invented images of America reflect complex processes of both idealization and denigration of America in which the inventor's self is itself invented as an other. In Lacanian language, the Latin word "imago" mainly stands for the ideal ego or the visualization of the subject's self which he or she (mis)recognizes as the core of identity through a process of identification with an other where the subject perceives an ideal image of himself. The formation of the ideal ego, in Lacan's words, "inaugurates, through identification with the imago of one's semblable and the drama of primordial jealousy ... the dialectic that will henceforth link the *I* to socially elaborated situations" (*Écrit: Complete Edition* 79). In other words, identifying with another's image and internalizing the image as the ideal ego, launches a lifelong dialectic of irrevocability and untenability. The modeling of the self as indistinguishable from, yet threatened by and aggressive toward, the other *alienates it from itself* as it oscillates between an imagined individuality and a deceptive association with the other. The figure of the father as a castrating figure – as a model to be admired and at the same time as an adversary – plays a major role as the other. The subject's acquired sense of self also points to perceiving a prior phase of fragmentation – confirmed by a feeling of incompleteness that does not show in the imago – in which the human subject is nothing more than "an inchoate collection of desires" (Lacan, *Psychoses* 39). In short, the complexity of the imago lies in the idea that it oscillates between two fundamental and paradoxical desires on the part of the subject: one for the connected whole of being one with its surroundings as in the narcissistic stage of non-being where the self *is* the other, and the other for individual perfection.

The imago can therefore be defined within Lacan's conception of imaginary being as "[the subject's] construct in the imaginary [that] disappoints all his certainties. For in this labor which he undertakes to reconstruct *for another*, he rediscovers the fundamental alienation that made him construct it *like another*, and which has always destined it to be taken from him *by another*" (*Écrits: A Selection* 46). An imago thus points to both the ideal and the deformed, the whole and the fragmented, identity and non-identity. In its essence, an imago is that which can be thought of as gained only in terms of being always already lost. Since it comes out of fragmentation, its perceived wholeness is not only threatened by fragmentation but is ultimately defined by it. It belongs to that middle ground between the symbolic and the real in which it is torn between the anticipation of being "there" in the symbolic order and the ultimate commitment to the oblivion of the real. It is in this sense that the term imago is used in the present book, not strictly as ideal ego but as an image which paradoxically reflects idealization and deformation, admiration and denigration, wholeness and fragmentation, being and non-being.

In light of this, the present book argues that how America is perceived in certain texts reveals not only the idealization or condemnation of it but, much more than this, *a constructed image, an imago, of the perceiver as well*. Because the unconscious is at the heart of articulating America, inventing America is tied with inventing subjectivity. In its analysis of this intrinsic relationship between conjuring up an object of imagination and contriving subjectivity, the book shows two things: First, that America, read by different readers/writers *seems* to fit in the structure of the castrating figure in psychoanalysis, and secondly, that it *reads back the unconscious of its readers/writers*. The aim of the book is to establish the idea that the presence of the corpus of idiosyncratic literature about articulating America paradoxically points to *an acute failure to articulate it*.

In the course of this, it will also be shown that texts which particularly focus on demonstrating how other texts about America communicate an unreliable message *themselves communicate an unreliable message*. Imagos of America are invented and reinvented reflecting an ongoing process of radical idealization/deformation. The ambiguity of the term imago in the present book thus becomes clear: Imagos of America refer to both idealized/deformed images of America constructed by the perceivers of America and to the imagos of the perceivers themselves constituted by their very act of reading America.

It must be mentioned, therefore, that it does not seem as a coincidence to the present writer that one of the most ideological as well as romantic definitions of America as the creation or the re-creation of the individual self seems to correspond in a fundamental way with the structure of subjectivity in psychoanalysis. It should be understood then that this book by no means says everything about America. No book can ever cover that. It talks about America only insofar as it is created in a process of creating subjectivity. By the same token, this book also does not, and cannot, adequately cover any of the various writers it deals with. It talks about the writers only insofar as they relate to America.

As the chapters of the book discuss readers or writers of America, each chapter also explains and uses one or more than one Lacanian formula. The formulas start from the notion of the imago in this introduction, through the psychotic phenomenon in Chapter 1, the barred subject in Chapter 2, castration and the "Che vuoi?" question in Chapter 3, identification with a sinthome in Chapter 4, subjectivity and the desire for death in Chapter 5, female subjectivity in Chapter

6, the objet petit *a* in Chapter 7, imaginary and symbolic identifications in Chapter 8, and "das Ding" in Chapter 9.

Both parts of the book end in a play of identifications which take place between the level of the barred subject at the bottom right hand side of the Lacanian graph of desire indicating the void beyond subjectivity, and the level of *jouissance* which is at the top of the graph. Thus, modernist perceptions culminate to Adorno's rejection of America, while postmodernist representations culminate to Said's enjoyment of America and Hassan's radical identification with it. The choice and the sequence of these three thinkers themselves follow a certain structure. Adhering to the modernist tradition of interpreting everything in the world, Adorno interprets America and at the same time represents a case of an acute inability to identify with it. Complying with the postmodernist tradition of standing against interpretation, Said enjoys America and at the same time is torn between his imaginary identification with Palestine and his symbolic identification with America, while Hassan neither interprets America nor seems to enjoy it. He sublimates it to the empty place of the Thing or "das Ding".

The three thinkers, therefore, in this particular sequence, seem to be near perfect examples of three different stages of denial which Lacan describes as "psychoanalytic effects" in his "Seminar on 'The Purloined Letter'" (*Écrits: Complete Edition* 6). Adorno represents a "Verneinung" or a rejection taking place at the level of consciousness; in other words, he rejects the imagined castrating power of America. Said represents a "Verdrängung" or a repression of America's castrating power, which entails its recurrent return in the form of a certain castrating feminine figure. Hassan represents a case of "Verwerfung" or foreclosure. He does not only repress America's threat of castration, he represses the fact that he had to repress something. Put in other words, Hassan does not only annul his cultural memory, but annuls the memory of that annulment itself. Since this idea of Verwerfung or foreclosure is discussed in the analysis given to Kafka's *Der Verschollene* in Chapter 3, Kafka makes a certain return in the final chapter. This foreclosure is itself where this book finally comes to a certain close.

It remains to say that there are two reasons why this particular field of study has been chosen. The first is observing a certain chasm, a belief that analysis of representations of America, outside the European and American spheres, is obviously lacking. In spite of the fact that the world today, as once put by Edward Said, is "literally held in the grip of an extraordinarily unbound power" ("The Other America") that we all recognize and name as America, it seems that apart from spotty and slapstick references to the master signifier called "America" in films, theatrical performances, TV serials, newspaper and magazine articles, jokes, and so on, serious non-European and non-American studies dealing with America either as a philosophical concept or as a trope in literature seem to be astonishingly rare.

The second reason is that since desire is always at play, this writer must confess that the temptation of articulating the inarticulable – America – has proved itself irresistible to him, too. America is far from a realized idea. Like democracy itself which, in a Derridean way, always "remains to come" or remains "the theme of a non-presentable concept" (Derrida, *Politics of Friendship* 306), America seems to always reside in the future. It should be stated then that this book about America, in a fundamental sense, also represents its writer's dream of a better Egypt that is finally free of both the chain of "secular" autocrats who ruled it from 1952 up to the 11 February 2011 when the worst of them bowed to the will of the Egyptian people and stepped down, and their underlying side-effect – the violent Islamist fanatics aiming at the complete Islamicization of its society and its politics. It is a work about America which, in a way, looks desperately forward to a democratic Egypt that is free of a long standing tradition of authoritarian bureaucracy as well as free of a long standing public sense of disheartenment and frustration, of an Egypt that is finally free of the state-owned national media filtering down what should be heard and what should be read, as well as irrevocably free of its disreputable Emergency Law which simply replaced *the* law whenever it chose to do so for 30 years, of an Egypt which believes in democracy as a *culture* and not just as a system of government or as some dramatic show of voting and balloting in order to create a spectacle of presidential nomination.

In short, if read closely enough as it progresses towards its end, it will become plainly evident to the reader that this book about America, which represents a dream of democracy, holds on *fanatically* to that impossible dream with no possibility of relinquishing it, and thus, oddly enough, still carries the unmistakable authoritarian stamp of the land of the Nile. It is as if the work makes its own Lacanian loop of imagining America then U-turns in order to fall back into its writer's dream of a free Egypt. So, as far as this study is concerned, producing some work that this writer sees as an unconventional attempt to penetrate what unavoidably penetrates his own imagination – America – exceeds, by far, his first reason.

PART I
Modernist Perceptions

Chapter 1

The Epical American Self and the Psychotic Phenomenon

"I admit that I saw in America more than America" (19)

Alexis de Tocqueville

In his essay "Reconstructing America: The Symbol of America in Modern Thought", James W. Ceaser argues that European thinkers "have seized on the word "America" and made it into something more than a place or country. They have converted it into a concept of philosophy and a trope of literature". Ceaser calls this abstraction of America "metaphysical America" or "symbolic America". His main point is to clearly distinguish between that literary creation of Europe and, in his own words, "the real America, by which I mean the country where we live, work, struggle, and pray, and where we have forged a system of government that has helped to shape the destiny of the modern world" (6–8). The second main point is the commonsensical idea that the symbol must have been created out of the reality of the country, i.e., that America was physically there before Europeans started to transform it into a symbol – a symbol, it must be made clear, that is not equivalent with the self-made image of America which has been created by Hollywood, the American mass media, or the prevalence of American commercial or cultural products.

At a closer look, however, things do not seem to be as simple as Ceaser suggests. America, as the latest comer of human civilizations, seems to have been *historically* preceded by its symbol. It can be argued that America existed as a certain symbolic power and a specific signifier that manifested itself strongly in the mind of Europe before it became aware of itself as a country. In his essay "A Roof without Walls: The Dilemma of American National Identity", John M. Murrin writes that it was the British, "not the settlers", who "imagined the possibility of an independent America […] the British worried about the whole because they did not understand the parts, and they reified their concerns into a totality they called America … In a word, America was Britain's idea" (339).

It is not therefore an exaggeration to say that America was created by the word of Britain. A symbol in language was invented before the country started to be literally *voiced* by its own people through the Declaration of Independence, the making of the Constitution, the Articles of Confederation, and the war for independence. Symbolic America thus seems to have been created before America as a political power came into existence, and has persisted beyond the political entity until the present. It is largely in this symbolic being of America where discourses about America's exceptionalism seem to reside, i.e., America seems to be indeed exceptional – far beyond what is seen as its ahistoricism, its ideological foundation, and its present economic and military supremacy – by the sheer power of its symbolic presence in the consciousness of the world.

Some classic American texts about America's exceptionalism contribute greatly in the creation and recreation of America's imagos. In those texts the American Self assumes a kind of epic quality that is peculiar to it. It is largely in discourses of American exceptionalism, individualism and pragmatism that this epic self becomes most animated. Just as epic is based on individual heroism, canonical ideological texts, like Ralph Waldo Emerson's "The American Scholar" and "The Young American", tend to create an American subjectivity which can only fit in a metaphysical work of art. Emerson, who paved the way to the emergence of pragmatic thought as an American public philosophy, draws an image of the American individual as a subject who is not constituted by the Other, the symbolic network, but who conversely constitutes his whole external world: "The world is nothing, the man is all; in yourself is the law of all nature, and you know not yet how a globule of sap ascends" (201–2).

Reason, to Emerson, is like raw material lying there inside this epic American Self, waiting to be excavated and made use of in the furthest possible sense: "In yourself slumbers the whole of Reason; it is for you to know all, it is for you to dare all". Man – who in this case must be bearing typical American characteristics – is made the centre of the universe by the sheer power of his instincts: "If the single man plants himself indomitably on his instincts, and there abide, the huge world will come round to him". In fact, Emerson seems to believe that men and even nations never existed before the emergence of this epic American Self: "A nation of men will for the first time exist, because each believes himself inspired by the Divine Soul which also inspires all men". Women seem to be excluded from this privileged disposition. America, and only America, is seen as the home of such self: "One thing is plain for all men of common sense and common conscience, that here, here in America, is the home of man" (201–2). It is as if non-Americans are excluded from Emerson's idea of humanity since the "home of man" seems to be nothing but America.

The point about Emerson's text is that it seems to have been written with an overwhelming passion. Every statement in it seems to be accentuated with a kind of absolutism. It certainly demonstrates all along that its writer is a man who strongly believes in what he says. This is no more evident than when he implores God to protect American individualism against homogenization:

> Is it not the chief disgrace in the world, not to be an unit – not to be reckoned one character – not to yield that peculiar fruit which each man was created to bear, but to be reckoned in the gross, in the hundred, or the thousand, of the party, the section, to which we belong; and our opinion predicted geographically, as the north, or the south? Not so, brothers and friends – please God, ours shall not be so. (201–2)

Emerson was a man who loved the America he created as he loved himself. And in his overwhelming love and passionate reasoning, he could not see that this epical American individualism he so anxiously wanted to create, *if* actually bestowed on every American, would precisely result in the very homogenization he was trying to ward off. The ensuing lines speak for themselves:

> We will walk on our own feet; we will work with our own hands; we will speak our own minds. The study of letters shall be no longer a name for pity, for doubt and for sensual indulgence. The dread of man and the love of man shall be a wall of defense and a wreath of joy around all. A nation of men will for the first time exist, because each believes himself inspired by the Divine Soul. (201–2)

It is not difficult to see what this "nation of men", each of which "believes himself inspired by the Divine Soul" would look like.

Underneath the discourse of American exceptionalism which seemingly can only be talked about through the power of America's created imagos, lies a kind of disbelief that society really existed in America in historical terms. In such discourse, America seems to be able to define itself or be defined by the other only in epic-like terms. Peter Conrad, for example, explains why America and the American way of life posed a problem for Victorian novelists – Dickens is Conrad's major example – who were not able to write a novel in America, ascetically because America's epic quality seemed to be incompatible with Victorian novel writing:

> Ever since Homer's account of the fashioning of Achilles' weapons, epic has been an image of industrial process. It does not imitate the decorative surfaces of things, but dramatizes their manufacture. Novels describe the leisure of society: the refinements of private life and emotional association. Epic describes the work of society: the creation of wealth which subsidizes that novelistic leisure. This is why America is such a problem for the Victorian novelists, because its obsession with work censures idleness and with it the cultivation of mental privacy which makes the novel possible. (90)

America's industrialism, worship of work, or, the dynamism that is usually seen as peculiar to American society thus seems to derive its force from a conception – which may seem certainly odd to most people – that America is no place for social leisure. This seems to have everything to do with the view that America never experienced the stage of civilization the way other civilizations did. In his essay "Aesthetic America", Conrad states: "Conservative critics of America proverbially say that it has passed from barbarism to decadence, bypassing the stage of civilization which ought to come between; but for the aesthetic critic, this is the wonder of it. Like a corrupt infant, it cannot wait to grow up before embracing venery" (P. Conrad 69).

Either conservatively criticizing this notion or aesthetically praising it is not the issue of the present book. The issue lies in the view that what seems to be held as the truth behind America's dynamism is that it moved from the chaotic directly to the decadent, bypassing "the stage of civilization" which cannot be thought of but in structural terms. This short circuit accentuates the structure of the master signifier in language; America is as an incomplete symbolic being with a fundamental fracture that needs constantly to be covered up by all kinds of fantasies – of which the cinematic ones are the most common.

In his essay "American Exceptionalism – A Double-Edged Sword", Seymour Martin Lipset puts an emphasis on ideology as to what America *actually is*. Such a defining idea, though quoted to serve his discourse of American exceptionalism, amounts to fantasizing the country altogether. Lipset writes:

> As historian Richard Hofstadter has noted, it has been our fate as a nation not to have ideologies, but to be one. In saying this, Hofstadter reiterated Ralph Waldo Emerson and Abraham Lincoln's emphases on the country's 'political religion', alluding in effect to the former's statement that becoming American was a religious, that is, ideological act. (40)

But to be ideology is to be based on fantasy and, in this case, a fantasy that dictates what being is. Lipset's discourse of exceptionalism starts by referring to Tocqueville's *Democracy in America* in which, in Lipset's words, "Tocqueville systematically compared the United States and France" (40). Being American thus seems to be about being ideologically different from the old world, and that is largely Europe more than any other place. Being American requires, more than anything else, differentiating what is American from what is European, in particular, since it is America's European start that frequently puts America's independent identity in doubt. It is significant enough that a discourse of exceptionalism such as Lipset's bases itself on a text which is written by a European. Again, America gets articulated by Europe, even when it is thought to be exceptionally different from Europe.

Lipset argues that "American exceptionalism is defined by the absence of a significant socialist movement in the United States" and this is mainly due to the fact that "class has been a theoretical construct in America" (44). It is precisely the astounding ability to state that "class has been a theoretical construct in America", and not a reality that manifested itself in the history of black Americans, Hispanics, Indians, and other American minorities, that firmly places the writer's argument in the realm of the ideological, in other words, the fantasy of which the proper role, according to Žižek's Lacanian analysis, is to cover up a gap in the symbolic (*Sublime Object* 33). In fact, stating that class has been nothing but a theoretical construct in America, again, amounts to suggesting that society never existed there. Moreover, the influence of the American Communist Party and the Industrial Workers of the World Union as resonant socialist movements in American history in the first half of the twentieth century cannot be ignored – even if they were systematically weakened and nullified. It is commonplace that some scholars tend to state that class, in its Marxian European sense, though it seems to be wooed by American labor history, never really existed in America outside theory. But this is just beside the point. The point is that this would-be absolute absence of class can never be explained except as a gap in America's socio-symbolic network that has to be compensated for by ideological fantasies.

In other words, this ideological absolute absence from the socio-symbolic network is also absolute presence – a presence that manifests itself radically and racially in all the traumatic moments of America's history of Native American annihilation and Black slavery and persecution.

In showing how America is "the most religious country in Christendom", Lipset argues that the morality of the American Self is determined by its "own sense of rectitude, reflecting a personal relationship with God" (41). As freeing as it is from institutionalized religion, a "personal relationship with God" is nevertheless not exactly a trouble-free idea, for it implies replacing the mediation of culture, history and the human dimension in religion with pure linguistic correspondence with the master signifier "God".

That such an elimination of ties with the human other of cultural exchange – being itself a reflection of the self – in favor of creating a relationship with the divine big Other is related to the psychotic phenomenon is an established discourse in Lacanian psychoanalysis. This is not to suggest that Lipset's idea of the American Self can be an instance of the psychotic. In fact, imagining a personal relationship with God and bestowing the privilege on the national self cannot be just an American peculiarity. The suggestion is rather that such an ideological discourse, in its very awareness of its phantasmal premise, can in fact help in explaining the psychotic phenomenon. The following tries to explicate Lacan's theory of the psychosis in light of the idea of a "personal relationship with God", as well as to illustrate how such an imagined relationship works as a mechanism by which the bits and pieces of the ideological discourse of the epical/national American self are made to fall into their right places.

In 1910, Freud wrote his "Psycho-Analytic Notes upon an Autobiographical Account of a Case of Paranoia" in which he discusses Daniel Paul Schreber's own account of his mental illness, which the latter published in 1903 in the form of a book entitled *Memoirs of My Nervous Illness*. In his discussion of Freud's analysis of the Schreber case, where Schreber's delusional experience is owed back to the fact that he regretted not having had children, Lacan explains the difference between neurosis and psychosis by stating that:

> In neurosis, inasmuch as reality is not fully rearticulated symbolically into the external world, it is in a second phase that a partial flight from reality, an incapacity to confront this secretly preserved part of reality, occurs in the subject. In psychosis, on the contrary, reality itself initially contains a hole that the world of fantasy will subsequently fill. (*Psychoses* 45)

It can be concluded, then, that neuroses remain inside the symbolic order, precisely because erotic relations with the other, or, that which is a reflection of the self, remain in them. In fact, Lacan says that the neurotic subject not only identifies himself in language, he loses his own being in the signifying chain; he transforms himself into a signifier and becomes language (*Psychoses* 155). The Neurotic phenomenon thus seems to be inherent in culture since the "normal" human subject does transform himself or herself into a signifier on daily basis. Transforming oneself into a signifier maintains the whole system of symbolic exchanges that define one's daily life and regulate all his or her relations with the other.

By displaying a cultural code, the subject sends a message to the other, which means that he turns himself into a signifier. In all societies, people transform themselves into signifiers every day. For example, if a man completely shaves his moustache and grows his beard, most people would think that he belongs either to a certain fundamental school of Islam or to the American Amish Christian community which mainly lives in Ohio and Pennsylvania. So, by this gesture which is nothing but his sheer appearance he would be transmitting a message to the other. This is one clear example, but there are many others because all human subjects, consciously or unconsciously, display cultural codes all the time. Because, according to Lacan, "the law of man has been the law of language since the first words of recognition presided over the first gifts" (*Écrits: A Selection* 67), it can be argued that human culture is by definition neurotic, or, even more precisely, that neurosis is in fact the very condition of culture.

The "second phase" in which the subject becomes incapable "to confront this secretly preserved part of reality" is itself the return of the repressed which, in the case of neurosis, takes place within the signifying chain, totally determined by the symbolic sphere, no matter how concealed that repressed material can become. It can disguise itself beneath a mask, or beneath various masks, but it always "reappears *in loco* where it was repressed, that is, in the very midst of symbols" (Lacan, *Psychoses* 105). The psychotic phenomenon, on the other hand, is marked by a "hole" in reality, a gap in the subject's symbolic order and, more importantly, it is an unbridgeable gap, a moment of total breakdown which renders the subject's whole signifying chain an inarticulate mess. A delusion thus results from an encounter with the real, or, with that which can neither be represented by language nor does it appear in the register of the imaginary. The "second phase" in such a case, i.e., the return of the repressed in the case of the psychosis, takes place "in altero, in the imaginary, without a mask" (*Psychoses* 105).

The difference thus between neurosis and the psychotic phenomenon is that while neurosis is still based on an erotic relation with the other within a system of symbolic exchange, the psychotic phenomenon is marked by a fundamental impairment to that relation and, in Schreber's case, by conceiving an imagined relation with God, the ideological big Other, or the symbolic almightiness of the Name-of-the-Father. In the psychosis, the relation with the imaginary other, with all the aggressivity that it carries, and which originates initially in the formation of the ego in the mirror stage, is essentially disrupted. Instead of symbolic exchanges within the symbolic network, the entire signifying *system* is reorganized/disorganized and brought into play in its totality, that is, in its ultimate representation – what Lacan calls the Name-of-the-Father. Consequently, while the discourse with the other, which is also the self, fades out, the psychotic subject contrives a discourse with the "imaginary father", "the basis of the providential image of God" (Lacan, *Ethics of Psychoanalysis* 308) – a discourse that, according to Lacan, is defined by a "mobilization of the signifier as speech, ejaculatory speech that is insignificant or too significant" (*Psychoses* 321). One might add here: insignificant, because it does not exactly belong to the world, since it does not constitute a discourse with the other, and, too significant, because it is overloaded with the notion of a correspondence with God.

To imagine a correspondence with God, a personal correspondence with God, in which God becomes an active participant, does not plainly come about because of an overzealous religiousness. In Schreber's case, Lacan illustrates a certain detour which starts with the lack of the signifier "being a father" and ends up at filling the lack by fantasy via the delusional way of "being the female correspondent of God" (*Psychoses* 77). Being a father is being a father in language since "before the name of the father, there was no father" (306). The natural father is actually nothing but that unfortunate subject who is destined to carry the heavy symbolic load of the name of the father, the castrating figure and, at the same time, the basis of the superego. This is why Lacan states that "the sum of these facts – of copulating with a woman, that she then carries something within her womb for a certain period, that this product is finally expelled – will never lead one to constitute the notion of what it is *to be a father*" (293).

In Schreber's case, thus, the lack of the signifier "being a father" is of such complexity as to arouse the Lacanian fundamental question: "Che vuoi?" (*Écrits: A Selection* 345–6) signaling an incomprehension on part of the subject as to the desire of the big Other, with no satisfactory answer. What does it mean to have all the characteristics of virility and yet not become a father? The psychotic in this case bases itself on this encounter of the void behind the desire of the big Other – the unrepresentable and ultimately unexplainable real which violently floods the subject through the fissure in his symbolic world. Delusional discourse follows in which, in Lacan's own words, "the signifiers begin to talk, to sing on their own" (*Psychoses* 294), creating the illusion that there is a discourse between two entities. It is in this discourse that the psychotic subject begins to transform himself into the object of desire of the big Other, in other words, compensates for the lack of being a father/bearer-of-the-phallus by transforming *himself* into a phallus.

The important point to be made here is that this transformation indeed also marks a sort of decline from the psychotic high tides to the less turbulent waters of paranoia. Žižek uses a famous scene from Steven Spielberg's *Empire of the Sun* to demonstrate how paranoia serves as an escape from falling into the psychotic. Little Jim coincidentally answers the light signals of the Japanese warship from a window in his room just before the ship drops a shell that shakes the building. His father dashes into the room. Jim, convincing himself that he is responsible for the assault, says to his father: "I didn't mean it! It was only a joke!" Žižek writes:

> His first, automatic reaction to this loss of reality, this encounter with the Real, is to repeat the elementary "phallic" gesture of symbolization, to invert his utter impotence into omnipotence, to conceive himself as *radically responsible* for the intrusion of the Real.

In other words, Jim hangs on to his symbolic world, which is his world of "reality" by incorporating his encounter with the Real into his world of play, a world that he masterly controls. Žižek argues that:

> This "phallic" inversion of impotence into omnipotence is invariably associated with an *answer of the real*: there must always be some "little piece of the real", wholly contingent but perceived none the less by the subject as a confirmation of his supposed omnipotence. (*Žižek Reader* 23–4)

The difference between psychosis and paranoia then becomes most vivid by comparing Schreber to Jim. In Schreber's case, the slow realization of the lack of the signifier "being a father" establishes itself through repeated encounters with the Real leading up to the subject's utter submission to the psychosis. In Jim's case, the symbolic world suddenly and *momentarily* collapses causing the subject to instantly incorporate this fracture in the symbolic, which already belongs to a most recent past, into a rounded-out symbolic whole that belongs to the present. While Jim immediately avoids falling into the psychotic depths by repeating the paranoiac "'phallic' gesture of symbolization", Schreber takes the whole delusional detour of the psychosis before reaching the much safer shores of paranoia.

It only remains to read Lacan on the relationship that Schreber's delusional mind creates between himself and God in order to notice the resemblance between its traits and the peculiarities of the ideological discourse of a national self that is made to be in direct contact with God:

> According to this conception which, moreover, gives him a certain mastery over his psychosis, he is the female correspondent of God. Henceforth, everything becomes understandable, everything works out, and I would even go so far as to say everything works out for everybody since he plays the role of intermediary between a humanity threatened to the very depths of its existence and this divine power with whom he has such special ties. Everything works out in the Versöhnung, the reconciliation, that positions him as the woman of God. His relationship with God, as he conveys it to us, is rich and complex, and yet we cannot fail to be struck by the fact that the text includes no indication of the slightest presence, the slightest fervor, the slightest real communication, that would give us the idea that there really is a relationship here between two beings. (*Psychoses* 77)

Lipset's text, as one clear example on drawing an epical self that is in direct correspondence with God, does show how everything becomes perfectly understandable. In his description of the "American Creed" he writes that it "can be described in five terms: liberty, egalitarianism, individualism, populism, and laissez-faire" (41). Five terms, fair and square, no more and no less, all positive ones, framing what America is in a way that sees no other side to any of these traits. The imago of the American Self created by Lipset seems to be definitely at an undisturbed peace with itself. Its supposed privileged position of having a "personal relationship with God" gives it an unusual confidence of itself based on the general belief in, in Lipset's own words, "the perfectibility of human nature" (41). It also indicates that God, being the source of this perfectibility, is its benevolent protector – *whose desire is always known*. There is no question here about the desire of God; America itself is made to be his object of desire, therefore, everything seems to be in place.

It can be concluded then that the tendency by which many writers on America seem to feminize it does not come from nowhere, since what is often taken as America's self-image according to texts canonical to American ideology, like Emerson's and Lipset's, seems to connote a kind of femininity. After all the aforesaid, this should not come as a surprise to the reader. For in spite of the fact that those extremely judicious texts seem to be soggy with masculine stresses, the supposed association with the castrating big Other, God, reflects a trial of avoiding the threat of such castration by what can be described as a sort of pre-emptive emasculation of the self.

Chapter 2
D.H. Lawrence's Radical Criticism of America

D.H. Lawrence's critical work *Studies in Classic American Literature* is one of the richest European texts ever written on symbolic America. In spite of what seems to be its highly personal onslaught on America, and precisely because of that, Lawrence's collection of essays powerfully puts a symbolic America that is made up out of his unusual imaginative powers in sharp relief. The created imago, however, is not just an account of how the writer perceived America in the first quarter of the twentieth century. It also reveals how the perceiver is himself perceived through his own creation.

In his analysis of Melville's *Moby Dick*, Lawrence demonstrates how he sees the white American psyche as a threat to itself. The white whale to him symbolizes the white race, which is "hunted by the maniacal fanaticism" of the "white mental consciousness" (169). It is not as easy as it might seem to be to locate where the writer exactly belongs in such a hypothesis. For though he apparently draws a sharp line between America and Europe all along his *Studies*, the most intensive moments of his critique of America seem to remove all barriers between America and Europe. At such moments, the America that he invents, though supposed to be a radical image of the other of Europe, is also Europe itself. At no point does the reader become unequivocally clear whether this "maniacal fanaticism" belongs to an American "white mental consciousness" or a European one, or both. Not to mention that the issue can be taken beyond this exclusively Western division if it can be considered that it is not only necessarily the white psyche that is a threat to itself.

America is criticized, it seems, because it represents for Lawrence an extreme example of duality, moral lip service combined with inner evil commitments. Yet this seems to be precisely why Lawrence's imago of America is a radical instance of compromise with the rules of symbolic exchange, the identification to the letter with the arbitrary rules of the symbolic order. In other words, America drives one mad – Lawrence himself is perhaps the most vibrant example – because it appears to be most abiding by the Law and at the same time the major transgressor of it. Thus, when he writes that Hector St John de Crèvecœur "helped his neighbors, whom no doubt he loved as himself, to build a barn" (30), it is difficult to ascertain whether Lawrence states this in a cynical way or actually means what he says.

For beyond Lawrence's American experience and his analysis of classic American texts, Crèvecœur's love of his neighbors as himself, taken seriously, is no less problematic than the same love, taken cynically. In fact, given Freud's and Lacan's theories about the biblical commandment "Thou shalt love thy neighbor as thyself", Crèvecœur's love of his neighbors as himself, if a true one, would be far more hypocritical than his love of his neighbors as himself, if a pretentious one. Freud sees the commandment "Thou shalt love thy neighbor as thyself" as an impossible demand of civilization that is imposed on man's aggressive instincts which necessarily run against it. He writes: "If this grandiose commandment had run 'Love thy neighbor as thy neighbor loves thee', I should not take exception to it" (*Civilization, Society and Religion* 300). Therefore, the loving of one's neighbor is supposed to be happening at the level of pure symbolic exchange, because what is at stake in it is no less than *jouissance*. Lacan says:

> To say that the retreat from "Thou shalt love thy neighbor as thyself" is the same thing as the barrier to *jouissance*, and not it's opposite, is, therefore, not an original proposition. I retreat from loving my neighbor as myself because there is something on the horizon there that is engaged in some form of intolerable cruelty. In that sense, to love one's neighbor may be the cruelest of choices. (*Ethics of Psychoanalysis* 194)

It is the proximity of one's neighbor, who is supposed to be the object of one's neighborly love, which constitutes not just a drawback to *jouissance*, but a repulsion which gets instantly created by the very nearness of the neighbor. As Žižek puts it, "the problem arises at the moment when [the neighbor] comes too near us, when we start to feel his suffocating proximity – at this moment when the neighbor exposes himself to us too much, love can suddenly turn into hatred" (*Enjoy Your Symptom* 8). The nearness of the neighbor allows perceiving what Lacan calls his "harmful, malignant *jouissance*" which "poses a problem for [one's] love" (*Ethics of Psychoanalysis* 187). The forbidden coveting of the neighbor's belongings comes out of a desire to enjoy in his place. Yet, because the object of the neighbor's desire constitutes one's own, the neighbor is always already perceived as enjoying in one's own place.

Thus, for Lawrence, the attraction of loving the neighbors as oneself implies that what Crèvecœur always wanted may be the good for his neighbors provided that it reflects upon his own self – purely a symbolic exchange that did not cost him his precious *jouissance*. Yet, this cannot be an abnormality within the American psyche, since this fluctuation between the symbolic elevation of the neighbor as an object of love and turning away from his hideous *jouissance* is constitutive of the human condition. That is why Lacan states that the biblical commandment "Thou shalt love thy neighbor as thyself" is the "terminal point" (*Ethics of Psychoanalysis* 96) of Freud's *Civilization and Its Discontents*. No wonder that America, this profound master signifier which often seems to constitute the "terminal point" of human civilization, finds itself caught, if only by its symbolic religious pledge, in the fundamental duplicity of such a commandment. America's postmodern beginnings, divisive identity, controversial history of murdering a nation of aborigine inhabitants, black slavery, introduction of democracy and freedom to the world as well as an unprecedented accumulation of wealth and a ruthless drive to power seem to correspond with Lacan's idea that "the two notions, the death of God and the love of one's neighbor, are historically linked" (193), and that is why the latter seems inhuman to both him and Freud.

Lawrence writes about America's "Spirit of Place" as the macabre ghostly spirit of the "Red Indian"[1] which possesses the land. To him, the white race is doomed in America, and the white American psyche is destabilized because it is haunted by the restless spirits of the exterminated original inhabitants of the land, the "Red Indians", which are "causing the great American grouch, [...] which amounts almost to madness". This madness, according to Lawrence, manifests itself in the American contradictory wish to wipe out the Indian race and venerate it at once (41).

Although these words cannot be completely devoid of any truth, what is so blatantly remarkable about them is that the point from which the writer is observing the ghost of the "Red Indian" identifies itself with him in relation to America. To Lawrence, the "Spirit of Place" is marked by "the fact that no place exerts its full influence upon a new-comer until the old inhabitant is dead or absorbed. So America" (40). But if the old inhabitant of America is dead, the European immigrant seems to be either put into the position of the living dead by annulling his European identity in an endeavor to be assimilated, or imagining America from a European point of view, creating an imago of it. It can be argued that while writing the *Studies* in America, Lawrence's European sense that the history and the civilization of Europe were being radically thrown into oblivion by America, in spite of the vexed debt America owes to Europe, seems, by far, to overshadow the fact that the civilization of the original inhabitants of the land has been obliterated by the European settlers. This seems to be most evident when Lawrence states that America's "Americanizing and mechanizing has been for the purpose of overthrowing the [European] past" – an act against which he emphatically urges Europe to "let Hell loose, and get [its] own back" (27).

The ghost of the "Red Indian" thus seems to be diminished by a much more unappeased ghostly being seeping through Lawrence's text, and so evidently giving it its personal taint as well as its poetic quality. It seems that it is the European Self, which *Lawrence's* America seems to be so keen on making ghostly, that touches upon the horrific real of the void at the very core of the writer's subjectivity. Unlike the Native American who is left with nothing but the choice of death, either physical or civilizational/cultural, in face of the radical ideological founding of America, the European is put into the position of being the inhabitant of both Europe and America, acknowledging his own dual identity and at the same time never quite comfortable in either Europe or America. Thus the point that Peter Conrad makes about Lawrence's sense of America in his essay "Primitive America": "In Europe, he uses America against Europe; in America, he invokes Europe in denunciation of America" (174).

In stating that the Americans "dodge their own very selves" (7) in the introductory chapter of the *Studies*, Lawrence seems to be suggesting that American literature is

---

[1]   I use Lawrence's own term here.

particularly misleading. Thus, one can argue that lying through literature to him is a particularly American characteristic. But literature always lies, especially when it becomes so keen on conveying the truth. Literature is that realm where the self tries its utmost effort to touch upon its own core ultimately with no avail. The law, the foreclosure of the literary text, including even Kafka's which is largely about this very law itself (Derrida's "Before the Law"),[2] is linked in a fundamental way to the inaccessibility of that core. This inaccessibility, however, does not mean that there is something behind a closed door other than an utter void.

When Pierre Klossowski writes about the "act to be done" in his essay "The Philosopher-Villain" where he analyzes the phenomenon of monotonous repetition in Sade's works, he points to that impossible transgressive act which always remains undone, even in Sade's monotonic description of what *seems* to be most transgressive (41). What always remains undone is precisely the *knowing of the self* which is, in Lacan, at its most reaching limit, an encounter with the most horrific real – the very nothingness on which the human self is based. For at the most preliminary stage of ideal ego formation, the Lacanian mirror stage, in which that tacit process of imaginary identification, the foundation of a subjectivity that is fated never to find its own tangibility, the self, to use Lawrence's word, has to be both "dodger" and "dodged".

The problem of imaginary identification, or that which stands in waiting to be symbolized, is that it never realizes what it sees out there as the basis of its construction. This means that identification at the level of the mirror stage, though it belongs to the imaginary register, is always already prefigured by the symbolic one'. The most fundamental struggle then that defines the life of any subject becomes the sum of all its failed attempts to return to the narcissistic stage prior to identification in which the self *was* the other. This struggle explains the fantasies by which it develops identifications with others clearly different from it, reducing the differences ingeniously to make the identifications possible, up to the point of forming an ideal ego, an imago that is paradoxically "identity" and "non-identity". When Lacan says that the biblical commandment "Thou shalt not lie" is "among all ten one of the cornerstones of that which we call the human condition" he means that the human self *is* the Lie par excellence. What does it mean then to dodge one's own very self? What does it mean to lie about a lie? Lacan says that in lying, language "also speaks some truth" (*Ethics of Psychoanalysis* 82) – in spite of itself.

In his analysis of Richard Dana's *Two Years before the Mast*, Lawrence writes one of his most insightful philosophical thoughts:

---

[2]   This essay by Derrida deals with one of Kafka's texts, "Vor dem Gesetz", in which Kafka deals directly with the idea of the law, but, almost all of Kafka's short stories, parables and novels seem to carry the germ of the same idea, "Before the Law", *Acts of Literature*, edited by Derek Attridge, New York and London: Routledge, 1992, pp. 181–220.

> Knowing and Being are opposite, antagonistic states. The more you know, exactly, the less you *are*. [...] It will always be a great oscillation. The goal is to know how not-to-know. (121)

Thus, when Dana took that "great step in knowing: knowing the mother sea", it was also a step towards "his own undoing. It was a new phase of dissolution of his own being. Afterwards, he would be a less human thing. He would be a knower: but more near to mechanism than before" (121). Lawrence's implication seems to be that the American Self at large tends to sacrifice being in favor of commitment to knowledge. Later, in his analysis of *Moby Dick* he writes:

> You would think this relation with Queequeg meant something to Ishmael. But no. Queequeg is forgotten like yesterday's newspaper. Human things are only momentary excitements or amusements to the American Ishmael. [...] Queequeg must be just "KNOWN", then dropped into oblivion. (156)

Lawrence's text, again, arguably against his personal desire, penetratingly reveals the writer's identification with America itself. His critical analysis of America's literature assumes the position of knowing America, framing it in a certain frame and, "as Americans themselves do", dropping it into oblivion after securing the knowledge. The question thus which he poses in his *Foreword* with regard to the authenticity of American literature: "Where *is* this new bird called the true American?" (3) and which is implicitly answered by almost every paragraph in the *Studies* as "there is no new bird called the true American, not in any sense of what is called truth" seems to be a rhetorical question which bases itself on a conclusion that he seems to have reached after going through the process of knowing/understanding America through its literature.

It is remarkable that his own experience in America does prove his insightful thought; the more the European writer "knows" America, the more it feeds on his being. His advice "the goal is to know how not-to-know" seems to be an advice that he couldn't resist going against. The temptation of knowing America, of defining what constitutes the American, proved itself irresistible to him. What he actually did was know too much and then, just as the typically American attitude he describes, drop the American imago that he invented into oblivion. After all, as Peter Conrad states, New Mexico "proved to be no more than an expedient resting place in a harried, vagrant career" (193). It was just one amongst a number of places that Lawrence visited between 1919 and 1925 before returning to Europe after his health continued to deteriorate in America.

The essay on Nathaniel Hawthorne's *The Scarlet Letter* seems to be by far the peak of Lawrence's onslaught on America. It is also a peak which fundamentally corresponds with the text's deepest reach at its writer's perceived problem of subjectivity faced with the creation of his own imagination. Throughout the *Studies*, the reader comes across many short, successive, and apparently disconnected statements, but the one on *The Scarlet Letter* definitely stands out in this regard.

Capitalized words, letters, phrases, imperatives, vocabulary innovations and
repetitions follow each other like successive cinematic images that are edited out
in such a way as to tell a long story by the shortest crosscutting way through the
writer's genius but clearly troubled mind:

> *A*. The Scarlet Letter. Adulteress! The great Alpha. [...] American! *A*. Adulteress!
> Stitched with gold thread, glittering upon the bosom. The proudest insignia. Put
> her upon the scaffold and worship her there. [...] The Woman, the Magna Mater.
> [...] America. (94–5)

His later attack in the same essay on woman as such makes it clear that Lawrence's
America seems to be gendered as a woman. This, however, is not Lawrence's first
association of America and Woman in the *Studies*. Earlier, Fenimore Cooper's
character Eve Effingham "had pinned herself down on the *Contrat Social*, and
she was prouder of that pin through her body than of any mortal thing else. Her
IDEAL. Her IDEAL of DEMOCRACY". America, just like Eve Effingham,
"pushed a pin right through its own body, and on that pin it still flaps and buzzes
and twists in misery" in an effort to "destroy Kings and Lords and Masters, and the
whole paraphernalia of European superiority" (49). The "destroying of masters"
thus implies the destroying of a hierarchical as well as patriarchal Europe. In the
"Spirit of Place", Lawrence writes: "Somewhere deep in every American heart
lies a rebellion against the old parenthood of Europe" (10). Europe seems to be
identified with the father figure while America, being the self-imposed historical
"heiress" of Europe, as well as the radical other of Europe, is thought of as a
deviant child as well as a cunning, hypocritical, and ultimately sinful woman.

In Lacanian theory, being a woman raises the question of *being* as such. In his
seminar on the psychosis, Lacan says:

> Becoming a woman and wondering what a woman is are two essentially different
> things. I would go even further – it's because one doesn't become one that one
> wonders and, up to a point, to wonder is the contrary of becoming one. The
> metaphysics of the woman's position is the detour imposed on her subjective
> realization. Her position is essentially problematic, and up to a certain point it's
> inassimilable. (*Psychoses* 178)

Woman's position is "problematic" and "inassimilable" because she lacks a
signifier of her own; she resists inscription into the symbolic order. But this is not
the whole story. In "The Subversion of the Subject and the Dialectic of Desire in
the Freudian Unconscious", Lacan states: "such is the woman concealed behind
her veil: it is the absence of the penis that turns her into the phallus, the object of
desire" (*Écrits: A Selection* 356). Woman thus does not exist because she resists
symbolization due to her lack of signifier/penis, yet it is this lack itself which
"turns her into the phallus, the object of desire". The intensity of her being the
phallus is paradoxically set against her non-existence. She is a non-being which

has gone missing in the symbolic world, or, which has been repressed, only to re-emerge in an altogether different register – in the real of man's desire. This is why Lacan states that "repressed and symptom are homogeneous" (*Four Fundamental Concepts* 176).

Woman's status is thus fundamentally interconnected with subjectivity in Lacanian theory. If the subject is a barred subject or a subject that is essentially split by the violent admission into the symbolic order and therefore never consistent with its own signification, then it can be argued that woman is the subject par excellence due to her inadmissibility into that sphere. It is in this sense that Žižek writes that "it is precisely woman that "exists", that persists as a residue of enjoyment beyond meaning" (*Žižek Reader* 31). If woman's existence is this intrinsically problematic non-being, man's existence on the other hand, as Lacan puts it, is a "being of non-being [...] conjugated with the double aporia of a true survival that is abolished by knowledge of itself" (*Écrits: A Selection* 332). Lawrence's assault on woman and on America as woman seems to be the peak of his critical essays in the *Studies*, where his yells become loudest and his sentences shortest as he tries to approach the kernel of his own being only to be traumatized by its perceived radical instability. So, "where is that new bird called the American?" For Lawrence, the new American bird, *just like woman*, "did not exist".

Studies in Classic American Literature does not only show, in accordance with Lawrence's desire, that Europe is the symptom of America; it also shows, arguably against the writer's desire, that America is the symptom of the European Self. Upon approaching it, the European subject seems to get in contact with this traumatic void at the core of its own subjectivity. It is significant enough that at some point in his essay "Fenimore Cooper's Leatherstocking Novels", Lawrence couldn't help writing this confession:

> It is perhaps easier to love America passionately, when you look at it through the wrong end of the telescope, across all the Atlantic water [...] than when you are right there. When you are actually *in* America, America hurts. (56)

The beauty of Lawrence's highly creative and frenzied text lies in the fact that it is brutally honest, and at the same time revealing of the psychotic threat that lies so near to the very formation of the subject's ego even at the level of meaning, far behind reaching the level of enjoyment. His incomparable ability to write a thought such as this one: "men are freest when they are most unconscious of freedom. The shout is a rattling of chains, always was" (12) without hearing his own loud shouts in the text and the rattling of the chains of his own unrealized being as a barred subject makes his text exceptionally romantic and particularly human.

Chapter 3

The Fiction of the Castrating Power of America: Kafka's Dream

Every human being has the right to pursue happiness. That much seems to be certain. Jefferson's iconic words, which became cornerstones of the law on which an independent America was founded, "hold these truths to be self evident": "That all men are created equal; that they are endowed by their Creator with certain [*inherent and*] inalienable rights; that among these are life, liberty, and the pursuit of happiness" (24). Out of these three notions, however, it is the "pursuit of happiness" that sounds most challenging to the human condition. It does not only assume that man knows what "happiness" is, it also presupposes that (s)he "knows how to pursue it".

On one level, this concept seems to connote a process of acculturation, liberation from culture, or a demolition of the idea of culture as differentia. On another, it may be thought of as an end to discourse as such, an end of the thinking process itself, or an end of the philosophical quest. The very indefinability of the idea seems to stand still at the symbolic mandate of man as a construct of language without indulging him as the ever questioning being about the desire of the big Other or, to put it in another way, as the very denial of existence by way of contemplating the reason behind existence. Yet, it is this non-indulgence in the philosophical discourse itself that makes the idea of the pursuit of happiness so appealing. Its appeal seems to derive from sacrificing reflection upon the ontological self for the continuous development of the animate self through its everyday existential challenges.

When V.S. Naipaul writes about the idea of the pursuit of happiness in his essay "Our Universal Civilization", he seems to be fascinated by something which somehow remains elusive to definitions and cannot possibly be talked about in any way other than a set of generalizations: "It is an elastic idea; it fits all men. It implies a certain kind of society, a certain kind of awakened spirit". Naipaul then tries to give the idea some substance by assorting together a group of sundry, but specific, concepts: "So much is contained in it: the idea of the individual, responsibility, choice, the life of the intellect, the idea of vocation and perfectibility and achievement". But the question is: Cannot such a list be extended endlessly? What about the idea of the family, companionship, integrity, freedom, love, desire, the life of the body, vacation, etc.? Unsurprisingly, Naipaul rapidly goes back to the safety of general statements: "It is an immense human idea. It cannot be reduced to a fixed system. It cannot generate fanaticism. But it is known to exist; and because of that, other more rigid systems in the end blow away" (*City Journal*).

It cannot be denied, however, that, looked at today out of its historical social context, the mystery and the indefinable excess of this fundamental Jeffersonian idea, in its abstract, also seems to mark a certain drive towards cultural death in various discourses. What seems to be at least historically indubitable is that the idea of the pursuit of happiness started with an historical America that once was tearing itself free in order to articulate itself outside British imperial definitions and ended with a living discourse of symbolic America in various imaginations.

As the leader of the happiness-pursuing modern world, symbolic America, as a philosophical concept, seems to provoke a kind of negativity about articulating it. America is perceived as exceptional, assertively religious, multi-cultural – the most advanced, most democratic, most powerful, most enlightened, most tolerant, freest, and richest country in the world. The superlatives attributed to the master signifier "America" create an excessiveness of all sorts. This very multi-faceted excessiveness seems to point to a kind of absolutism about America which sets it apart as a historical civilization. The problem here is that heterogeneous intellectual approaches, in spite of their differences, seem to confer on America an air of finality of the human experience as a whole – a finality which a humanist would perceive as mass culture and technology destroying intellectual and cultural traditions, while a Marxist would call it capitalism and imperialism totally canceling out the agency of the human subject, a nationalist would call it globalism destroying nations and countries, abolishing their cultures as well as their local economic potentials, while a postmodernist would call it the hyper-real, the cinematic, the fictitious, or the simulacrum.

Yet somehow America remains ineffable. This very fact, at the background of which lies a huge corpus of literature which has made it its concern to articulate America, seems to elevate it to a status of an idiosyncratic power. This power is not just political, economic, military, or even cultural. At the core of America's invented imagos lies the fiction of its castrating power. Symbolic America as a castrating power seems to be the main rhetoric that lies behind America's many interpretations. It is also the most illuminating of all pensive manipulations of it, since it seems to get to a certain denominator across various discourses on America.

In these discourses, it can be argued that in whatever way America is thought about, including the most optimistic and positive ways, the shadow of a castrating figure seems to emerge behind the thought. Even the liberal democratic view, though the most right-wing and conformist one, throws it in what can be seen as an after-castration world of melancholy, a totally seemingly contented but actually desexualized world in which all eroticism is a thing of the past. For example, who is Fukuyama's citizen of liberal democracy or "that individual who … gave up prideful belief in his or her own superior worth in favor of comfortable self-preservation" (301), if not Horkheimer's and Adorno's "sacrificial victim … the self which incessantly suppresses its impulses"? (43) One needs to add the word "erotic" to "impulses" for all impulses are necessarily erotic. What is eroticism, if not the egoistic love/hate relationship between the subject and what it sees as part of itself in others, that which is measured by nothing but a "prideful belief in his or her own superior worth"? What is Fukuyama's "comfortable self-preservation" in such a case, if not a total *annulment* of the self?

A look at the history of the Enlightenment reveals how the idea of castration came to be associated with imagining America. In old times, European colonial powers thought of themselves as enlightenment on the move, reaching out in all directions to enlighten all the "dark" places on earth. Such was the law. Joseph Conrad's beautiful image of those powers shows how that enlightenment was as much a form of castration as a process of illumination or eyes opening:

> Hunters for gold or pursuers of fame, they all had gone out on that stream, bearing the sword, and often the torch, messengers of the might within the land, bearers of a spark from the sacred fire. What greatness had not floated on the ebb of that river into the mystery of an unknown earth! [...] The dreams of men, the seed of commonwealths, the germs of empires. (17)

It can be argued thus that America, alternatively, perceived as "utopia achieved" (Baudrillard, *America* 75), with all the European dreams, achievements, successes and failures finally put to rest, represents a castrating enlightenment with a great absorbing power rather than a penetrating one. In such a view, the sword stays, as does its most natural displacement, the torch. It is significant enough that Kafka's *Amerika* opens with "Karl Rossman" entering New York harbor on board a liner, greeted by a Statue of Liberty whose "Arm mit dem Schwert ragte wie neuerdings empor" (*Amerika: Roman* 9) ("arm with the sword rose up as if newly stretched aloft") (*Amerika* 1). The idea seems to be "newly stretched aloft" in order to castrate another one of those new comers. As if this is the most natural requirement that the immigrant must fulfill before entering the land of the most mythologized country on earth, ironically enough, before penetrating the love object of his dreams. It is as if this must be the precondition to a much sought after and over-valued assimilation, an assimilation that takes the form of a cultural ahistoricism which is thought to be particularly American.

Because the melancholic notion of the very disappearance of the immigrant as a subject lies at its root sense, the discourse of the castrating power of America becomes related to what Lacan calls the Freudian "Verwerfung" (*Psychoses* 149).[1] That is to say, in order to be American, the immigrant is required not just to annul his cultural history but, more importantly, *to annul the memory that he had to annul his cultural history*. In other words, to completely foreclose – which is neither to negate nor to repress – the threat of America's castrating power. If America is thought about as a castrating power, then this cannot be something that the immigrant subject negates or represses. For what is negated must be unconsciously

---

[1] Also in "Marginal Comments", *The Ethics of Psychoanalysis 1959–1960*, edited by Jacques-Alain Miller, translated by Dennis Porter, London: Routledge, 1999, p. 131, and, "Seminar on 'The Purloined Letter'", *Écrits: The First Complete Edition in English*, translated by Bruce Fink, New York and London: W.W. Norton and Company, 2006, p. 6.

recognized as present, and what is repressed entails a return of the repressed. If there is one certain proof to Lacan's assertion that the castration complex "is not a myth" (*Écrits: A Selection* 351), it is precisely the fact that it is neither negated nor repressed by the subject; it must be completely shut out.

Going to America in such a sense would be like inscription into a totally distinct register, a different reality. Castration here could be thought about as the violent tearing out from the old register. Karl's suffering in America can thus be seen as his own refusal of the very condition on which he is admitted to it. His situation in this case seems to be similar to a particular Lacanian subject who "refuses access to his symbolic world to something that he has nevertheless experienced, which in this case is nothing other than the threat of castration" (*Psychoses* 12). It is not exactly surprising that Kafka, the writer of *Vor dem Gesetz* (Before the Law), could sense the law of castration in an America that came completely out of his imagination. Like his hero, the countryman who spent his life before the law dreaming about admittance to it without ever being admitted by its doorkeeper, Kafka must have dreamt about being admitted to America. Yet, looking at the very imago he created out of America, he knew precisely what was at stake were he given the chance. No other text more than Klaus Mann's preface to Kafka's *Amerika* shows how America in Kafka's mind was such a powerful figure of castration, even though the preface was obviously written with the aim to demonstrate the opposite – that Prague was Kafka's permanent nightmare, while America was a beautiful dream and a hope for the future.

Mann writes: "He suffered not only from his disease, but from life itself – life as a Jew, in Prague, in the tumultuous period of World War and Revolution" (vi). Mann seems to suggest that Kafka's far-seeing thoughts on the law, human destiny and unexplained suffering stem from his living conditions in Prague and that his dream to go to the New World emerges as an escape from the city to the open spaces of America. Thus Mann confidently writes:

> The city of Prague meant to him, in a weird and definite way, the microcosm in which he recognized the tragedy and struggle of mankind. Prague was actually *all he knew* – his entire world, his paradise and his prison. He yearned for other landscapes, for a lighter and brighter beauty. (vi)

The argument suggests that the imagined visually correct landscape of America in Kafka's mind stood for freedom compared with the tiny prison Prague was. Mann then moves on to the point that although the atmosphere of solitude prevails in *Amerika* like its equivalents *The Castle* and *The Trial*, "*Amerika* […] is the only one of Kafka's fragmentary novels on the last pages of which a confident mood prevails" (x). He then concludes his essay by demonstrating how Kafka's dream of going to America ends upon writing the last pages of the novel, after which his mind sadly returns to Prague:

> Kafka's excursion to the New World has come to an end. The gloomy streets of Prague, the familiar background of his suffering, welcomes her prodigal son:

Here you are – our son, our prisoner, our poet; this is Europe – your chain, your curse and your love. (x)

Yet a closer look at Kafka's *Amerika* can show that it is probably the gloomiest of Kafka's works. For if the other works of Kafka focus on the question of the law, *Der Verschollene* ("The Unheard Of", or, "The Man who Disappeared"), later entitled as *Amerika*, is the one that creates a fantasy by which that question is repressed. The amazement of the subject in front of his symbolic mandate, which he cannot even begin to understand, in *The Castle* or *The Trial* for example, is replaced by a kind of unquestioning submission to what is perceived as the castrating power of America. While K can ask himself the erotic "Che Vuoi?" question, uncomprehending the desire of the ideological big Other, and standing open to all the fantasies he can make up so as to make sure he *misses* the answer every time, Karl Rossman's relation to America seems to be devoid of any erotic questions. He does not ask himself why he is there because he thinks that he wants to be there, as if his desire has been disciplined by the master signifier America is. While K's desire transforms itself to a query about the desire of the Other, Karl has been taught what to desire. Karl's "Amerika", like Susan Sontag's heroine Maryna Zalezowska's "Hamerica", is "supposed to repair the European scale of injury or simply make one forget what one wanted, to substitute other desires" (*In America* 209).

It seems that Kafka's solitary heroes, instead of their gloomy solitude and their suffering under the yoke of the law, can still be enjoying a certain kind of eroticism in their relation to the law – the masochistic enjoyment of playing the victim of an ideological big Other. In fact, this seems to be one of the reasons why readers of Kafka enjoy his works immensely. K's role is always to enact a role for the big Other. The fact that he does not even know what role exactly he is supposed to enact adds to the arbitrariness of the big Other's mandate, its capricious demands. Yet it must be made clear that K's being-for-the-Other can also be a form of being for himself. K can fit in the structure of hysterical neurosis in which the subject, according to Žižek, "is himself already symbolically identified with the gaze for which he is playing his role" (*Sublime Object* 106). Karl, as a Kafkaesque hero, seems to be fundamentally different. In spite of all his hardships, America does not seem to be more eager to impose any specific role on him than to dumbfound him by its very heterogeneity and open choices – that is to say, out of which he can really choose none. K suffers under the ultimate dictatorship: a dictatorship of total authority which seems to hold him absolutely still and uncomprehending as to what exactly is required of him. Karl, to his astonishment, suffers in what seems to be a total democracy.

The concluding chapter entitled by Max Brod as "Das Naturtheater von Oklahoma" ("The Nature Theatre of Oklahoma"), arguably contains the lightest and most optimistic prose ever written by Kafka. The Theatre, in which Karl finds a new job and a new life, supposedly stands for a promising America. There are writers, however, who interpret Kafka's symbolic America in its totality as a threat of castration and total disappearance for the European subject. That is to say that the only hope of reconciliation in Kafka's last chapter is still conditioned by castration. In his essay "The States and the Statue: Kafka on America", Jeremy Tambling seems to express this view, although from a strictly European cultural sense that seems to be more concerned about America's historical competition with Europe rather than the problems that symbolic America poses as a master signifier in language. He discusses how Kafka's Statue of Liberty is at one and the same time a feminine figure of castration where "liberty and justice meet contradictorily in one goddesslike single figure who asserts the impossibility of both or of either", and a sign which points to the "interpretation of signs – which includes interpreting the Statue of Liberty – as European paranoia" (187–94).

Although this double reading of the Statue of Liberty does not seem to reflect a conflict emerging from two different points of view that can be reconciled in any way – for the two readings are necessarily contradictory – the two readings need each other in order to make sense to themselves. In other words, although adopting one of the two is nothing but the very fallacy censured by the other, looking at the issue from the point of view of "European paranoia" does not seem to effectively cancel out reading America as a castrating power rather than dialectically enhance the existence of the discourse of the castrating power of America.

Commenting on the last chapter, Tambling argues that "plural narratives and the two possible fates of Karl Rossman imply several Americas [...] that which, under the pressure to compete with Europe, has tried to play out a dream of everything being better and nothing impossible, while being at the same time subtly coercive" and "the America whose difference from Europe questions it with the possibility of a minor literature". It is the first America that concerns us in the present context. Tambling continues:

> The first America creates a utopia that seems to promise reconciliation, yet always, in its bourgeois construction, it has exclusionary principles behind it, implied in the Statue of Liberty's sword and glanced at in the implications behind Rossman's irrevocable change of name to "Negro". (197)

So, America as utopia, in this particular reading, is still conditioned by a castrating law. I would argue though that even the America invented by Kafka still lives by principles of inclusion, however problematic they may be, rather than exclusionary ones. More precisely, it is not that Karl is excluded from what constitutes an "American community", but that the sense of solitude in a festive world is what defines everyone in that community.

It seems, however, that it is with an uncompromising view which sees only positivity in America's historical welcoming of all European immigrants as compared to Europe's intimidation of its own religious communities that Klaus Mann wrote his preface to *Amerika*. As a German who was stripped of German citizenship by the Nazi regime because of his Jewish origin as well as his homosexuality – thus becoming a Czechoslovak citizen in the mid-1930s, then an American citizen in the early 1940s – Mann's own biography seems to have influenced his preface greatly. So, Karl "arrives in New York, welcomed by 'the free breezes' of America and a Statue of Liberty furnished most surprisingly with an upraised sword" (viii). As if this 'most surprising' image does not quite fit in what Mann interprets as Kafka's most optimistic literary work. Quoting Kafka himself, Mann writes:

> With an enigmatic smile he declared that his young hero, Karl Rossman, might well find again, "in this almost boundless theatre", his profession, his security and freedom, and perhaps even his homeland and parents – "as by a celestial spell". (ix)

One could imagine Kafka with this "enigmatic smile" on his face and wonder what it really meant. Did it only mean that Kafka was optimistic about Karl's future in America or was there something deeper than that behind his smile? Could Kafka's smile also have signified Karl's final resignation to the castrating power of America or a total identification with it? Is it not telling that Kafka "declared" that Karl might find profession, security, freedom, homeland and parents, but not particularly love? Why is not a beautiful wife or a sexual partner, for example, one amongst the good promises that await Karl in the future? Kafka's words, backed by an "enigmatic smile", promise Karl mainly economic stability, yet this seems to be conditioned by the cruelest of all deprivations. The economy of desire is to be sacrificed for the economic.

Kafka's enigmatic smile in such a view would not be one of simple optimism, and his look upon his hero would not be that of tenderness. It is true that he relieved Karl from his suffering, but only by pushing him over, suddenly, into an abyss in which the erotic becomes history. Karl's whole experience in the Theatre of Oklahoma seems to be written in order to be interpreted as a dream. At the end of chapter seven, he falls asleep in Brunelda's house. At the beginning of chapter eight we see him in a different world in which everything seems to be hallucinated. The most interesting moment in that dream is when the female appears. Fanny, an old friend of Karl's, stands on a high pedestal, dressed as an angel in a white robe with great wings on her shoulders. The pedestal and the ladder leading up to it are concealed by the long draperies of the robe she is wearing so that she appears to be unnaturally tall. In what seems to be a representation of sexual intercourse, Kafka describes how Fanny "schlug die Tücher auseinander" (*Amerika: Roman* 226) ("parted her draperies") (*Amerika* 256) for Karl to come up the ladder. After a brief chat, Karl climbs down the ladder and arranges the robe over the ladder again as it had been before. Fanny nods her thanks for his gesture. Even if the language, the gestures, and the movements all suggest sexual activity, the image of the female as a winged angel and a sublime being, whose lower part is depicted as an instrumental apparatus, creates an atmosphere that is depressingly asexual, removing any erotic potency from this supposedly sexual dream.

According to Max Brod, "Ganz unerwarteterweise unterbrach Kafka plötzlich die Arbeit an dem Roman. Er blieb unvollendet" (*Amerika: Roman* 260) ("Kafka broke off his work on this novel with unexpected suddenness. It remained unfinished") (*Amerika* 277). If the last chapter was actually written as a dream, we are not given the privilege to know how Karl felt after waking up. It is not uncommon that what is experienced as a happy dream can actually seem to be a nightmare when pondered in waking life. The same lines quoting Kafka's excitement about his last chapter of *Amerika* are written by Max Brod in his afterword to the novel. With what appear to be slight differences, Brod writes:

> "Mit rätselhaften Worten deutete Kafka lächelnd an, daß sein junger Held in diesem "fast grenzenlosen" Theater Beruf, Freiheit, Rückhalt, ja sogar die Heimat und die Eltern wie durch paradiesischen Zauber wiederfinden werde". (*Amerika: Roman* 260)

> (In enigmatic language Kafka used to hint smilingly, that within this "almost limitless" theatre his young hero was going to find again a profession, a stand-by, his freedom, even his old home and his parents, as if by some celestial witchery). (*Amerika* 277)

The enigma in Max Brod's account was not in the smile, it was in Kafka's language itself. This difference which appears to be a secondary issue in fact changes the whole story. It is as if Karl's unconscious linguistic puzzle declared itself on his writer's tongue. Whereas Klaus Mann's text talks about a writer who looks upon his hero from an external point, Max Brod's account draws the image of a writer who identifies himself *completely* with his fictional character.

Concerning the chapter entitled "Das Naturtheater von Oklahoma", Max Brod reports that it was "ein Kapitel, dessen Einleitung Kafka besonders liebte und herzergreifend schön vorlas" (*Amerika: Roman* 260) ("[a chapter that] particularly delighted Kafka, so that he used to read it aloud with great effect") (*Amerika* 277). Kafka and Karl obviously had the same dream. Yet, he "broke off his work on this novel with unexpected suddenness". Why would Kafka break off his work suddenly and unexpectedly on a novel which made him "cheerful and confident"? (Mann, vii). Why would he discontinue writing that particular chapter of which he was "especially fond"? (ix). Perhaps Karl, or Kafka, realized that as the dream progressed towards its end, the dreamer approached, with accelerating speed, an encounter with the real of his desire manifested in his dream before he wakes up – terrified. For the dream, to quote Lacan, is "essentially [...] an act of homage to the missed reality – the reality that can no longer produce itself except by repeating itself endlessly, in some never attained awakening" (*Four Fundamental Concepts* 58). To rephrase Lacan, the dream is a compensation for that which cannot be articulated or symbolized in waking life thanks to the metonymic structure of desire. It is only in a dream that the subject comes face to face with the real of his desire. On the dream of the ill-fated father who recounted to Freud seeing his burning child in his dream, Lacan says: "Desire manifests itself in the dream by the loss expressed in an image of the most cruel point of the object. It is only in the dream that this truly unique encounter can occur" (59).

And it is precisely from this point that Lacan argues that it was not the excess of the external element – the smoke coming out of his son's bedroom which was actually on fire – which awakened the father, it is rather the horridness of the fact that his dream has searched out the real of his own desire, which he can never articulate to himself in waking life, and put it right in front of his eyes. So, Kafka dreamt of going to America and, as Karl, he did go to his own version of it in his dream. Yet at some point his dream seems to have turned into a nightmare. What started with a powerful and at the same time playful image in "Der Heizer" ("The Stoker") about the castrating power of America – the Statue of Liberty equipped with an upraised sword – ended with what could be felt or even experienced as real castration in Kafka's unusually penetrating mind: total disappearance and loss of identity and cultural or even sexual death in "Das Naturtheater von Oklahoma". Kafka stopped writing his "Amerikanischen Roman" (Brod, *Amerika: Roman* 260), as he used to call his *Der Verschollene*. He "broke off his work on this novel with unexpected suddenness". Even though in his letter of November 11, 1912 Kafka wrote to his fiancée Felice Bauer that *Der Verschollene* is a "Geschichte, die allerdings ins Endlose angelegt ist" (*Briefe an Felice* 86) ("[story written] in such a manner that it will never be completed" (*Letters to Felice* 35), somehow, Max Brod's line does not sound as if the sudden cessation of writing happened out of a desire to stop working on the novel. It seems that Kafka could not go on dreaming. The imago that he himself created finally got to him.

On the chapter entitled "Ein Asyl" ("A Refuge"), where Karl suffers from his servitude and humiliation in Brunelda's house, Mann writes:

> The grand and appalling chapter [...] represents the burlesque and moving climax of the adventurous story. But as though the author found it intolerable to continue this macabre report, he suddenly breaks off his narrative, and when Karl re-appears – months, perhaps years later – he is looking for a new job, and finds one in *The Great Nature Theatre of Oklahoma.* (ix)

But macabre tales are not exactly alien to Kafka. The Kafka of "Ein Asyl" is the writer as he is widely known and read. It is the Kafka of "Das Naturtheater von Oklahoma" who does not seem to be himself. If *Der Verschollene* is a dream of going to America, "Das Naturtheater von Oklahoma" is a dream within a dream. It sounds particularly uncharacteristic of Kafka to break off his narrative in Brunelda's house because he "found it intolerable". It is, in fact, the seemingly democratic and festive world of the Theatre of Oklahoma, built at the expense of total castration that *even Kafka* found intolerable. He was completely destabilized by the America he invented without ever leaving Prague.

"Mein Roman geht ja wenn auch langsam vorwärts", wrote Kafka once to Felice about *Der Verschollene,* "nur *ist sein Gesicht dem meinen schrecklich gleich*" (emphasis mine) (*Briefe an Felice* 179) ("My novel is progressing, though slowly ... the only thing is that *it looks terrifyingly like me*") (emphasis mine) (*Letters to Felice* 103). Out of Kafka's works, it is *Amerika*, the one text written about a place which he never really experienced, that looked like him – *terrifyingly*. It is as if in his other works, Kafka was writing texts from which he could more or less detach himself as a creative writer exercising full mastery over his narratives. In the case of writing *Amerika*, however, the text he invented seemed to look back at him with the terrifying threat of fulfilling the real of his desire.

Perhaps, some readers will conclude that America is only a signifier for Kafka or that Kafka's problems remain his and, if they speak to us, as they do, there are valid reasons for that. I am in complete agreement with these statements. However, to say with complete assurance that the master signifier America is holds no power over writers on America, or the writer and the readers of the present book, simply cannot be true. In other words, it is not only that the castrating power of America is fictitious; it is also that writers on America somehow do not seem to be able to escape its fictitious castrating power. Is America's power thus only for show? Needless to say that such a notion would be as much erroneous as stating callously that America "is actually a castrating power".

Perceptions of America may differ, yet there is always a discourse of irresolution on how America is to be represented. America is beautiful, but also imperialistic. America is a source of hope, but also of fear. America is an attraction, but also a danger. On the surface of it, it is not difficult to see how this nicely fits in the structure of the castrating figure in psychoanalysis. The figure of castration is a model to be admired, and at the same time an adversary. The father is "the castrating father, on the one hand, and the father as origin of the superego, on the other" (Lacan, *Ethics of Psychoanalysis* 307). On castration as such, Lacan says that "it conditions the narcissistic fear. To accept castration the subject must pay as elevated a price as this reworking of the whole of reality" (*Psychoses* 312). Does not going to America also require a reworking of the whole of reality? The law of castration in this sense is that it conditions access to a certain symbolic world where the immigrant never attains the status of being consistent with his own place in it.

But America, as previously elaborated, seems to be even more complicated than that. If there is anything we can conclude from the texts written on America, including the present text, it is that America belongs more to the imagination than to reality. A confession by Jean-Philippe Mathy indicates that the "rhetoric of America" is something that survives even beyond experiencing the country itself. In his essay "The Rhetoric of 'America'", Mathy writes:

> As a French man living in the United States, I could not deny that my study reflects a personal experience of uprooting and acculturation. Still, the question of the specificity, of the "exceptionalism" of American society and culture started to puzzle and interest me long before I decided to live in this country. Once I did emigrate, however, I experienced what many travelers, immigrants, and exiles have gone through.

One might expect that what follows will refer to how the writer had preconceived ideas about America which changed later on after living there for a long time. One might expect that the "uprooting and acculturation" eventually resulted in assimilation. Yet, Mathy continues:

> As I was revising the long held views and familiar clichés I had inherited from my French upbringing, American culture, paradoxically, became more foreign to me, although I was growing accustomed to it and was even getting better at living in the midst of it. (14)

Is there a stronger testimony than this one that the whole world, including America itself, imagines America all the time? What is perceived as the castrating power of America does not belong to it as a country or even as a political and economic superpower. It has nothing to do with what is commonly referred to as America's ahistoricism or even with what Baudrillard calls "power of unculture" (*America* 78). The fiction of the castrating power of America seems to be generated and sustained by its multifarious imagos which are invented and reinvented in innumerable imaginations, including the imaginations of its founding fathers themselves, who were occupied by the *idea* of a country more than the country itself as a reality. As Peter Conrad puts it, "they saw the new kind of state they were creating not as a fact but as a formula, not a natural growth of history but the actualization of an idea" (3).

The fact that this idea belongs to language, and in America's case it is perceived as a particularly ideological, pragmatic, and chillingly rational language, gives the sense of a melancholic castrating mandate that conditions inscription into America's registers. Yet, in spite of the powerful fiction of America's castrating power, symbolic America remains a certain problem, a certain unrealized being, or a certain forbidden knowledge. It persists. It remains even for the totally American (immigrant). Once it occupies the mind, which is something that does not even require going to America at all, the mind never really regains its freedom from it, even after becoming totally "American".

Chapter 4
Adorno's Fascist America

In the preface to the Italian edition of the *Dialectic of Enlightenment*, written in 1962, twenty years after Adorno and Horkheimer began writing the German text of the *Dialectic* itself as a fragment, the following statement appears: "In keeping with its theme, our book demonstrates tendencies which turn cultural progress into its opposite. We attempted to do this on the basis of social phenomena of the 1930s and 1940s in America" (xiii). If one thus poses the question "why does America continue to exert such a fascination on the world?" one of the most valid answers may be this: Because it is the country said to have provided the social phenomena upon which the most melancholic intellectual work of cultural theory based itself.

Even though it was the fascist movement in Europe which provided Adorno's work with a concrete origin, European fascist rule does not seem to be his focal point of analysis. The corpus of Adorno's work in its totality seems to suggest that social domination is more at home in the capitalist apparatus itself on top of which America dwells. In *Minima Moralia* he writes: "Fascism is itself less 'ideological', in so far as it openly proclaims the principle of domination that is elsewhere concealed" (108). That is to say that fascism, in its historical German and Italian materialization, was considered by Adorno less ideologically coercive – hence less dangerous in the long run – to human freedom than the potential of social domination that he saw lying in America's commodified culture, its films, its music, radio serials, and even its astrology columns.

Adorno's construction of an American imago, however, is not conditioned by any American phenomena from the present work's perspective. Adorno's America seems to have a much deeper background that has to do with his relationship to Walter Benjamin – his life, his thoughts, and his suicide. Specifically, Adorno's American imago comes out of identification with Benjamin's poignant idea of conditioning the experience of the present with the "dialectical image" where "image", in Benjamin's words, "is dialectics at a standstill" or "that wherein what has been comes together in a flash with the now to form a constellation" (*Arcades Project* 462). This constellation is identical with the "monad", the "historical object" (475), or the indivisible historical traumatic event on which Benjamin bases his idea of materialist historiography. To refigure this Benjaminian idea of conditioning the present with the dialectical image in a Lacanian way, I am persuaded to call it "constructing the present out of contemplating the psychotic moment of history", where the psychotic moment of history stands, with no doubt, for the "real" of history.

In what follows, I will look first at the idea of reassessing Adorno's relationship to America in light of the changing Adorno scholarship – a point that I will have to return to at the end of this chapter. This, and discussing a number of insights by Adorno on enlightenment, fascism, cinema, jazz, individualism, mass culture, anti-Semitism, and the trace of America in all of these, will serve as an introduction to analyzing the Benjaminian influence on Adorno's thought, in particular, his invention of an American imago out of contemplating the psychotic moment of history.

With the increasing interest in the writings of Adorno over the past two decades, it became important to reassess Adorno's relationship to America. The image of the unapproachable, pessimistic elitist who detached himself from American society even while living in the midst of it has been effectively altered. A seminal essay which helped to change the face of Adorno scholarship is Martin Jay's "Adorno in America" which appeared in *New German Critique* in the winter of 1984. In it, Jay seeks to take Adorno's relationship to America beyond the "anecdotes" of the "sensitive European mandarin" who is "shocked and bewildered by the commercialism, vulgarity, and theoretical backwardness of his temporary home". He argues that these anecdotal views seem to turn Adorno into "an elitist mandarin merely pretending to be a Marxist or an aesthetic modernist with only residual nostalgia for the world he left behind" (158–61). Jay's counter argument is that just as the European experience affected Adorno's views about America, his American experience affected his views about Europe, especially in the realm of democratic politics. In conclusion he states:

> As an American, [Adorno] was obviously a displaced European, while as a European, he was deeply affected by his years in America. As a result he was able to remain in permanent exile from both contexts, and still does after his death. (181–2)

There is no doubt about the strengths of Jay's argument insofar as it remains within the discourse that Adorno himself established on the idea of exile of the intellectual émigré. This is used by many writers on exile, for example, Edward Said, who writes about it extensively in "Between Worlds", "Reflections on Exile", and in his book *Out of Place* as the controversial "form of freedom" (*Out of Place* 295) for the critic who is always in some form or another of exile. In the case of Adorno himself, however, it does not seem to go without problems. It is not the point of the present book to return to an earlier estimation of Adorno's relation to America in particular as entirely hostile and unforgiving. Such a view simply cannot be true, just as the exaggerations of Adorno's disposition in America must be downright laughable. Some of these exaggerations are characterized by Detlev Claussen in his essay "Intellectual Transfer: Theodor W. Adorno's American Experience", where he writes:

> In Europe, anti-Americanism has long distorted accounts of Adorno's view of America. On the American side, the clichéd image of Adorno as an intellectual whose myopias supposedly made him less than normal dovetails with a highly distorting anti-intellectualism. Thus Adorno, we are told, had no clue about

sports, blindly hated jazz, and never enjoyed himself at the movies, in front of the television, or anywhere else. (6)

The problem, however, seems to be that this new historical analysis of Adorno's American experience presumes at its very point of premise that America, in Adorno's mind, names something that is clearly distinguishable from Europe. It does not consider the possibility that Adorno's *creation* of an America that is as authoritarian as fascist Europe can, in effect, confuse the two. The Adornian "trope of chiasmus" (Jay, "Adorno in America" 181) which Jay makes good use of in order to describe Adorno's complex relationship to both America and Europe is not just about the impossibility of dwelling for the intellectual émigré. It is also about Adorno's unfaltering stand by his negative dialectics, which problematizes the very core of humanity's enlightened reason epitomized, no doubt, by America.

Looking closely enough at the idea of mythical regression at the very heart of progress makes Jay's attempt to determine whether it is America's culture industry or Europe's fascist experience that is the "original source of the damage" behind Adorno's subtitle to *Minima Moralia* (Reflections from Damaged Life) quite fruitless. The issue does not even seem to be adequately articulated by what Jay describes as Adorno's "pessimism about the universality and irreversibility" (161) of the crisis of European culture during the Nazi era. In fact, if Adorno's negative dialectics and his critique of enlightenment are taken as the major markers of his thought – and they certainly are – it may be more appropriate to suggest that for him Europe's striving to follow America's steps of modern progress could have created the Nazi era in the first place.

The philosophical argument that "thought is being turned inescapably into a commodity and language into celebration of the commodity" (Horkheimer and Adorno xiv), which appears in the preface of the 1944 and 1947 editions of the *Dialectic*, seems to be historically connected to America's coming out of the Second World War as the triumphant superpower with a lot of ideological and cultural commodities to sell to the world for many years to come. Thus, conditions of late capitalism seem to be formulated in and by America more than anywhere else in the world. It can be argued therefore that the human regression that the *Dialectic* sees as inherent in the concept of enlightenment, and which inevitably makes enlightenment self-destructive is meant to allude more to "thought in its headlong rush into pragmatism" (xvi) – pragmatism being mostly an American tradition – than to the barbaric regression into myth that marked the Nazi era in Europe. To Adorno, the belief in God seems to play its role as one among the factors which give the Enlightenment its regressive character. In "The Concept of Enlightenment", the *Dialectic* states:

> In their mastery of nature, the creative God and the ordering mind are alike.
> Man's likeness to God consists in sovereignty over existence, in the lordly gaze,
> in the command. Myth becomes enlightenment and nature mere objectivity.
> Human beings purchase the increase in their power with estrangement from that

over which it is exerted. Enlightenment stands in the same relationship to things as the dictator to human beings. (Horkheimer and Adorno 6)

By likening enlightenment, which is supposed to be a human quest to come out of myth, to dictatorship and authority – concepts inseparable from the man-made images of God – the *Dialectic* seems to be melting a barrier between religiosity and the spirit of modernism, a process that can be argued to have been possible only within the tradition of American pragmatism in modern times. The argument that enlightenment as authority seems to be subtly linked to America's ideological mixture of progress, capitalism, religion and the market, signifies a love for authority and mastery – a theme that is fully developed in *The Authoritarian Personality*, in which Adorno draws what seems to be a highly questionable fascist picture of the American psyche.

It is true, however, that the *Dialectic*'s distrust of "faith" and its degeneration into "bad conscience" (14), as well as its perceptive reference to a "secret alliance" (32) between progress and culture in order to obliterate truth, seems to describe a recent state of affairs in the world. A secret alliance often takes place between two entities that appear to be antagonistic while secretively aware of a common base that shapes their actions. The recent "war on terror" seems to be a perfect example. It was a war launched by the American president on underground terrorist organizations, mainly "al-Qaeda", headed by Osama Bin Laden. On the surface of it, it seems that the conflict was one between one who claims to stand for the fundamentalist backlash of the marginalized of today's world and one who claims to stand for freedom, progress and, if need be, American "democratization" of the world.

What is striking, however, is the set of similarities between those two "enemies". Both are well known capitalist figures. Both are oil-rich. Both believe in the good-versus-evil idea. Both divide the world arbitrarily into two camps, the believers and the infidels, or, those who are "with us" and those who are "against us". The war on terror itself seems to have had the effect of promoting Islamist radicalism rather than eliminating it. In that sense, there seems to be a kind of undeclared or even unconscious alliance between enemies to repress the role of capital in all this and cover everything by bragging about ideology.

So, at one level, Adorno saw the Nazi movement as a nightmare where political radicalism rides on capitalist means and the mythical violence and criminality of human nature return after being repressed, coupled with enlightened modernity. At another level, his argument concerns itself not with the regressive moment of European fascism, but with the birth of a cruel world that follows it: The American "administrated world" in which "there is no longer dignity in poverty" and "not even any longer the possibility of modestly surviving the winter for a person who loses his position" (*Culture Industry* 119), in an era where reason will completely regress to being a mere instrument of power. This is the world that backgrounds all of Adorno's major works, which he actually wrote while being in America including *Dialectic of Enlightenment*, *The Culture Industry*, *The Stars Down to Earth*, and *Minima Moralia*. It is a world in which human agency is completely cancelled out by a universal system of domination in which "power confronts the individual as the universal, as the reason which informs reality" (*Dialectic of Enlightenment* 16). The only identity allowed to anyone living in the "administrated world" is the one given in order to be functional in the capitalist apparatus.

To Adorno, the historical European era of the infatuation by authoritarian charismatic leaders and the identification with the authoritarian state served as an introduction to something more complicated and even far less human: A world in which "freedom is manifested only ideologically, as talk about freedom, in stereotyped declamations, not in humanly commensurable actions" (*Minima Moralia* 145). And it is precisely because the illusion of freedom is included in the very fabric of the "administrated world", that "The world wants to be deceived" (*Culture Industry* 103) by the culture industry. If America is not explicitly shown to be the producer of the culture industry, the implied connection is always there. About 40 years later, Baudrillard expresses the same idea when he writes that American culture "fascinates those very people who suffer most at its hands, and it does so through the deep, insane conviction that it has made all their dreams come true" (*America* 77).

By looking at works like *Dialectic of Enlightenment*, *The Culture Industry*, *The Authoritarian Personality*, *Minima Moralia*, *The Stars Down to Earth* and *Prisms*, it can be argued that what Adorno sees as social mutational vicissitudes of mass culture may be related one way or another to America. So, it is in America, the inventor of motion pictures, that "the elimination of the distinction between image and reality has already advanced to the point of a collective sickness" (*Culture Industry* 64). In other words, the real major achievement of American cinematic production is producing America itself. Americans carry "faces of which one no longer knows whether the film has alienated them from reality or reality has alienated them from the film, as they wrench open a great formless mouth with shining teeth in a voracious smile" (47).

It cannot be a coincidence that Baudrillard writes about the same American "toothpaste effect" (34) in his book *America*. Between the 1940s and the 1980s the Marxist approach to America changed considerably, but how it sees the American smile seems to be a fixed idea. To Adorno, cinema itself is one of the main tools by which the capitalist apparatus imposes the view that identities are mere social functions and nothing more. As for its effect on its audience, the "worst bourgeois sadism" (*Complete Correspondence* 130) actually replaces what might be misrecognized as revolutionary in their laughter.

It is well known that Adorno's attack on jazz goes beyond his attack on cinema. As a musicologist, he was obviously more sensitive to music than to the visual. If cinema converts subjects into what seem to be heterogeneous social functions, jazz to Adorno does nothing less than a castrating homogenization. In his essay "Perennial Fashion – Jazz" he writes:

> The aim of Jazz is the mechanical reproduction of a regressive moment, a castration symbolism. "Give up your masculinity, let yourself be castrated", the eunuchlike sound of the jazz band both mocks and proclaims, "and you will be

> rewarded, accepted into a fraternity which shares the mystery of impotence with
> you, a mystery revealed at the moment of the initiation rite". (*Prisms* 125)

If one speculates that cinema to Adorno was thought of as a social activity by
which society itself is reproduced and identities are manufactured, jazz was seen
by him as an omnipresent threat implying a direct political anti-revolutionary
message:

> [It] collaborates in the "technological veil" through its rigorously repetitive
> though objectless cultic ritual, and fosters the illusion that the twentieth century
> is Ancient Egypt, full of slaves and endless dynasties [...] Timelessness is
> projected on technology by a world-order which knows that to change would
> be to collapse. (129)

It can be argued thus that when Adorno wrote "On the Fetish Character in Music
and the Regression of Listening", it was with a belief that America is the main
producer of regressive music and regressive listeners, a culture that eventually
infected Europe and the rest of the world. Regression in Adornian thought is
regression to myth, something which paradoxically marks enlightened progressive
bourgeois society. There seems to be, then, common ground between Adorno's
analysis of jazz and his earlier analysis of Wagner's music. This common ground
is the idea of regression to myth itself which Adorno sees as manifesting itself in
Wagner's music dramas where "law is unmasked as the equivalent of lawlessness"
(*In Search of Wagner* 106).

To Adorno, Wagner adopts this idea "not just as subject-matter, but in its
innermost aesthetic consequences [...] in his eyes all musical being is Being-for-
another, it is "socialized" in the process of composition itself" (107). Wagner's
music, to Adorno, "establishes the primacy of exchange over the organization and
internal progression of the work of art: it becomes the incarnation of the processes
of exchange in society as a whole" (108). Although Wagner as an individual is seen
by Adorno as a "profane person" who "offended against myth", his irreverence,
though it may be seen by many as a form of expression of individuality through
music, destroys the category of the individual by committing itself to the principle
of exchange:

> [Wagner's] regressive aesthetic practice is not a matter of individual choice
> or psychological accident. He belongs to the first generation to realize that in
> a world that has been socialized through and through it is not possible for an
> individual to alter something that is determined over the heads of men. (108)

Wagner's music then, like jazz, represents social homogenization in its worst
form: homogenization which gives the illusion of individuality and individual
choices. To Adorno, the supremacy of such social homogenization is perceived
by the individual as a "metaphysical mystery" of which force he inevitably sides

with. This is how Wagner, in Adorno's mind, "has devised the ritual of permanent catastrophe. His unbridled individualism utters the death sentence on the individual and its order" (108).

Consequentially, in view of his theory on cinema and jazz as means of social coercion, American individualism, in Adorno's mind, is molded into one of its most extraordinary representations. If Dickens's hero "Martin Chuzzlewit", according to Conrad, thinks that the Americans' "common worship of individualism has ended by effacing their individuality" (P. Conrad 57), Adorno thinks that it is their common masochistic submission to commercial necessities unreservedly manipulating their very identities that erases their individuality and leads to a cultural "pretence of individualism which necessarily increases in proportion to the liquidation of the individual" (*Culture Industry* 40).

That is why "Simple Simon" is seen by Adorno as the best instance of American individualism as well as the complete fully assimilated American citizen. When Adorno writes about the immigrant tout court, there can be no doubt that the meant personality is what mainly constitutes the immigrant society America has always been. "Simple Simon" is not just one of the "individualities imported into America, and divested of individuality in the process" (*Minima Moralia* 135). To Adorno, he is also the perfect bearer of American ideology itself; the true representation of what is taken to be its well-meaning altruism as well as its politics of sentimentality. "Simple Simon" is thus supposed to be the manifest image of American innocence, with all the intrinsic problems that notion raises. At the same time, he is also that masochistic subject upon which American ideology exercises its full power. He is a manipulator and a victim at once.

Between November 1932 and August 1933, five years before his departure to America, Adorno wrote the libretto "Der Schatz des Indianer-Joe" (The Treasure of Indian Joe) as an operatic comment on Mark Twain's *Tom Sawyer*. Commenting on the libretto in his letter to Walter Benjamin, dated 4 March 1934, he wrote:

> About "Tom" [...] The hearty language is not the heartiness of real children, so much as that encountered in the literature written for children [...] I am using the childlike imagery to present some extremely serious things: in this connection I am far more concerned with presenting this image of childhood than I am with invoking childhood as such. (*Complete Correspondence* 25–6)

This particular "image of childhood" is drawn from a point from which Adorno obviously saw a peculiarity to American childhood taken from Mark Twain's fictional account of it. Adorno could sense that behind the childish innocence of Twain's boy hero, there is a kind of chilling pragmatism that has nothing to do with naivety or childish pride. More than a decade later, in America, he wrote in *Minima Moralia*: "If across the Atlantic the ideology was pride, here it is delivering the goods. This applies also to the products of the objective spirit" (196). Thus, Adorno's America is highly selective in its European heritage. Whatever is taken from Europe has nothing to do with things like identity, roots, history, or culture.

What is taken from Europe is taken only in so far as it can serve as a platform for the taking off of marketable products. Everything is thoroughly searched for the particular capacity of being commodified and put on sale.

In this regard, in one of his most perceptive moments, Adorno seems to touch upon Lacan's *objet petit a*. A familiar or a successful product has a "poetic mystery" in which it is "more than itself" (*Culture Industry* 63). It is not taken for what it is but for that which it most certainly can never be: the unattainable compensation for the fundamental lack forming the economy of the subject's metonymic desire. Moreover, the "poetic mystery" of the particular reflects the mystification of the general. The secret of a particular successful product is itself the secret of American cinema, jazz, radio serials, and mass culture in its totality, which has this self awareness which enables it to look at itself in the mirror and see that it is "always the fairest in all the land" (67). The point from which Adorno sees the impossibility of having freedom and democracy coupled with bourgeois capitalism is the point from which Snow White and the ugly queen can be seen as one and the same character, or, more precisely, the point from which the queen is seen as the only real character, dreaming up Snow White who does not really exist. It is notable that Adorno's sense that the particular is marked with the enormity of the general seems to extend to the American landscape as well. The only difference, however, is that here this is seen by him as a beauty: "Beauty of the American landscape: that even the smallest of its segments is inscribed, as its expression, with the immensity of the whole country" (*Minima Moralia* 49).

Adorno's version of America reaches its ultimate negative imago in *The Authoritarian Personality*. Although this is a study "whose uneasy mixture of empirical methods and Critical Theory was very atypical of his work as a whole" ("Adorno in America" 158) as Martin Jay correctly states, the work without doubt carries some of Adorno's most insightful ideas. One of these is his analysis of the liberal approach in politics, which "hides the conviction that there is no objective truth in politics, that every country, as every individual, may behave as it likes and that the only thing that counts is success". Adorno believes that "it is precisely this pragmatization of politics which ultimately defines fascist philosophy" (726). So, fascist philosophy is that of a man or a woman who measures everything happening in the present with a pragmatic eye on what he or she counts as a successful final material gain in the future, and who remains totally apathetic to everything else that falls outside the frame of this economy, even if this is to be against his or her own desire.

To Adorno, this "pragmatization of politics" goes perfectly with the use of religion in the authoritarian psyche as a "practical aid in the mental hygiene of the individual", or as "something 'to hold on to'". In such a case, religion seems to have nothing to do with the belief in God, but with what Adorno calls the "abstract belief in power" (734–8). It is revealing to see how this is manifested in the contemporary popular song "When You Believe" by Mariah Carey, which is used in the sound track of Disney's production *The Prince of Egypt*. It is a song which accompanies the great exodus of the Jews out of Egypt and which is supposed to be about the belief in the one God of the people of Israel. Yet somehow the word "God" is nowhere to be found in it. In fact the opening line goes: "Many nights we've prayed with no proof anyone could hear", which means that the prayers are not supported by the belief in an existent god, but by the psychological dependence on the hope that someone or something might one day serve as a proof for filling in this gap. Yet, even when the proof (or the prophet) comes, the main choral line carrying the core message of the song comes along with it with the empty idea of believing as such, without mentioning what it is exactly that one is supposed to believe in: "There can be miracles when you believe". What you believe in is shrewdly left open, partly because it does not sound particularly trendy to insert the word "God" in a modern popular song, but more significantly because what is unconsciously implied here is that what you believe in is ultimately what gives you power, be it God, money, America or – why not? – a fascist dictator.

There is no doubt, however, that *The Authoritarian Personality*'s chief concern is to record the unconscious and the ways people rationalize the irrational far more than it measures American pragmatism. Yet, this is precisely what makes Adorno's work in *The Authoritarian Personality* highly problematic. He seems to take a psychoanalytic approach which arguably applies only too generally to the human psyche and applies it narrowly to what he considers to be a certain type of people – all of them in the study are apparently Americans. In his analysis of the personality which is seen as authoritarian, Adorno takes a detour via the Oedipus complex and the incest taboo in order to reach a conclusion which seems to say nothing more than that the fascist, or the "high scorer" on the "'f' scale" is a sadomasochist. The taboo which controls love for the mother results in the adversarial love-hate relationship with the castrating father. To Adorno, in the psychodynamic formation of the authoritarian personality, part of the aggressiveness against the father "is absorbed and turned into masochism, while another part is left over as sadism, which seeks an outlet in those with whom the subject does not identify himself: ultimately the out-group" (759).

It can be argued, however, that this is neither an abnormality nor does it seem to be adequate as a basis for either fascism or racism. This is not just to suggest that the "F" scale and the whole empirical method which is used to establish a psychoanalytic theory of fascism are obviously unreliable means by which to assess authoritarian tendencies. The allusion is rather to point to what seems to be Adorno's major blind spot in the study, which is the fact that he arbitrarily ties fascism with ethnocentrism. While fascism for him is partly based on the "pragmatization of politics", ethnocentrism is blown out of proportion as an abnormal psychological deviation that necessarily leads to the fascist authoritarian personality. In fact, there do not seem to be adequate reasons, psychoanalytic or else, to suggest that ethnocentric non- identification with the other necessarily leads to fascism or any authoritarian tendencies at all. Not to mention that from a Lacanian perspective, if the subject is constituted by language, he is all the more alienated from his very self before being alienated from the other. Ethnocentrism, unlike fascism, is something that bases itself within the human psyche at a very early stage. This seems to be one of the things that Lacan hints at when he talks about the "discourse in the universal movement in which [the subject's] place is already inscribed at birth, if only by virtue of his proper name" (*Écrits: A Selection* 163).

In their "Foreword to Studies in Prejudice", the editors of the massive project to which *The Authoritarian Personality* belongs, Max Horkheimer and Samuel Flowerman, write:

> Our aim is not merely to describe prejudice but to explain it in order to help in its eradication. That is the challenge we would meet. Eradication means re-education, scientifically planned on the basis of understanding scientifically arrived at. (vii)

It is needless to point out that it seems particularly odd for a thinker like Adorno, who wrote the *Dialectic of Enlightenment* in collaboration with Horkheimer himself and who intellectually parted ways with the latter due to his own uncompromising stand with regard to the negative dialectics which he saw as inherent in the concept of enlightenment and the regression at the very core of its progressive process, to trust scientific planning and understanding which is "scientifically arrived at". In the preface to the *Dialectic*, Adorno and Horkheimer state that "in the present collapse of bourgeois civilization not only the operations but the purpose of science have become dubious" (xiv). What is regarded as highly susceptible in the *Dialectic of Enlightenment* seems to be over-trusted in *Studies in Prejudice*.

In fact, it can be argued that the idea of Adorno himself, in his essay "Research Project on Anti-Semitism: Idea of the Project", to empirically research anti-Semitic tendencies in different states in America by showing certain films and observing the reactions of the audience to them in order to study the "distribution of anti-Semitism in the United States" (*Stars Down to Earth* 215), inadvertently implies that Adorno is almost imposing an anti-Semitic image on the American psyche in general. It is only long after he returned from his American exile and got resettled in his home country that he could write something like this:

> The author could wish for nothing better than that the English version of *Prisms* might express something of the gratitude that he cherishes for England and for the United States – the two countries which enabled him to survive the era of persecution and to which he has ever since felt himself deeply bound, (*Prisms* 8)

In order to get to the core of Adorno's America and the psychodynamic processes behind his adversarial relation to it, a close look at his relationship with Walter Benjamin may be particularly useful. To begin with, Adorno's departure to America seems to have been principally tainted by feelings of guilt – particularly towards Benjamin. In his letter to Benjamin dated 27 November 1937, a few months before his departure to America, Adorno wrote:

> Our move to America has now become an immediate prospect […] I am very conscious of what this abandonment of my position in Europe – in the double sense – will mean. You will know that my thoughts about you were uppermost in my mind, and it is only to underline the seriousness of my decision if I add that I must also reckon with the real possibility of never seeing my mother again if I leave for America. (*Complete Correspondence* 227)

He then goes on to ask about whether Benjamin's financial situation has improved after the agreement with the Institute of Social Research in New York to offer him a monthly grant in American dollars instead of the then badly devalued French franc. Adorno then writes: "I am also thinking of how we can also bring you over to America as quickly as possible", even though he himself was not in America yet. The split already created between the two friends by Adorno's prospect of going to America made him stress their intellectual closeness and that they are somehow united in their philosophical isolation: "The fact that we have no 'heirs' rather fits in with the general catastrophic situation" (230). His ending one of his earliest short messages to Benjamin later from New York by "lots of love from your not so distant Teddie" (244) seems only to stress how far distant he really felt.

In fact, Adorno's early letters to Benjamin seem to show a kind of an attempt to obliterate the difference that he felt *then* between America and Europe. In one of them he writes:

> It is, sérieusement, much more European here than it is in London, and 7th Avenue, which is very close to where we live, rather gently reminds us of boulevard Montparnasse, just as Greenwich Village, where we live, similarly reminds us of Mont St Geneviève. (241)

In another he writes: "We have found an exceptionally pleasant location here: on an island resembling something between southern France, Rügen and Cronberg" (265). While this can be a way to convince himself that America is familiar and European by looking for traces of Europe in America, it can also be a way by which to suggest to Benjamin that they are still living in the same world, that there is no real divide between a European who lives in America and another who lives in Europe – not the least because the one living in America will try to create his small European world around him. Perhaps Gretel Adorno was less eager to bestow a European atmosphere on America when she wrote to Benjamin her impressions about the country: "One is faced everywhere by the contrast between the extremely modern and the downright shabby. One does not have to search for surrealistic things here, for one stumbles across them all the time" (241).

Apart from the various intellectual discussions taking place between the two thinkers in their correspondence between 1938 (the year Adorno arrived in America) and 1940 (the year Benjamin took his own life), the subject of *saving* Benjamin from Europe and getting him over to America backgrounds the whole correspondence. Although he was trying to be naturalized in France, Benjamin's letters to Adorno show unmistakable evidences that his chief desire was to go to America. When he writes "it is a familiar old thought of mine that I wish to be seduced by new cities" (*Complete Correspondence* 243), there seems to be no doubt about the message that he wants to pass to Adorno: to step up his efforts and use his influence in the Institute of Social Research in order to accelerate his move to America.

In another letter, he demonstrates that he is in touch with America by advising Adorno and his wife to visit the American Folk Art Gallery in New York, and by asking them if they know about the work of Herman Melville (260). At a certain point, however, Benjamin's "wish to be seduced by new cities" turns into what seems to be a more pressing demand to leave the *suffocating* atmosphere in Europe. In one of the letters he writes to Adorno: "I do not know how long it will still physically be possible to breathe this European air" (277). His daydreaming about being in America, and significantly nowhere but in the street where Adorno's house is located, is a kind of fulfillment of a wish to be there and in such close proximity to Adorno: "I glance every now and then at the town plan of New York, which Brecht's son Stefan has mounted on the wall, and stroll up and down the lengthy street on the Hudson where your house is situated" (279).

While the correspondence between them shows how focused they were on their respective writings and how interested they were in each other's feedback, Benjamin's letters must have had their effect on Adorno when it comes to this particular "side issue" of wishing to be in America. His dependence on Adorno's help with that must have weighed on the latter in ways which are not yet fully explored. Mentioning that he has started to take English lessons in one of his letters to Gretel Adorno was probably even more touching than directly expressing his wish to move to America (324–5). Benjamin's worsening situation in Europe and the fears that apparently led finally to his suicide are revealed in the letter he wrote one month before his death. This is where he also wrote briefly but unreservedly about his dependence on what is being done for him in America by his friends:

> The complete uncertainty about what the next day, even the next hour, may bring
> has dominated my life for weeks now. I am condemned to read every newspaper
> (they now come out on a single sheet here) as if it were a summons served on me
> in particular, to hear the voice of fateful tidings in every radio broadcast [...] I
> remain dependent on what all of you are doing for me from abroad. (339–40)

He singled out Adorno as the one who should receive his curriculum vitae and as the one upon whom he actually counted: "You will be getting my *curriculum vitae* via Geneva – which is also how I shall probably be sending these lines [...] It is a great comfort for me to know that you remain "reachable" in New York, and *constantly watchful, in the deepest sense, for me*" (emphases mine) (340). Less than two months later, Benjamin took his own life in a village in the Pyrenees close to the border between France and Spain. His last words, written to Henny Gurland in order to be passed to Adorno, were:

> In a situation with no escape, I have no other choice but to finish it all. It is in a tiny village in the Pyrenees, where no one knows me, that my life must come to its end. I would ask you to pass on my thoughts to my friend Adorno and to explain to him the situation in which I have now found myself. I no longer have enough time to write all those letters I would dearly have written. (342)

The exemplary interpretation of Benjamin's suicide has mostly remained within the widely accepted view that it was an escape from the fate of being handed over to the Nazis. The main reason behind his suicide is taken to be either fear or a final gesture by which he takes some agency and control over his own life instead of submitting to the sadistic other. Yet, this final act by the philosopher who theologically undermines the notion of the sacredness of human life definitely deserves a deeper look. In his "Critique of Violence" Benjamin writes:

> However sacred man is (or that life in him that is identically present in earthly life, death, and afterlife), there is no sacredness in his condition, in his bodily life vulnerable to injury by his fellow men. What, then, distinguishes it essentially from the life of animals and plants? And even if these were sacred, they could not be so by virtue only of being alive, of being in life. It might be well worth while to track down the origin of the dogma of the sacredness of life. (*Reflections* 299)

This insightful critique of humanism, however, is put forward from an intrinsically problematic mystic position which gives an upper hand to what it sees as the expiatory nature of divine violence, often substituted with the less critical notion of "divine power", over mythical violence which is seen as man-made and merely destructive: "If mythical violence brings at once guilt and retribution, divine power only expiates; if the former threatens, the latter strikes; if the former is bloody, the latter is lethal without spilling blood" (297). This binary opposition between divine and mythical violence is seriously undermined by Derrida who observes how this Benjaminian idea of the bloodless and fatal divine strike can easily incarnate the idea of the Nazi gas chamber. Thus, he finally frames Benjamin's text itself as violent and even complicit in a number of discourses that are, to quote Derrida, "too Heideggerian, too messianico-Marxist or archeo-eschatological", discourses which anticipated and even ultimately helped in the realization of that "nameless thing that one calls the 'final solution'" (*Acts of Religion* 298).

This is not the right place to look closer at Derrida's claim or at the vexed debt he himself owes to Heidegger, which can potentially render Derrida himself "too Heideggerian" in his own way. However, it is notable that the way Benjamin took his own life is itself the same bloodless way of killing the self by making it disappear, without violence or mutilation of the body. He took an overdose of morphine tablets. Oddly enough, as his last words indicate, this was for him a "final solution". But a final solution to what? The fact that Benjamin's life has always seemed to him to be a series of rejections and psychological defeats opens up the possibility of being finally in a situation which gives the perfect opportunity to do something that he perhaps always wanted to do anyway. In such a case, the idea of suicide would probably have been something which played on his mind for a long time before he finally decided to execute it.

It can be argued that while his own series of personal career failures led up to it, the sense of desecration and pointlessness surrounding the act of his suicide can be traced back to the dual suicides of his friends, the poet Fritz Heinle and Rika Seligson, in protest against Germany's First World War. Yet, Benjamin's suicide seems to be so marked by that symbolic gesture of being committed on the border between two countries, so accentuated by being registered as to have been committed where "no one knows me". It seems that it was the sense of being treated by the world as an excess that stood behind Benjamin's final act; his hyper self-awareness by which he was convinced that, as an intellectual, he was being rejected by Europe and at the same time, not really needed by America.

And thus, he leaves life on a note to Adorno, expressing the request to pass his thoughts to the latter, even though his letter to Henny Gurland is probably the shortest letter he ever wrote and hardly expresses any thoughts but the allusion to his suicide in a strange place, and the fact that his time has run out. His final sentence "I no longer have enough time to write all those letters I would dearly have written" pertinently shows the double sense by which he perceived "all those letters" in the last hours of his life – they were dear ones, but they were also in a sense useless. Benjamin's suicide thus can be categorized as what Žižek calls the subject's "suicide '*in* reality'" which "remains caught in the network of symbolic communication" (*Enjoy Your Symptom* 43). By committing suicide in this particular manner, Benjamin seems to put a note in a bottle and throw it into the sea. He "attempts to send a message to the Other" (44), to make a statement of protest to the world. His message seems to be reinforced by his actual written letter to Adorno.

Of all his letters to Adorno, Benjamin's last indirect message must have had the greatest effect on Adorno, something that the latter seems to have repressed out of a sense of guilt about his failure to help Benjamin in time. In his essay "A Portrait of Walter Benjamin", written more than twenty years after Benjamin's death, Adorno writes about Benjamin as a philosopher and as an unusual thinker, but with a particular muteness about their very close relation shown in the twelve years of correspondence between them. The essay significantly opens with that which by then had become an established standard interpretation of Benjamin's suicide: "The name of the philosopher who took his life while fleeing Hitler's executioners" (*Prisms* 229), which seems to rule out any other speculations about the cause behind it, or even any other partially responsible causes. He writes about Benjamin's intellectual relation to Proust and to Kafka but avoids his relation to Theodor Adorno.

The idea of being close to Benjamin is expressed only in general terms, and behind exaggerated metaphor, like, for example, describing how those who were drawn to Benjamin felt like children gazing at a glowing Christmas tree through a hole in a shut door (229). In fact, there are moments of describing Benjamin's intellectual powers in relation to radioactivity and even "atomic fission": "Everything which fell under the scrutiny of his words was transformed, as though it had become radioactive […] his intellectual energy might well be described as a kind of mental atomic fission" (230). It is as if Adorno wants to compensate for what is officially seen as Benjamin's final act of helplessness against "Hitler's executioners" by drawing this semblance between Benjamin's intellectual power and that cutting edge of atomic power by which America finally passed the message to the world that war must be over forever – or else.

The effect which Benjamin's experience in Europe and his suicide have had on Adorno's writings seems to insinuate itself in the same essay where he writes: "Benjamin, who as subject actually lived all the "originary" experiences that official contemporary philosophy talks about, seemed at the same time utterly detached from them" (230). Although this is written in order to show how Benjamin's philosophy is distinguished by its unusual concretion through which individual experience is transformed into general knowledge, it also seems to draw unconsciously a comparison between Benjamin and Adorno himself. While Benjamin had to actually live the "originary" experience of being threatened by fascism in Europe up to the point of taking his own life, Adorno, who lived safely in America during the most critical period of Nazi persecution, seems to have imaginatively transferred the whole idea of fascism to America, reconstituting the whole trauma in order to live it like the Jews who actually went through it as a real experience in Europe.

It can be argued that his own sense of guilt about not being able to save Benjamin in time could have played a major role in the fact that almost all of Adorno's writings in America are marked by that imposition by which he convinces himself that the fascist potential exists in America too, a kind of wish fulfillment by which to suggest that he and Benjamin always lived in the same world, in which the American culture industry and fascism amount to the same thing. The answer to Benjamin's weighty expectation, "I remain dependent on what all of you are doing for me from abroad" (*Complete Correspondence* 339–40), came later imaginatively in almost all of Adorno's writings after Benjamin's death as: But there is no abroad in the administrated world of the culture industry, everybody is persecuted everywhere. The whole world is living the nightmare of authoritarianism.

To Adorno, how Benjamin seemed "utterly detached" from the experiences that he lived is attested to by Benjamin's well-known sensitivity to the constructed image, his tendency to avoid philosophical argumentation and to "have the meanings emerge solely through a shocking montage of the material" (*Prisms* 239). The uncompleted *Das Passagen-Werk* is the most appropriate example, in which Benjamin's intention, as put by Susan Buck-Morss, was to "construct, not a philosophy *of* history, but philosophy *out* of history, or (this amounts to the same thing) to reconstruct historical material as philosophy" (55). This is why, to Adorno, Benjamin "had nothing of the philosopher in the traditional sense"

(*Prisms* 229). He is a philosopher who cannot be categorized as one. On the other hand, Benjamin's celebration of the anti-auratic revolutionary potential of popular culture seems to constitute some kind of identification with that which Adorno staunchly opposed: mass culture's ideological mandates. This celebration itself can be considered as a feel for what America stood for in opposition to what is often seen as the "cultural originality" of Europe. It can be argued thus that Benjamin identified with America, of which he daydreamt, more than Europe, from which he always seemed to be detached, while Adorno never actually left Europe in spite of the fact that he lived in America for about fifteen years, during which he never seemed to melt into American society.

While Benjamin took his own life in desperation over missing that life which he wanted to live unthreatened by the ideological Other, Adorno had to more or less conform, at least to some practical extent, to that which he opposed unwaveringly. Fully aware that the intellectual émigré has to "eradicate himself as an autonomous being if he hopes to achieve anything or be accepted as an employee of the super-trust into which life has condensed" (*Prisms* 98), Adorno fiercely resisted this eradication on an individual level and yet must have had to sacrifice something of his being in order to achieve something in America. His continued attachment to Europe, even though Europe was the place of a historically proven record of fascism and anti-Semitism, reflects his discomfort as an immigrant intellectual whose attempts at resistance to America's culture industry are set against his very dependency on living out of that resistance.

In fact, it can be argued that Benjamin's suicide itself, as contrasted to his theological tendencies, seems to symbolically express a sense of the insignificance and disposability of the individual life of the modern subject and seems to resemble the mindless process of production/consumption of numberless goods in the capitalist apparatus. In contrast to this, Adorno's uneasy coping with life in America and his attempt to restore the sense of wholeness in the face of the thorough fragmentation of everything by the culture industry, including the human self, show far more established theological beliefs. It can be argued that while Benjamin used/philosophized theology in his penetrating gaze on historical material, Adorno actually lived saintly according to it, even though he was made to play the devil himself in Alfred Sohn-Rethel's uncompleted manuscript, "A critical Exposure of Philosophical Idealism. An Investigation into the Method of Historical Materialism", which is something that Adorno mentions casually – but perhaps proudly – to Benjamin in one of his letters (*Complete Correspondence* 271–2).

In his essay "Adorno and Authoritarian Irrationalism", Stephen Crook writes: "Overall, however, Adorno's star has waned. In a curious irony his theologically inclined protégé Walter Benjamin was taken up as a more appropriate model for a 'materialist' culture theory" (32). It is obvious enough that calling Benjamin Adorno's "protégé" seems to reverse their real relationship – and not the least because of the age difference between the two men – in Benjamin's favor. In fact, Jay's essay "Taking On the Stigma of Inauthenticity: Adorno's Critique of Genuineness" shows how Adorno's critique of genuineness in *Minima Moralia*'s aphorism 99, entitled "Gold Assay", in which he attacks the notion of authenticity and even links it to fascist philosophy, "was itself deeply indebted to Benjamin's defense of mechanical reproduction against the aura and to his notion of the mimetic faculty". Jay argues that "many of Adorno's 'own' ideas betray precisely the kind of inauthenticity that he defended against jargon". Adorno's own inauthenticity then, according to Jay, "shows the nonauratic authenticity of the intellectual who knows himself not to be in full possession of his own ideas" (30).

The fact that Benjamin is given more credit than Adorno by those who are engaged in cultural theory seems to go even beyond the stress being put on the importance of the materialist view of culture as such. If the ultimate aim of the materialist view is resistance to ideological discourse, Benjamin's celebration of anti-auratic popular culture carries in itself a possibly successful resistance to ideology through the unexpected identification with its arbitrary mandates. In contrast, it can be argued that Adorno's oppositional resistance to mass culture and his attempt to uncover its deceptions fall into the trap of ideology which he himself analyzed so correctly. In "On the Fetish Character in Music and the Regression of Listening", for example, he observes how the listener who serves as a representative of the denial of commercialized music himself becomes part of the culture industry's scheme to establish the authority of commercialism over musical taste: "The seductive power of the charm survives only where the forces of denial are strongest: in the dissonance which rejects belief in the illusion of the existing harmony" (*Culture Industry* 33). Adorno's stance with regard to popular mass culture seems to be the strongest force ever of its denial and thus the greatest witness to its established authority. His whole theory of culture seems to precisely comprise an acute "dissonance which rejects belief in the illusion of the existing harmony" created by the homogenization which popular culture seems to impose on modern subjects.

Another example is to be found in his essay "The Stars Down to Earth: The Los Angeles Times Astrology Column", in which he links the absolutely serious social implications of reading astrology columns, namely psychological dependency, to the very fact that astrology is not meant to be believed or even taken seriously at all. While appearing to be a harmless social phenomenon, astrology, in Adorno's words, is "an *ideology of dependence* [...] an attempt to strengthen and somehow justify painful conditions which seem to be more tolerable if an affirmative attitude is taken towards them" (*Stars Down to Earth* 155). The "painful conditions" are certainly those imposed on the modern subject by the merciless capitalist apparatus. The important point that Adorno makes, however, is that this disguise of serious ideology in the cloak of what seems to be benign entertainment is not misunderstood by its victims; it is taken exactly for what it is: a disguise. The fact that astrology continues to play its commercialized social role in spite of the basic disbelief in what it presents makes this disbelief itself its underlying support:

> This alienation from experience, a certain abstractness enveloping the whole realm of the commercialized occult may well be concomitant with a substratum

of disbelief and skepticism, the suspicion of phoniness so deeply associated with modern big time irrationality. (49)

Similarly, however, it can be argued that Adorno's intellectual project in its totality, insofar as it is an attempt to show how social freedom does not really exist except in ideological terms, comprises that critical last stand by which the deceptiveness of mass culture is both revealed and yet given its ultimate authority over freedom.

It seems thus that the role which Benjamin's thought *and* suicide play in Adorno's America is greater than has ever been yet explored. In his discussion about Benjamin's attachment to culture and reification as two major features of his thought, Adorno writes:

> He was drawn to the petrified, frozen or obsolete elements of civilization, to everything in it devoid of domestic vitality no less irresistibly than is the collector to fossils or to the plant in the herbarium. Small glass balls containing a landscape upon which snow fell when shook were among his favorite objects. (*Prisms* 233)

Although this seems to be written in the general context of paying tribute to Benjamin and his thought, it is this particular feature in Benjamin which is precisely at crossroads with Adorno. To Adorno, one of the most dangerous characteristics of mass culture is that it takes reification beyond its metaphoric sense. It is not just that the products of mass culture illusively reify objects of dreams and fantasies, but that people themselves "resemble products [...] they assimilate themselves to what is dead" (*Culture Industry* 95). What is reified comes as a result of searching for identity in the wrong place and, in the course of this, acquiring some sort of a pseudo-identity. That is why Adorno writes to Benjamin in one of his letters that the "reification of the cinema is all loss" (*Complete Correspondence* 129). While the character on the screen defines the human subject strictly in terms of his function in a capitalist society, the spectator assimilates himself to what he sees on the screen. That is to say that; first, the human is transformed into dead material. The dead material is then endowed with humanness.

To Adorno thus the products of American mass culture are not exactly anti-auratic. The lost aura of high art is compensated for by what he sees as the seriously flawed over-identification with products of low art or mass culture giving them a "human aura". In "The Stars Down to Earth" he states:

> The kind of retrogression highly characteristic of persons who do not any longer feel they are the self-determining subjects of their fate, is concomitant with a fetishistic attitude towards the very same conditions which tend to be dehumanizing them. The more they are gradually being transformed into things, the more they invest things with a human aura. (*Stars Down to Earth* 100)

Some restless associations now seem to form themselves: This kind of retrogression, the loss of self-determination or the fear of not being the master of one's fate, seems to correspond with what Benjamin suffered particularly in the last two months of his life before committing suicide as a final gesture by which to retain that which is thought lost. In fact, Benjamin's gaze on the petrified landscape inside the glass ball seems to resemble the gaze on the either lost or imagined world of cinema. It could ultimately be a search for what might be thought of as a human trace, constituting – consciously or unconsciously – the same "fetishistic attitude" by which pseudo-artistic products are invested with a human aura. And finally, this transformation into a "thing" seems to strikingly exemplify what is previously discussed as Benjamin's potential feeling of being treated as an excess by universities in both Europe and America – "to their disgrace" (Adorno, *Prisms* 232).

In spite of the fundamental differences between the two thinkers, however, it is most gripping to the point of dizziness to see how particularly after Benjamin's death, Adorno's thought in its totality has been conditioned by *his own petrified gaze* on the fascist moment of history. In his view of the Enlightenment as the frighteningly ruthless project of humanity towards its own death, Adorno himself is frighteningly persistent and non-compromising. It is as if he stopped at Benjamin's monadic moment of history, the real of history, and kept contemplating it for the rest of his own life. With such an act, Adorno, following the very core idea of Benjaminian thought, refused what Benjamin called "historicism".

In order to explain what historicism is Walter Benjamin's seminal essay "Theses on the Philosophy of History" as well as some fragments from his unfinished magnum opus, *Das Passagen-Werk* or *The Arcades Project*, are exceptionally useful. What Benjamin means when he writes about the "monad" in thesis XVII could be that intensive moment of history where historical time seems to stop. The symbolic structure of history, or that which is constructed in a specific way in order to serve the ideology of the present, is broken by the psychotic moments of history where humanity seems to get in touch with the real of its nihilistic desire. Benjamin believes that the materialistic historiographer should take up what has been suppressed by the ideological construction of history and engage it actively in the present. In other words, the materialistic historiographer should inscribe the monadic moment of history into the present, or condition the experience of the present with it. This, however, is not as easy as it sounds, because it amounts to a wish fulfilment for the "ich kehrte gern zurück" of the "angel of history" of thesis IX whose desire is to "stay" and "awaken the dead" – if only he could resist the "wind" of progress (*Illuminations* 245–55).

Dealing with the whole debris of history on the other hand without being selective of monadic moments would be "historicism" which is an ultimately negative word in Benjaminian thought, indicating thinking about history as a linear, logical and, at the same time, utterly meaningless series of events. Benjamin's point here is that, without a materialist construction of history, the traumatic past gets covered up by an ideological or illusionary futurism that makes a deceptive experience out of the present as well as a fictitious narrative of progress out of the course of history, or, in Susan Buck-Morss's words, by a "futurist myth of historical progress (which can only be sustained by forgetting what has happened)" (95). The suppressed traumatic event, to Benjamin, is the only historical fact that can make the present truly comprehensible because "materialist historiography does not choose its objects arbitrarily", it chooses the object of history of which "monadological structure" where "all the forces and interests of history enter on a reduced scale" calls for it to be "blasted out of the continuum of historical succession" (*Arcades Project* 475).

Benjamin's materialist historiography realizes that "in order for a part of the past to be touched by the present instant <Aktualität>, there must be no continuity between them" (470). This "seemingly brutal grasp" of history accomplishes the essential "process of rescue" of the monadic moment out of historicism's coercive and unquestionably capitalist drive to forget (473). To put it in Lacanian language, Benjamin's call for attention to the "monad" can be summed up as "to deal with the real of history", to contemplate the psychotic moment of history. In such contemplation, the trauma undergoes a process of perpetual reconstitution. This is how Adorno himself took the fascist anti-Semitic moment completely out of its socio-historical European context by putting forward the argument of a psychical authoritarian personality, which implies that the distribution of anti-Semitism is utterly unpredictable.

Therefore, anti-Semitism to Adorno is not foreign to modern society but inherent in it and "hatred of the Jews [...] is capable of flaring up anew at any moment" (*Stars Down to Earth* 181–2). Because the present is thought of strictly in terms of the horrible experiences of a certain historical moment, America could have never been outside this imaginative economy. Adorno's American imago then comes out of an imagination which preconditions all experience of the present by the fascist moment of history. And, to him, the fascist moment of history is neither exactly timed nor affiliated to a certain country or people, that is to say, it is not simply European.

Like Antigone, whose ethical judgment of choosing death uncompromisingly is based on acting in conformity with her desire (Lacan, *Ethics of Psychoanalysis* 314), Adorno, both saintly and perversely, did not give way on his desire either. The difference, however, lies in the fact that his desire is precisely that of Benjamin's angel of history: To stay, to awaken the dead, to contemplate the monadic moment forever and condition all experience with it because it is judged as the real amidst the symbolic chain of historicism. Adorno did try to resist the wind of progress in every sense. After all, his life could not progress in America and he had to go back to Germany, as if the angel physically returns to that debris of fascist history to awaken the dead. Staying in America meant to him moving along by forgetting the past, by betraying the monadic moment of history, by committing that paranoiac act of including the real into one's symbolic world unceremoniously as if nothing of significance has happened. The angel's "ich kehrte gern zurück" (Benjamin, *Illuminations* 249) never left Adorno while he was in America, until that day when he had the chance to actually go back to Europe, particularly to Germany and, ultimately, to Walter Benjamin.

Because the years which Adorno spent in exile seem to have been dominated by his imago of an anti-Semitic American society, Jay's reassessment of Adorno's American experience, which seems to take it beyond the clichés about Adorno's elitist position by stressing the positive side of his relation to America, still simplifies that relation considerably. In his previously mentioned essay, "Intellectual Transfer: Theodor W. Adorno's American Experience", Detlev Claussen writes:

> Unfortunately, despite Jay's warnings to be on guard against anecdotes and clichés about either Adorno or the German émigré experience, those clichés have come to dominate the very idea of Adorno and America. In the centenary of Adorno's birth, 2003, the German arts and culture media did their part to perpetuate the old legends. The ostensible literature of remembrance thus tells us yet again how the intellectual elites of Weimar escaped the Nazis by fleeing into the cultural wasteland called America, and how, after finding a place for themselves in the paradise of California during its golden age, they seemed to want nothing more than to return to their Germany, the land of *Dichter und Denker*. (5–6)

In the case of Adorno, however, the issue of his relation to America and his return to Germany seems to go beyond the discourses of both the German arts and culture media and the new direction the Adorno scholarship has been taking since the early 1980s, trying to create some sort of reconciliation between Adorno and America. To Adorno – precisely since Benjamin's suicide and the subsequent years which witnessed the traumatic experience of Europe's Jewish community – America was not named something distinguishable from Europe, nor was his return a return to Europe, but rather a return to the *place of the massacre*, to the place which witnessed Benjamin's prophetic and ominous thought of the "one single catastrophe which keeps piling wreckage upon wreckage and hurls it in front of [the angel of history]'s feet" (*Illuminations* 249), to the place which witnessed the horrid reification of the idea which, by far, dominated Adorno's thought than any other and which Claussen correctly describes as "the appearance of barbarism in the midst of culture" (13).

Adorno's response to America's charm cannot be even categorized as a reaction. Because he seems to have provided for himself a preconceived reading of it all at an early stage, he contrived a certain mechanism of resistance even before touching upon the experience of seduction. In his critique of Aldous Huxley's *Brave New World*, Adorno comes across the novel's treatment of the "erotic collision of the two 'worlds'" of the "polished American career woman" and the "savage who loves her" even though he pretends to resist her seduction. The relationship between the seductress and the reluctant lover clearly describes the adversarial relationship between America and the immigrant European intellectual. While the lover is this "shy, aesthetic youth, tied to his mother [which is Europe] and inhibited, who prefers to enjoy his feeling through contemplation rather than expression and who finds satisfaction in the lyrical transfiguration of the beloved", the beloved seductress (America) treats him with a "matter-of-fact abandonment". This degradation of his transcendent love makes him run away from her. Adorno's argument is that the falsity of Huxley is particularly revealed at the point where he presents the "artificial charm and cellophane shamelessness" of the American seductress as having an un-erotic effect on her European lover. To Adorno, it is precisely the "highly seductive" influence of her very artificiality and shamelessness that the lover gives in to at the end of the novel (*Prisms* 105).

Although it can be argued that it is actually hard to determine how much of this love affair applies to Adorno's own relationship to America, the fact remains that he judges Huxley's critique of America as hypocritical and neurotic, because it conceals an erotic love for that which it pretends to criticize. For Adorno, although he must have wanted to love America by virtue of being the country which protected him during Europe's Nazi persecution, his authoritarian version of it seems to have always already impeded that love before it took any substantial form. To him, America's problematic is not that it wants to be authoritarian but, like the seductress whose every gesture is "part of a conventional ritual", *is* authoritarian "down to her very core" (105). He later writes that "Huxley is well aware that Jews are persecuted because they are not completely assimilated and that precisely for this reason their consciousness occasionally reaches beyond the social system" (106). The evidences which support Adorno's statement seem to be beyond doubts. Quoting Thorstein Veblen, Jorge Luis Borges comes across the second part of it in his essay "The Argentine Writer and Tradition" where he argues that Jews "are outstanding in Western culture because they act within that culture and, at the same time, do not feel tied to it by any special devotion" (218).

But Adorno's statement also implies that he seems to have expatriated himself from America even before setting foot in it. The "subjective and objective reasons" behind his return to Germany, which Jay quotes from Adorno's radio talk "Auf die Frage: Was ist Deutsch?" even though stated by Adorno himself as "the slight to his self-esteem dealt him by an American publisher" and "his desire to write in his native tongue" ("Adorno in America" 157–8) are far from convincing. For it seems unbelievable that Adorno would give such weight to the critical comments of a publisher – American or not – on one of his works. And what is it exactly that prevented him from writing in his native tongue from time to time while being in America if he wanted to? In fact, Claussen's suggestion that Adorno "needed to return to Germany to complete the circuit, for only there could he bring Benjamin's work to press" (8) seems to be much more relevant to Adorno's real reasons for return. The sum of all this indicates that in Adorno's imagination, that "America" which he always already expatriated himself from goes far beyond just the country which gave him refuge during the era of Nazi persecution. But that is not all. On the other side of Adorno's imago of fascist America lies another imago: a portrait of Adorno himself, carrying distinctive Benjaminian features.

PART II
Postmodernist Representations

Chapter 5
America: A "Stereotype" and a "Beautiful Imperialist"

There are texts that perceive America and misrepresent it; others that perceive how America is misrepresented by other texts. One of the main points of the present book is that both kinds of texts contribute to the discourse of symbolic America in which the fictitious castrating power of America is manifest. At the background of such discourse lie the problems of catching up with America's giant steps in all fields of human knowledge for the rest of the world, the problems of how to achieve what America has achieved without becoming American, or, simply, how to imitate America – ultimately, the problems of perceiving America for various writers. The result is that the discourse of the fictitious castrating power of America is empowered by the very resistance to it. The following mainly examines two texts. Each of them is written by a contemporary American writer. The two writers seem to have more or less the same concern: Mainly to reveal how non-Americans perceive America, how certain texts about America invent their own "America" and, therefore, communicate to their readers an unreliable message. One of the arguments of the present book, however, is that those particular texts which try to reveal misconceptions about America themselves fall into other misconceptions.

In his thesis, *America in France's Hopes and Fears, 1890–1920*, Charles W. Brooks illustrates how French intellectuals created a stereotype of America before the First World War and continued to feed that stereotype afterwards. Brooks' thesis looks at different pieces of French literature on America between 1890 and 1920 in order to reconstruct out of his historical material a French-perceived image of America that turns out to be revealing more of France than of America. He argues that for the French, America was "a place where they could cast, and witness the ravages of, their own sins and excesses, while they themselves remained in their own eyes fair and pure" (41). The symbol that is created out of America in this account is nothing but a receptacle for the French people's desperations about what they consider to be their own flaws. The image is evidently a negative one, and the America created by French literature on America in that period, which had to be reconstructed by Brooks, is in fact a source of more fears than hopes for France.

Brooks argues that this stereotype the French constructed as "America" before the war "remained largely and serenely impervious to vastly improved international communications and mutual understanding" (17), which means that the French kept the created image of America untouched and unaffected by new knowledge about America. In fact, he notices that although there is a huge corpus of French literature on America, most of it seems to be "weary, stale, flat, and unprofitable" because it is "second-hand and derivative" (28). According to Brooks, a series of articles entitled *Outre-Mer*, which was written by the French writer Paul Bourget during his visit to America in 1893, and which came to be published as a book in France in 1895, remained the main source of information for other French writers who wanted to write about America. Once the French American stereotype was created, literature kept feeding it regardless of the changes new methods of communication caused in reality – the refutations or challenges they posed to the stereotype.

Brooks' thesis shows that the image the French created of America radically changed within less than a century. What Tocqueville saw in America sixty years earlier to Bourget was a model of democracy that Europe was bound to follow because it was "coming under the imminent and inevitable dominion of the principle of democracy" which was "already complete" in America. Alternatively, what Bourget expected to see in America was a possible escape from Europe's "irreconcilable antagonism of races" – an escape that didn't work because, he claimed, the New World has not "escaped it to any greater degree". This and other statements made by Bourget drove Brooks to conclude that "it was the European, and not the American, racial antagonism that he had in mind" (93). Hence what Brooks describes earlier as "a place where they could cast, and witness the ravages of, their own sins and excesses" (41). That is to say, in summary, that the other is (mis)recognized as the self, a self that is perceived as lacking in all the necessary ways that make it cast its shadow on the other in order to deny difference except, strictly speaking, in negative terms.

Yet Brooks' historical approach seems to implicitly suggest that if the constructed imago of America praises American ideology, it can be thought about only in positive terms, while if it is critical of America, it must be stereotyping. Thus, on one level, Tocqueville, according to Brooks, "saw and sought the Old World's destiny in the new", that is to say, in the positive terms that indicate that America was a great democratic, practical, and progressive model that France was bound to learn from and eventually follow, in order to reach, in Tocqueville's words, "an almost complete equality of condition" (65). On another level which seems to be semi-critical of America, Ernest Renan's thoughts according to Brooks, though connoting the same idea that France will inevitably have to follow the American model, point to French traditional resistance which Renan saw as "unavailing":

> The world [and naturally France] is marching towards a kind of Americanism
> (une sorte d'américanisme) which wounds our delicate susceptibilities but
> which, once we get over the initial shock, will, in regard to the one thing needful,
> namely the emancipation and progress of the human mind, be no worse than the
> order which it replaces. (68)

It seems that Renan – and Brooks' text seems to be in conformity with that – thought of Americanization as a bitter yet necessary medicine for France's ills. On a third level, a purely critical one, Bourget's expressed disappointment in the New World, according to Brooks, amounts to downright stereotyping of America.

Judging the French-invented American imago, in Brooks' work, seems to be determined by how far Americanization is accepted by the French. In other words, the French American "stereotype" seems to be confused with the various imagos that the French created – are creating – out of America, while in fact they are two separate things. The stereotype, as Brooks correctly argues, is consistent, flat, unaffected by changes, and, above all, altogether manageable. Stereotyping is a way of articulating the other from a privileged position of what seems to be "true subjectivity". Examples of it are abundant in Edward Said's theory of Orientalism, and perhaps one of the best is the picture he draws of Ernest Renan himself as an Orientalist who is:

> Surveying as if from a peculiarly suited vantage point the passive, seminal, feminine, even silent and supine East, then going on to *articulate* the East, making the Orient deliver up its secrets under the learned authority of a philologist whose power derives from the ability to unlock secret, esoteric languages. (*Orientalism* 138)

The imago is in fact precisely the opposite of that: contingent, changeful, restless, and, above all, completely unmanageable due to the fact that it is always dreaded and at the same time recognized as a model by its inventor. It is not difficult to see that the point from which Renan *surveys* the East is authoritatively different from the point from which he *perceives* America. While the stereotype serves as a confirmation of its inventor's subjectivity, who may be, at least partly, aware of all its vacuities and the repressions that it emerges from, the imago is an invention that has the power of putting its inventor's ideal ego into question, and thus, destabilizing his very being. Simone de Beauvoir puts it beautifully in her four months diary *America Day by Day*. In the heart of America, sitting on a bench overlooking Brooklyn in 1947, Beauvoir's existence seems to have been more threatened by a preconceived idea of America than by being simply lost in an American city: "Brooklyn exists, as does Manhattan with its skyscrapers and all of America on the horizon. As for me, I no longer exist" (13).

In short, while the stereotype may be easily discarded as dead material, the imago is an ever living fantasy by which the self deceptively answers the Lacanian "Che vuoi?" (Lacan, *Écrits: A Selection* 345–6) with regard to the desire of the Other. In the case of the stereotype, let's say, the Orientalist's East, the desire of the other is not only marginalized, it is not even wondered about in the first place. The question about it is never raised. While in the case of America, it can be argued that it is with the initial speculation of what America desires that Renan goes on to articulate what France should do.

This is not to say that "what America wants" is something that is clearly defined. What America wants, in the imagination of its perceiver, must be unclear. This is due to the fact that what it wants is evoked only by the "Che vuoi?" question and, therefore, exists only as an answer to that question. The answer to the question of "what does the Other want of me?" can only be articulated in a phantasmal way.

So, the created imago of America fits into the Lacanian formula of fantasy. The function of this fantasy is that it relieves the perceiver from the anxiety of the "Che vuoi?" It is not accidental that the formula of fantasy, in Lacan's completed graph of desire, brings the subject back in the direction of – but not at all in – the imaginary realm. The stereotype completely belongs to the imaginary. Why? Because it is mainly a deformation that holds no power on its creator's ideal ego. The stereotype is not a phantasmal response to the anxious "Che Vuoi?" In fact, as previously mentioned, in the case of the stereotype, the question of the desire of the other is not raised at all. By accentuating the stereotype, mainly to show how it reflects French psychic turbulences and, in effect, helps to evoke them in the first place, Brooks elevates it to the status of the imago, and this fundamentally contradicts stereotypic traits.

Another idiosyncratic study in the early 1990s was made by David Shambaugh on how China perceived America between 1972 and 1990. At the time Shambaugh wrote his study, *Beautiful Imperialist*, China had "multiple sources of information and intelligence about the United States emanating from a sprawling community of approximately six hundred to seven hundred America Watchers spread throughout a complex civilian and military bureaucracy". The study defines an "America Watcher" as "an individual whose full-time professional occupation is to study and interpret events in the United States or American foreign relations for China's concerned elite or mass public" (5–7).

According to Shambaugh, Chinese (mis)perceptions of America came chiefly from the study and interpretation of it by this handful of individuals. He mainly argues that as a political superpower, the image of America created by its Chinese "Watchers" reflects a kind of detached admiration mixed with deep suspicion of America's imperial intentions. As a society, America's Chinese image according to Shambaugh reflects a "respect for American industrial and technological prowess" mixed with "depictions of a society beset by immorality, inequality, and racism" (137). Shambaugh concludes his study by stating that:

> No matter how well Chinese leaders understand the internal workings of the United States, its external behavior worldwide (and particularly toward China) will always be viewed with a great deal of suspicion. Given their historical experience and this perception of American hegemony, Chinese leaders simply do not trust American motives. (301)

He then sums up the core idea of the study by coming full cycle back to its title which is meant to encapsulate the "ambivalence – admiration and denigration – that distinguishes Chinese perceptions of the United States" (3): "For the Chinese, the United States remains a Beautiful Imperialist" (303).

Yet, it can be argued that the Chinese imago of America that Shambaugh's study puts in sharp relief shows not exactly an ambivalent perception, but a dialogic one. The difference is crucial. While an ambivalent position fluctuates between two opposites in search of a harmonious synthetic idea, a dialogic one paradoxically *believes* in opposites to the extreme. Ambivalence is marked by dialogue and can be illustrated through discourse, while dialogism stands in opposition to dialogue. No one other than Paul De Man made this Bakhtinian idea understandable. In his discussion of Bakhtin's thoughts on the novel in "Dialogue and Dialogism", De Man argues that dialogism is a "principle of radical otherness" the function of which "far from aspiring to the *telos* of a synthesis or a resolution, as could be said to be the case in dialectical systems, [...] is to sustain and think through the radical exteriority or heterogeneity of one voice with regard to any other" (*Rethinking Bakhtin* 109).

In other words, dialogism is about the radical acceptance of disharmony within the same discourse. Shambaugh's study aims to show how China is impressed, baffled and at the same time alarmed by America. Even though the ambivalent perception is talked about as the core idea, the study leaves the reader in no doubt that it is America's imperialism that worries China. "Beautiful Imperialist" manages to communicate a final message that America, perceived as an imperialist by its Chinese Watchers, is the main issue, while perceived as "beautiful" is beside the point. "Beautiful" is the contestable adjective that may or may not apply. Beauty is marginalized; it is dealt with as something that is altogether manageable while imperialism is depicted as the unmanageable threat.

Yet, if America can be really seen as an imperialist, then it must be the most surreal of imperialists that human history has ever produced. It is true that there are plenty of Asians, Iraqis, Afghanis and others around the world who have died because of its policies of intervention. Yet, half a century of American post-Second World War power seems to mainly demonstrate America's capability of being destructive when it so chooses, but at the same time, its incapability of changing what it sees as its lesser others forcefully or coercively. In most of the political arguments about the American empire, something fundamental seems to be missing – the exhibitionist character of America's relation to the world, what Jean Baudrillard called the "power museum" (*America* 27) America has become for the rest of the world to watch. It is not only that the unrestrained spending on military might cannot be directly transformed into power; what is more important is that America's wars in the second half of the twentieth century and the beginning of the twenty-first seem to be about staging a certain spectacle as well. What matters is the presentation and contextualization of the act of war. For example, the image of saving the world from "evil communism", or the image of combating "global terrorism", or the image of "finding and destroying weapons of mass destruction".

To say that China is not aware of all this would be naïve. Today, America is believed to be penetrated by the Chinese more than China's society or economy are penetrated by America in any sense. According to Stanislav Lunev, the highest ranking Russian intelligence officer to defect from Russia to the United States after serving in Singapore and China in the 1970s and 1980s, "Chinese military and political intelligence agencies are working overtime in the U.S. and have already stolen many of America's most precious secrets". In fact, Lunev claims that "at times Chinese intelligence operates so aggressively that it appears as if it already considers [America] part of its own backyard". Whereas drawing US investments and trade constitutes one major dimension of China's rapidly growing economy, infiltrating American capital markets, according to Lunev, goes "beyond the traditional ways of penetrating America", with a significant number of American investors "holding Chinese stocks and bonds, often without their knowledge" (*Newsmax.com*). China, like its America watchers, Marxists or non-Marxists, with or against China's callous capitalistic drive towards its own cultural death, seems to be only contented with the notion that it is on its way to becoming the world's superpower, that after history has completed a certain cycle, it is finally China that is pulling the carpet from underneath America's feet, or, if one is to put it in a Žižekan theoretical frame, instead of being "passive through the other" or, relinquishing to the other the factor of passive enjoyment, will be literally enjoying in the other's place (*Plague of Fantasies* 115).

It does not seem to be the case, as Shambaugh's study argues, that China's perception of America is an ambivalent one due to the fact that it acknowledges a certain benign attractive beauty in America which helps to tone down its "imperialism" which is seen as dangerous. The issue is much deeper than that. It is America's imperialism that seems to be invented in multifarious ways by China as a defense mechanism against the real threat, which is America's marginalized symbolic beauty, that which constitutes the real attraction as well as the real danger – its drive beyond the principle of the good, towards cultural death. Given China's new form of capitalism, the study seems to partly repress the fact that China is more *inspired* by America than susceptible of its imperialism. It seems to disregard the fact that, in the case of China, approaching America with discourses of moral and critical prudence is mixed by nothing but total commitment to America's ugliest principles – its merciless capitalism.

At the same time, China seems to be fascinated by its perceived image of America just as the audience is fascinated by Antigone – Lacan's Antigone – the one- dimensional ultimate martyr of uncompromising desire for death – even though it is more of a cinematic death. It is America's symbolic incarnation of the Western idea of nihilism which constitutes its dreaded beauty, which is precisely the beauty of the inhumanity of looking death in the face, the nihilism which seems to be an anti-life force but which at the same time gives life itself its only meaning in Western culture. The obsession of America's cinematic imagination with the idea of self destruction adds substantially to its infatuating Antigone image. The numerous Hollywood films which illustrate various scenarios of America's devastation show how cinematic America, like Antigone, lives "a life that is about to turn into certain death, a death lived by anticipation, a death that crosses over into the sphere of life, a life that moves into the realm of death" (Lacan, *Ethics of Psychoanalysis* 248).

It can be argued thus that the America that is perceived by the Chinese "Watchers" is more of an imperial beauty than a beautiful imperialist. The attraction to follow its steps to achieve what Baudrillard calls the American "power of unculture" (*America* 78) causes what *appears* to be a critical discourse of it to pale. At the heart of the invented Chinese imago of America, in spite of various criticisms of its details, there is something in the totality of it which seems to cancel out all criticism – the perceived beauty of America's theatrical ability to repudiate the good, to look as if it is crossing the realm of power which necessitates defending the seat of power, to what is beyond, namely, the total identification with the principle of nihilism. In America's imago as a "beautiful imperialist", it is the *beautiful*, that additional adjective, that "dangerous supplement" (Derrida, *Of Grammatology* 141–64) that really counts. It is the beautiful which is, according to Lacan, "closer to evil than to the good" (*Ethics of Psychoanalysis* 217) that constitutes China's fundamental problem in perceiving America.

Its unresolved position is not one that wavers between the view of America as an imperialist and as a model of economic and technological success. It is one that stands sure enough at the limit of the good, secure in the knowledge that it will eventually occupy its unrivalled place there, but faced with a critical question concerning *itself* and not America. The overriding question involves a certain crossing, and there is no doubt that it is a pseudo-cultural one: Will China be able to project itself, like America, beyond such a limit? Will it be able to live its imagined death beyond the principle of the good(s)? Can Antigone put on a Chinese face? The Chinese uncertainty which Shambaugh perceives in his work, even though created out of "watching" America and concluding that it is a "beautiful imperialist", does not seem to be more about how America is perceived at all rather than about the American anxious question: *What will exactly become of China?*

The sum of all this shows that what is more important than analyzing any text about America is looking at why there is a whole idiosyncratic literature about America in the first place. The question is not how different cultures, nations, or individuals perceive America. It is not even about whether the perceived image relates something truthful or not. Texts about America, including – one is tempted to say "particularly" – texts written with the specific aim to show how other texts about America consciously or unconsciously communicate an unreliable message, always communicate an unreliable message. Either telling the "truth" about America or inventing a "deformed image" of it seems to be subordinated by the fact that the linguistic message, whatever it is, depends on its fundamental power of inaccessibility. One comes face to face with one of Lacan's major ideas: that language "doesn't itself know what it is saying when it lies" (*Ethics of Psychoanalysis* 82). Literature about America in particular seems to be getting at something that is never really understood.

Chapter 6
America: The Invincible and the Surreal

In spite of the fact that America is, de facto and de jure, the most welcoming place for immigrants and different cultures, somehow it also seems to signify prior ideological completeness of a self-sufficient system that is closed upon itself and in no need of the world. The same can be said about cinematic America, or, the America created by Hollywood. The cinematic spectacle, especially in the case of America, is not just a cinematic spectacle – and never was. One classic example is D. W. Griffith's *Birth of a Nation*. The film's unmistakable racist message is only matched by its aesthetic quality as cinematic art – pioneering techniques in cutting, montage, lighting, camera movement, make up, costumes, massive casting, and so on. Its artistic form seems to serve its white supremacist content. White Americans in the film, regardless of the differences and antagonisms dividing the North and the South, seem to be bestowed with a certain dignity, composure, and integrity, while "true evil" belongs only to African Americans. At the height of their power in the South, after their newly acquired freedom, the black characters are shown as misfits in garments not their own. They are shown as people who do not know how to use power, they can only abuse it. In their short-lived state as the "new aristocracy", they are made to look not dignified but ridiculous and rowdy. Not to mention that the film's narrative obviously seeks to show that at the back of all political ambitions, the black man's principal desire is plainly the flesh of the white woman.

Whiteness is not only privileged by the narrative of the film which conclusively says that African Americans, as a race, need to be set apart, controlled, or segregated, it also seems to be advantaged by editing the shots in such a way as to connote antagonism between the good (white) and the bad (black), by the all too frequent and categorical positioning of black characters in the background of scenes with white characters focused in the foreground, by the cozy atmosphere and warm illumination of scenes with white characters which seem to surround them with an aura of calm composure and dignity, while scenes with blacks are mostly either dimly lit or carrying a sharp contrast of bright lighting and spotty shades casting a menacing air.

It can be argued that the film's disturbing content, though it belongs to a certain historical era that seems to have nothing to do with the present, together with its aesthetic form, do have a certain long-lasting ideologico-political influence which still manifests itself today in the general not-so-bright characterization of black Americans in Hollywood films. Films which do their best to put black and white on equal footing by showing how the white hero cannot really save the day without his "black brother" – like the *Die Hard* series – still always put the black American in second place. Quentin Tarantino's *Pulp Fiction*, which could be Hollywood's best attempt to put black and white in the same melting pot (and the black hero even appears in it as having more intellect, professionalism and composure than his white counterpart), had nevertheless to get the black gangster sodomized by the white cop in a mordant shot which seems to stand out in the film, no matter how quickly the black victim is saved by another white. So, the black is still both victimized and saved by the white.

On the other hand, the number of all-black-cast films and TV series produced in recent years seems to indicate that the white-black division somehow could not be cinematically bridged after all and had to be finally lived with or even reinforced by separating white films from black films. It can be argued then that *Birth of a Nation* is not just a film about the birth of a nation that needed to segregate black Americans in a certain way in a specific historical era. *Birth of a Nation* itself as a cinematic production – which represents black Americans with hardly any black cast in it, since almost all black characters are played by white actors with black-painted faces – seems to be the birth of a certain cinematic, white, and impenetrable America.

America seems to have moved swiftly from aboriginal pre-modernism to the postmodern without really experiencing the (European) stage of modernism. It moved from the unruly directly to the dissolute, bypassing the structural stage of slow historical progress. This short circuit accentuates the structure of the master signifier in language America is as an incomplete symbolic being with a fundamental fracture that needs constantly to be covered up by all kinds of fantasies – of which the cinematic ones are the most common – that not only try to illustrate how civilization has been built in America, but also how it will get destroyed and disappear in the future.

This may be one way to explain the obsession of American cinematic imagination, represented by Hollywood, with the idea of the destruction of America. As a symbol, though a living one, America in a way is a great civilization that lived, prospered, and has already perished – a frightful notion that needs to be constantly pushed away by the mechanism of reminding the self of it from time to time with illustrating cinematic accounts of different scenarios of destruction and disappearance. The idea of comparative decline, however, is often repressed or simply discarded. There seems to be extremely few cinematic representations of an America that declines, disintegrates, or loses its grip on power to another terrestrial civilization. America, in the world of the American films, does not decline – for instance, like the British or the French empires – it only gets devastated, submerged under water, destroyed violently by some natural catastrophe or attacked by aliens from outer space.

America's invincibility in American films is only matched by its sur-reality in non-American films. Hong Kong films, for instance, seem to provide one of the clearest examples of such sur-reality. Mabel Cheung's *An Autumn's Tale* and Clara Law's *Farewell China* stand out in that respect. In *An Autumn's Tale*, a young Chinese girl goes to America to be reunited with her boyfriend. There, she is met by her raucous yet kind-hearted cousin and learns that her boyfriend is having an affair with another girl. She falls into depression while her cousin falls in love with her. He helps her to mature, become independent and regain confidence in herself while all the time losing his own confidence as someone worthy of her love. In the more morose and unsentimental *Farewell China*, a Chinese couple get separated by the taxing process of illegal immigration to America. They suffer their lots individually as they live their daily lives in the most dreadful of circumstances, learning through destitution, humiliation, and the urban decay surrounding their existences that America is far from the land of opportunity they imagined it to be.

In the stories of both films, America is mainly about the problems of immigrating to America. For their two female protagonists, America initially means separation from the beloved. In Cheung's film, it also means maturing, growing up emotionally away from Hong Kong and the cushy way of life her heroine enjoyed before deciding to go to New York. The important point, however, is that America in both films seems to mainly provide an esoteric background to the human relationships that the films focus on. In spite of the fact that most of the action takes place in America, somehow America seems to be impenetrable to the Chinese men and women that the viewer sees on the screen. The American society does not really exist in both movies. Even the American characters in the film sound bizarrely unreal. The reality of the trashy slums and back alleys of New York in which the Chinese protagonists live is overlooked by the adjacent glowing skyscrapers of the city which provide a sort of a dreamland backdrop to their sufferings – the America that remains virtually sealed to them. It is as if that untried rich part of the city represents their failed aspirations and dreams about the Promised Land.

America as the "Promised Land" is a slippery notion. Who is America promised to? What makes it different from any other land? If America as the Promised Land promises departure from the Old World, its hierarchies and culpabilities, does this mean that the land of the free is free from guilt? The idea of the Promised Land seems to mainly connote an ideology of open opportunities for all without the presence of any class struggle or any racial antagonisms. Even if we assume that this is true now it cannot be thought about without seeing it as an ideological reaction to America's historical primal guilt: the almost complete annihilation of the aboriginal inhabitants of the land. In other words, the absolute absence of the Old World's injustices in America's present ideological mandates is also absolute presence if we are to look at it as America's paranoiac unceremonious inclusion of the real of its history in the ideological construction of its altruistic image. Its abolition of an entire primitive nation by means of more advanced weapons seems to belong to one of the most monadic moments of history.

According to David Stannard, "the destruction of the Indians of the Americas was, far and away, the most massive act of genocide in the history of the world" (x). Stannard even argues that in spite of the similarity between the "volumes of grandiloquently racist apologia for the genocidal holocaust they carried out"

(246), there is a categorical difference between the European and white American near total extermination of America's native inhabitants and the Nazi massacre of European Jews:

> On the one hand, much (though not all) of the European and American slaughter of American Indians – from fifteenth-century Hispaniola to sixteenth-century Peru to seventeenth-century New England to eighteenth-century Georgia to nineteenth-century California – was not driven by reasons of politics or plunder, nor by military strategy or blind expediency, but by nothing more than, to use Des Pres's phraseology, genocide for the sake of genocide. On the other hand, much (though not all) of the Nazi slaughter of Europe's Jews *was* driven by what the perpetrators of that holocaust regarded as rational motives – however perverse or bizarre or sick or hateful those motives appear to others. (150)

Motives and their rationality, nonetheless, are highly debatable. There can be no real standards or criteria by which they can be determined to be rational or irrational. Just as the Nazi's "rational motives" can be described as irrational by others, the European and American irrational slaughtering of Native Americans must have had its own "rational" justifications in the minds of its perpetrators. In both cases, what is rationalized by a genocidal apologia of a certain people in a certain time belongs to the irrational of human history as it is written according to dominant ideologies. What seems to be indisputable, however, is that the difference between the Nazi European holocaust and what Stannard describes as the largely forgotten "American holocaust" is that the former is documented, its evidences photographed and much written about. It seems to be even cinematically over-represented so as to include both the biographical formality of Steven Spielberg's *Schindler's List* and the slapstick joyfulness of Roberto Benigni's *La vita è bella*. In the case of the latter, however, "there was neither 'paper nor time enough to tell all that the [conquistadors] did to ruin the Indians and rob them and destroy the land'. As a result, the very effort to describe the disaster's overwhelming magnitude has tended to obliterate both the writer's and the reader's sense of its truly horrific human element" (Stannard x).

It thus seems that the only means by which history justifies setting the European fascist moment somehow outside the norm and including the violent act of founding America inside it is nothing but ideological fantasies which make it trouble-free to say, in Walter Benjamin's words, "'once upon a time' in historicism's bordello". It is painless to say it and commit to the wind of progress, which is precisely equivalent to the paranoiac act of moving along by the subversion or betrayal of history's monadic/psychotic moment and the unceremonious inclusion of it in the linear structure of what Benjamin calls "universal history". This seems to be the reason why Benjamin writes about being "man enough to blast open the continuum of history" in his thesis XVI (*Illuminations* 254). Dealing with the monadic moment of history, or fixedly contemplating it like the angel of history, would be, for a historiographer, something like identification with the real of history, which is psychotic since it lives precisely where universal history *breaks*. Yet, this could be also the price of a certain *jouissance* that is "beyond the pleasure principle",[1] a *jouissance* which Benjamin seems to hint to at the end of thesis XVII as a "blasting" but in the Hegelian language of Aufhebung (*Illuminations* 254).

As for writing the history of America ideologically, as Susan Sontag puts it in her book *Regarding the Pain of Others*, America's "tragic past does not sit well with the founding, and still all-powerful, belief in American exceptionalism" (88). Sontag's statement may appear in dispute with her fictional work *In America* in which she draws a portrait of an indeed exceptional place where dreams of self recreation come true. The sumptuous kitschy America portrayed by Sontag, its nineteenth-century mixture of capitalist spectacles and ardent attention to Shakespeare, as a background against which the dramatic and determinately willed self-transformation of her heroine Maryna Zalezowska to Madame Marina Zalenska – a remaking of identity which seems to correspond with Sontag's observation about the American "belief in the power of possibility of self-reinvention" (*Online NewsHour*) – are all themes that call for serious discussions. But what concerns our discussion here is Sontag's insightful summation of what America was to Europeans in the late nineteenth century and what it is to the world now. To Sontag, "you can't write a novel about the past that isn't about the present" (*Connection*). Thus, America was and still is a country which is "made too mythical by a suffusion of dreams, of expectations, of fears that no reality could support" (Sontag, *In America* 117). Yet America's unreality is paradoxically accentuated by the very realization of its overpowering existence and, at the same time, what seems to be an unfulfilled desire to actualize it:

> To be so struck that something really exists means that it seems quite unreal. The real is what you don't marvel over, feel abashed by: it's just the dry land surrounding your little puddle of consciousness. *Make it real, make it real!* (emphasis mine) (117)[2]

It is not an exaggeration to say that these three short sentences from Sontag's *In America* sum up everything about symbolic America as the Promised Land as well as the cinematic invincible, surreal, and impenetrable entity. In fact, they also touch upon another thornier issue, for it can be argued that the failure of articulating America itself resembles the failure of defining "Woman" or the failure

---

[1] Lacan explains how a *jouissance* that is beyond the pleasure principle is realized at a certain stage where the subject realizes "that his desire is merely a vain detour with the aim of catching the *jouissance* of the other". A *jouissance* that is beyond the pleasure principle thus seems to fall outside the metonymic structure of desire. "The Transference and the Drive", *The Four Fundamental Concepts of Psycho-Analysis*, edited by Jacques-Alain Miller, translated by Alan Sheridan, Penguin Books, 1994, p. 184.

[2] This statement about America is said by Sontag's heroine, narrator and occasional mouthpiece in the novel, Maryna Zalezowska or Marina Zalenska.

to determine whether there is actually a form of writing that can be recognized and described as "feminine". Consequently, it is also a failure which marks the destabilization of the subject position of the seemingly defined or symbolized writer. And, if one can talk about the imago of the male writer about America, or, that which comes out precisely from his reading of America, what happens when America is read by a subject who inadvertently assumes the position of someone who does not exist?

Coming from a woman with unusual visionary powers like Sontag, her insistent demand "make it real, make it real!" could have far deeper implications. Playing with the (un)reality of America could be, at its deepest level, a kind of unconscious hovering at an undefined verge of an abyss to which woman is ultimately committed, and upon which subjectivity as such bases itself by means of language. Going over Sontag's lines again about America, one is struck by the fact that they could as well be at the heart of Lacan's discourse about the inexplicability of the notion of woman or the impossibility of becoming one: *"To be so struck that something really exists means that it seems quite unreal. The real is what you don't marvel over, feel abashed by: it's just the dry land surrounding your little puddle of consciousness. Make it real, make it real!"* (all emphases mine) (117).

No wonder that Sontag's major concern during a period in which she was fighting against a second attack of cancer and had to stop her work on *In America* for a whole year was her despairing repetitive inner cry: "I've lost the book, I've lost the book" (*Online NewsHour*). It is as if losing *In America*, though it could have been thought of as the price for saving her life, itself amounted to losing her life. Writing, thus, is in a fundamental way an attempt to actualize a life, to "make it real, make it real!"

It is inevitable that one of the most important statements by Lacan should be repeated here:

> Becoming a woman and wondering what a woman is are two essentially different things [...] It's because one doesn't become one that one wonders and, up to a point, to wonder is the contrary of becoming one. The metaphysics of the woman's position is the detour imposed on her subjective realization. Her position is essentially problematic, and up to a certain point it's inassimilable. (*Psychoses* 178)

Becoming is becoming *in* the discourse. Wondering *is* the discourse. A dilemmatic question arises: How can the female writer be described as a woman if she engages, consciously or unconsciously, in the "wondering"? Put in its simpler yet no less unanswerable form, the question could be: Is there a writing that is feminine? It is because of that that the inassimilability of the woman's position not only puts her right in the middle of the void upon which subjectivity as such is based, but casts a serious doubt on the existence of the symbolized subject (man) as well. If woman is outside the discourse, this can only be explained by being its very instigator. In other words, while the presence of man is a symbolic possibility that does not actually explain either man or woman, the absence of woman, in its essence, is an impossibility, because it would be an absence that cancels out the presence of both genders – and the discourse.

It is worth mentioning here that it took Lacan nine years, between publishing *Écrits* in 1966 and publishing *Encore* in 1975, to say something on feminine sexuality – hence subjectivity – in a completely different seminar with a completely different mind. Žižek explains how Lacanian thought shifts radically from the notion of the "Other" to the notion of the "One" in *Encore*, from the signifier to the sign, from the symbolic network to the psychosis reflected in Lacan's effort in his last years which was "directed at breaking through the field of communication-as-meaning" (*Žižek Reader* 29). In short, from discourse to *jouissance*. This Lacanian shift also marks "the two opposed meanings of the word "existence" in Lacan". The first means "symbolization, integration into the discursive order [...] in which Lacan maintains that 'Woman does not exist'", and the second is the opposite meaning of "'ex-sistence', the impossible-real nucleus resisting symbolization" (31) to which Woman is ultimately committed.

The structure of subjectivity thus in the case of the female, even though she may initially take the same detour within a discourse that is predominantly written in the Name of the Father, is nevertheless fundamentally different by virtue of the female's connection to the notion of Woman. As Lacan puts it: "~~Woman~~ cannot be said *(se dire)*. Nothing can be said of Woman. Woman has a relation with S(A̶), and it is already in that respect that she is doubled, that she is not-whole, since she can also have a relation with Φ" (*On Feminine Sexuality* 81). In other words, the subjectivity of the female relates to Woman who does not exist in the system of symbolization yet exists at the level of *jouissance* where she as well as the big Other itself are crossed out. She is outside the system but she is defined as the very subversion of it. She is not threatened by castration, yet the lack of the phallus transforms *her* into a phallus, in other words, into man's real of desire as well as his very sign of castration.

Likewise, the invincibility of America, above its representations as an invincible entity in American and non-American films, is constituted by the very inability to articulate it, or to come to terms with its real existence, or to definitively distinguish between its reality as a country, its cinematic persona, its trope in literature, and its designation as the Promised Land or the dream of individual self invention.

Chapter 7

Dogville: Lars Von Trier's Desexualized America

Lars Von Trier's movie *Dogville* is one of the most interesting European takes on America. *Dogville* is largely a film about the film industry itself, in which the key word "illustration" – being so frequently mentioned by the narrator and the film's focus male character, Thomas Edison junior – plays a major part in communicating that idea to the viewer. Cinematic America is indeed *Dogville*'s major "illustration". The fact that the Danish director never visited the United States makes it altogether more fascinating. To be able to give such a strong statement about America, from afar, using mostly an American cast, attests to the fact that America, the symbol, the dream, the philosophical concept that goes far beyond the country, belongs to everyone aware of it on earth and to no one in particular at the same time. Though the movie might be understood as a critique of human nature in a universal sense rather than an anti-American onslaught, the director, unequivocally, cuts short the possibility of such interpretation by ending the film with a series of shocking photographs, presumably pointing to America's social injustices.

The argument that follows will show that what *Dogville* as a cynical as well as a Brechtian cinematic work says about America reflects a vision that tries to render America a desexualized mutant of Europe. Put another way, *Dogville* as a European text seeking to read America is in one way capable of doing so by arguing how America, seen as an inheritor of European civilization, desexualized itself to be different and non-European. In the course of this, the structural and conscious processes by which *Dogville* invents a desexualized America and relates this desexualization to the idea of murder will be revealed. The main point to be made, however, is that this anti-American European take on America, in spite of its outspoken aggressivity, seems to mark a certain unconscious erotic affair between the inventing European subject and the invented imago of America. This is precisely where the Lacanian intervention occurs. To summarize greatly, the main two questions posed here are *how* and *why Dogville* invents a certain imago of America.

In his essay "America First", Michael Wood writes: "Home is what we know we ought to want but can't really take. America is not so much a home for anyone as a universal dream of home, a wish whose attraction depends upon its remaining at the level of a wish" (40–2). It is exactly this that *Dogville* seems to aim at demolishing. For the America invented in it is in fact a home, but obviously only for a certain type of people. It is the "universal dream of home" that is targeted by indicting America's ideas of home, community, hospitality, and, above all, the altruistic democratic ideology represented by the writer character, Thomas Edison junior, who plays the enlightened philosopher, the possible instigator of social change and the one who is looked upon as a savior, *and*, at the same time, the one who turns out to be the weakest and most treacherous of all of Dogville's inhabitants. All of this makes Von Trier's film unapologetically cynical. But what kind of cynicism does one find in it? To what extent does this cynicism constitute a political position taken via artistic transgression? Or is it mere cynicism? Is there anything more to it than being a sign of paranoiac repression?

A cynical work of art always causes such controversy around its message and its usefulness in the field of cultural politics. Cynicism is always caught between being politically active through transgressive satirical laughter, unbound sensuality and body politics, and, being that "enlightened false consciousness" that Peter Sloterdijk describes in his *Critique of Cynical Reason* as the "modernized, unhappy consciousness, on which enlightenment has labored both successfully and in vain" (5). In its first instance, cynicism would take root in the Bakhtinian realm of carnival, and the cynical work of art would belong to that special political "antibody" which Michael Gardiner, as one of the Bakhtinian circle of thinkers, perceives through "Bakhtin's own bacteriological metaphor" as "living within a pathological social body, always threatening to rupture it from within" (37). In its second instance, however, it falls back into Sloterdijk's "enlightened false consciousness" and its dilemmatic postmodern condition of being "well-off and miserable at the same time" – a consciousness which "no longer feels affected by any critique of ideology" because "its falseness is already reflexively buffered" (5).

But somehow *Dogville* seems to be devoid of the carnivalesque sense. There seems to be an elaborate kind of satire as well as a sharp cynicism in John Hurt's tone and deliciously tortuous style of narration, but certainly, no satirical laughter. It "hurts", but from above, from what seems, or rather *sounds* to be, an aristocratic tower, and not from below, not from a carnivalistic sense of a social public sphere. From the very opening scene, Hurt's voice introduces the viewer to an obvious miniature representation of small town America living in a particular time that defined the future of modern America, the time of Thomas Edison. With an unfailing English accent that seems to reflect how America was seen by the aristocratic and socially hierarchical nineteenth century Europeans as simple, sentimental, honest, urbanly as well as urbanely primitive, Hurt starts his narration with:

> This is the sad tale of the township of Dogville. Dogville was in the Rocky Mountains in the U.S. of A., up here where the road came to its definitive end, near the entrance to the old abandoned silver mine. The residents of Dogville were good, honest folks, and they liked their township. And while a sentimental soul from the east coast had once dubbed their main street Elm Street, though no elm had ever cast its shadow in Dogville, they saw no reason to change anything. Most of the buildings were pretty wretched. More like shacks frankly. The house

in which Tom lived was the best though and, in good times, might almost have passed for presentable.

It can be argued thus that the all-seeing-eye view of the town of Dogville which the film opens with and which persists all along penetrating physical barriers that had to be made invisible, reflects a degree of contempt by which Lars Von Trier looks down upon his material. But it also communicates an unmistakable Brechtian message that advocates the alienatory way of creating art while being hostile to the illusionary way that targets the viewer's emotions rather than his or her intellect. It is relevant to the present discussion to mention some of the many subtle references to Brecht's works before discussing what America meant to Brecht himself as the most appropriate introduction to Lars Von Trier's "Dogvillian" America.

While the film's staging and style persistently detach the viewer and impede identification with the characters, the ghastly content evokes Brecht's *Die Dreigroschenoper* (*The Threepenny Opera*). The name of the town itself, Dogville, seems to play on the allegorical character of "Dogsborough" in *Aufhaltsame Aufstieg Des Arturo Ui* (*The Resistible Rise of Arturo Ui*). While the film obviously targets the vicious image that it invents as a collective American psyche which, it seems to claim, underlies an ostensible kindness and a deceptive simplicity of small-town America, "Dogsborough", in Brecht's *Arturo Ui*, is an American citizen who is "reputed to be honest" but whose "morals go overboard in times of crisis", "a hard-boiled broker, who takes a lawyer with him to his lawyer's" and, above all, someone who should be "educated" (12–14) by others who are more experienced in matters of life and human nature – in Brecht's symbolism: Europeans. Dogville's society, like that of *Der Gute Mensch Von Setzuan* (*The Good Person of Szechwan*), is portrayed as a society that rhapsodizes over virtue and generosity while its practice contradicts both. In the interlude following scene nine of Brecht's play, one of the three gods comments on such a society in a way that could as well describe Dogville's:

> What a world we have found here: nothing but poverty, debasement and dilapidation! Even the landscape crumbles away before our eyes. Beautiful trees are lopped off by cables, and over the mountains we see great clouds of smoke and hear the thunder of guns, and nowhere a good person who survives it! (*Good Person* 98)

Shen Teh, taking her mask off in scene ten, retorts back to the three gods' shocked reaction to her gesture by: "Your original order to be good while yet surviving split me like lightning into two people. I cannot tell what occurred: goodness to others and to myself could not both be achieved" (105). Shen Teh's disguise in most of the play and the taking off of her mask close to its end corresponds with Grace's hidden identity which is not revealed to the people of Dogville until the last scene of the film, where she transforms from the town's victim to its judge and prosecutor. Brecht's symbolism of the three gods disappearing in a mechanical pink cloud that descends from the ceiling of the theatre in scene ten after giving up the prospect of finding a single good person on earth is evoked in *Dogville* by the alternative dramatic appearance of a god-father in a "Cadillac series 355 C" in order to punish Dogville for not having a single good person living in it. Even using real life photographs as a background for the end credits evokes Brecht's ending of *Mutter Courage und ihre Kinder* (*Mother Courage and Her Children*), with documentary images of Lenin, Stalin, and Mao backgrounding the action on the stage.

What America meant to Brecht himself cannot but have a powerful influence on his followers and admirers, and Lars Von Trier is no exception in this regard. In his essay "America Before and After", one of the authorities on Brecht, James K. Lyon, writes:

> Much like a social scientist, Brecht tended to see the world in terms of "models" – in this case models constructed out of Marxist ideological views and out of his poetic imagination. His sociological model for America when he arrived was based on the assumption that it represented the most advanced form of capitalism and consequently the most uncivilized, inhumane form of human existence. (341)

As a socialist and anti-fascist, Brecht's experience in America after fleeing Nazi Europe was not seen by him as devoid of harassment due to his ideological commitment to communism and to his famous confrontations with the film industry which he perceived as capitalistically exploiting. His entanglement with Hollywood's film industry clearly marked an unhappy phase in his life as Martin Walsh argues in his essay "The Complex Seer: Brecht and the Film", where he writes:

> It is clear that Brecht regarded his work in the cinema as simply a means to earn his living. Hollywood was always eager to secure <<name>> writers, and Brecht churned out scripts, which were so chewed over in the studio factories that his ideas were invariably modified beyond recognition. (10)

Arguably, nothing could have made a writer like Brecht more bitter and resentful than altering his ideas so as to produce right-wing conformist works that he undoubtedly detested. Thus his sad lines in his poem entitled *Hollywood* which is cited by Walsh in the same essay:

> Every day to earn my daily bread
> I go to the nearest market where lies are bought
> Hopefully
> I take up my place among the sellers. (11)

Brecht's experience of exile in America has been epitomized by his being investigated as a witness in 1947 by the House Committee on Un-American

Activities, among nineteen personalities deemed unfriendly to American values and ideology. James K. Lyon cites his statement before that committee in which he said: "I am not a film writer, and I am not aware of any influence I have had on the film industry, either politically or artistically", a statement that Lyon sees as summarizing "not so much his view of himself as a writer, but the realities of his life in the film world" (71). Needless to say, contrary to Brecht's own words, he had an everlasting artistic imprint on the film industry, especially in Europe. *Dogville* is one of the most obvious effects of that. America seems to have been such a hostile place to Brecht – and he in turn such an intimidating figure to it – to the extent that even American Marxists themselves were not particularly on good terms with their European comrade. In "The Ideological Brecht", Lyon gives an account of the mood that defined Brecht's controversial relationship with members of the Marxist American left-wing:

> Joseph R. Starobin, an active member of the American communist party at the time, recalls an experience that captures the atmosphere that often prevailed. In the company of other Communists, he met Brecht and Gerhart Eisler at a soiree in New York City in 1943 or 1944. It was, Starobin says, "a painful evening, with Brecht lying astride a bed, contemptuous of everybody." The exile, he claims, shared the "general European self-centeredness and arrogance" that American Communists sensed in their European counterparts. (288)

Even the destruction of the town of Dogville in the film's last scene could be argued to symbolize the "destruction of America" that Brecht seems to have carelessly announced out of his political over-enthusiasm at some point during his life of exile in the United States. Lyon writes:

> In 1947 he strongly espoused the cause of Henry A. Wallace, who was emerging as a third party candidate for president. Bentley recalls hearing Brecht say that, if Wallace were not elected, the alternative for America would be World War III. There was no middle ground. And when the House Un-American Activities Committee launched its investigation of Hollywood in 1947, Brecht announced to friends the imminent destruction of America. (303)

Dogville thus, as a film that style-wise belongs to Brechtian cinema as well as one that obviously pays such a high homage to Brecht, his works, his ideology and his life, is obviously a work that tries to *mutilate* the image of America. And because an image is never just an image, or, to put it in a Žižekan way, "an appearance is never 'merely an appearance', it profoundly affects the actual sociosymbolic position of those concerned" (*Plague of Fantasies* 26), the invented imago, like fantasy, not only covers up gaps in the sociosymbolic network of its inventor, of which instance in the present context would be the destabilization of his or her very constructed subjectivity, but it can actually infuse or confuse reality with the phantasmal – either for its producer or its consumer.

A pertinent starting point would be the character of the philosopher/writer, "Thomas Edison". It is obvious enough where Tom got his name from. Thomas Alva Edison (1847–1931) is the celebrated American engineer whose great inventions substantially defined the modern age. Two of his most important contrivances are film projectors and motion pictures. The fact that this historical piece of information is almost forgotten seems to obliterate the notion that it is not just by Hollywood's hegemony over the international film industry that people tend to think of the world of movies as an American one. Cinema *is* an American invention, and the history of film is largely an American history. It is true that the French Lumière brothers developed the first commercially successful film projection system. Yet, their work was mainly inspired by Edison's earlier motion picture devices, like the kinetoscope and the kinetograph, where the idea of creating the illusion of movement out of successive pictures was first introduced.

One exceptionally revealing European text dealing with the character of Edison is Villiers de l'Isle-Adam's *Tomorrow's Eve*, in which the French writer (1838–89), who was actually a contemporary of Thomas Alva Edison, creates a fictional character of a scientist whose name is *Thomas Alva Edison*, "the man who made a prisoner of the echo" (7). Not so different from the Thomas Edison of *Dogville*, Villiers' fictional scientist is a man whose "favorite foible is to think himself ignorant, by a kind of legitimate naïveté. Hence that simplicity of welcome and the mask of rough frankness – sometimes even the show of familiarity – with which he veils the icy realities of his thought" (8).

Perhaps there is no better example in the present context on how the fictional problematizes the sense of reality in the case of anything related to America than the advice that the writer of *Tomorrow's Eve* gives to his reader as a preface to the main text. In "Advice to the Reader", Villiers makes an exceptionally meticulous effort to show the reader that his fictional character of Thomas Edison refers to the "legend" that "has sprung up in the popular mind regarding this great citizen of the United States" and not to the real American Engineer. And since the legend is completely separate from the real man, the writer seems to suggest, then it belongs to the world of literature.

So, with a Catholic sense of a must to eradicate all confusion, he starts his advice with: "It seems proper to forestall a possible confusion regarding the principal hero of this book". Yet, his repeated emphasis on the need to eradicate such confusion somehow seems to reflect how much he is himself confused. Later he writes: "The Edison of the present work, his character, his dwelling, his language, and his theories, are and ought to be at least somewhat distinct from anything existing in reality". The affirmative "are" is not only diluted by "at least somewhat distinct" but immediately undermined by the following skeptical "ought to be". It is as if Villiers is at odds trying to convince *himself* that the legend, in his mind, is truly something separate from reality. Even after making his point thrice, somehow his feeling that it is not established firmly enough persists. So, at the end of his advice he adds:

> Let it be understood, then, that I interpret a modern legend to the best advantage
> of the work of Art-metaphysics that I have conceived, and that, in a word, the
> hero of this book is above all "The Sorcerer of Menlo Park", and so forth – and
> not the engineer, Mr. Edison, our contemporary. ("Advice to the Reader")

This is his final statement by which he tries to convince the reader and himself that the judgment that the legend belongs to literature while the real belongs to the real world has been established. Yet as a conclusion arrived at after this most apologetic preface, Villiers' statement seems to be very shaky indeed, as if trying laboriously to suppress a fundamental suspicion: that the fictional might in fact still be more established than the real. If *Dogville* can be considered a film of any significance in the field of cultural politics, the questions that it would be posing in such a case would be of this kind: Is reality actually distinguishable from what has been created as a legend? Is America distinguishable from what has been created by Hollywood as cinematic America? Or, to take the issue further, how much of the reality of America has been created *by* cinematic America? None of these questions can have a clear-cut answer.

In *Tomorrow's Eve*, Thomas Edison creates a mechanical woman, *Hadaly*, who represents the dream of the ultimate romantic love. Edison's genius makes Hadaly look, move, and talk exactly like a real woman. Moreover, she is as eloquent and no less versed in managing a dialogue than a philosopher or a great poet. But what is really significant about Hadaly, according to her creator's expressed point of view, is that she is devoid of what men perceive in women as female pettiness and small-mindedness. The feminine conscience is what Edison was able to get rid of by inventing the android – for the usage of man.

As a female android, Hadaly seems to have everything except the soul and the Eros of a woman. She is a desexualized creature. Besides that, Hadaly's cinematic movements and gestures in the scenes in which she plays the heroine of a romantic love story are numerous and unmistakable. At the end of Villiers' eccentric novel, the android gets destroyed by an accidental fire on board a transatlantic liner on her way to Europe. It seems that by giving the celebrated American name "Thomas Alva Edison" to his scientist character, Villiers de l'Isle-Adam's text implies that his fictional scientist who wanted to invent a mechanical woman ended up, *in reality*, inventing only cinema instead. The displacement seems to suggest that cinema, as an American invention, is desexualized at birth, the implication of which brings to the surface a whole discourse that seems to be lying deep in a certain European subject's unconscious: that America, at its highest symbolic representation, is portrayed as a desexualized woman.

With a more or less the same Thomas Edison as a focus character among the inhabitants of Dogville, the strange atmosphere of anti-eroticism in the film shrewdly presents the sexual either in its most violent/sadistic form or as being entirely dominated by the economic. On the one hand, raping Grace is made to be the only way to have sex with her; on the other, all the town's inhabitants seem to be asexual creatures, each of them in his or her own way. The first rape scene could be considered one of the most disturbing rape scenes in the history of motion pictures. Lars Von Trier was actually able to put in it his whole perspective of the power discourse and its relation to sexual exploitation. The victimizer's suggestive short statements of vicious entrapping are contrasted to the victim's bewildered yet apprehensive questions:

> - I wouldn't try to run away
> - Why would I want to run away Chuck?
> - I wouldn't try to holler either
> - Why would I want to do that?

The persuasion takes its philosophical turn when Chuck tells Grace, "I need your respect Grace", to which she replies, "You have my respect Chuck". He follows up by repeating: "I want your respect". The demand for respect somehow verbally replaces the sexual desire, as if the metonymic structure of desire[1] assumes no disguise at all, in a clear message that defines the relationship conventionally assumed between the powerful and the powerless, the male and the female, the ruling and the ruled, the colonizer and the colonized, the master and the slave, or, in Marxist terms, the bourgeoisie and the proletariat.

When the direct talk of force starts to take place through Chuck's statement "I can force the flowers to bloom early in the Spring, I can force you", the camera, in one of the most cynical moments of the film that hardly fails to draw a suppressed titter, if not outright guffaw, moves to a contemplating Tom while he is taking a stroll "outside" Chuck's house. This is where the satirical factor in the film reaches its highest point. The lack of physical barriers seems to point to the classic role of the philosopher in human civilization – to contemplate while power has its way right in front of his eyes. And while Chuck's grim "practicality" unabashedly declares that friendship cannot exist between two people when one of them has the opportunity and the power to exploit the other, Tom's assumed position of the enlightened model of man, in spite of the fact that his own sexual desire matches Chuck's, makes him recoil from acting in the same manner. His pathetic position gets revealed by his brief awkward questions to Chuck and the latter's unruffled tone and suggestive invitation right after the rape scene:

> - Have you seen Grace?
> - She is at my place
> - She is busy?
> - Not anymore, go right in.

---

[1]   Lacan defines the symptom as metaphor and desire as metonymy in his essay "The Agency of the Letter in the Unconscious or Reason since Freud", *Écrits: A Selection*, translated by Alan Sheridan, London & New York: Routledge, 1989, p. 193.

Yet he opts to walk away after standing reluctantly at the invisible door of the house, a gesture attesting to his complete awareness of what Grace went through. Hurt's voice cuts in right after that only to add to the viewer's discomfort with his cynical, "Yet again, Grace had made a miraculous escape from her pursuers with the aid of the people of Dogville". For the truck driver, Ben, the sexual is attained only through the economic. He visits prostitutes when he has enough money to have sex, and when he rapes Grace in his truck he makes a point of assuring her beforehand that this is "not personal", philosophizing the whole situation according to the rules of the "freight industry". Grace, in fact, becomes a receptacle for the town's psychic troubles, an unpaid prostitute who not only suffers humiliation silently but who often masochistically defends her tormentors as well. As for Tom, the sexual, though sought after all along, counts for nothing compared to his desire to maintain a sense of "author-ity" over Grace and everybody else in the town, including his own self. The authority of being the "author" of everybody and everything around him.

This image of mastery upon the self and upon the other makes Tom the very representation of man striding forward on his way of human enlightenment. His leadership of the people of Dogville strikes a resemblance between the town and the image that Adorno and Horkheimer draw for Odysseus' ship filled with marines under his command as a representation of human civilization detaching itself from myth, or the sirens and their infatuating song.[2] The movie seems to represent a static moment, however, where the ship stops, takes aboard one of the beautiful sirens, and risks listening to the song for two weeks – needless to say with disastrous results. Tom, whom the film projects as some kind of small-time Odysseus, "complies with the contract of his bondage, and, bound to the mast, struggles to throw himself into the arms of the seductresses" (Horkheimer and Adorno 43) for whom Grace stands. His character is where the humanist, the artist, the savior, and the philosopher intersect, and it is exactly that character that carries the ultimate sacrifice and the ultimate guilt within. He seems to represent what Adorno and Horkheimer call "the introversion of sacrifice" (46) as what the history of human civilization always meant. Tom's life's project is to acquire an identity as an author, and for that he always proves capable of sacrificing anything. It is fitting, in the film's discursive narrative, that this particular character becomes the ultimate victim in the last scene of vigilante justice that Grace brings to the town.

Perceived as a cinematic critique of America and the American people, *Dogville's* main point seems to be to make the anonymous viewer ill-at-ease. For the "universal dream of home" (Wood 42), of liberty and democracy, that idea that epitomizes the human experience and its achievements to be at stake, ought to be a gloomy idea. There seems to be little doubt that *Dogville* does not view

---

[2]   This is the main theme of the chapter entitled "Excursus I: Odysseus or Myth and Enlightenment" in Horkheimer and Adorno's *Dialectic of Enlightenment*, edited by Gunzelin Schmid Noerr, translated by Edmund Jephcott, Stanford, CA: Stanford University Press, 2002, pp. 35–62.

America as just another civilization in the course of human history. As Hurt states in the opening scene, Dogville is "up here where the road came to its definitive end", in other words, where the human experience seems to be coming to a close. Yet it is the portrayal of the society of Dogville itself that is meant to make the viewer ponder over the question: Is this really where the road comes to an end? The satirical message of *Dogville* subtly suggests that it is certainly ironic that the road should come to its definitive end in such a place where hospitability, overcoming human selfishness, the ability to forgive and, above all, friendship are all impossible.

Dogville's inhabitants are portrayed as gregarious but not friendly. A gregarious person tends to associate with people of his/her type, which does give some sense of belonging to a group or a certain society or a family. But one of the main messages that *Dogville* seems to be communicating is that friendship demands more. Friendship demands acceptance of, and the erotic rivalry with, the other as such. This could be one of the reasons why the inhabitants of Dogville, in spite of their common human differences, are portrayed in such a way as to strike the viewer as outlandishly alike. A stark similarity can be observed between them and a group of people that Dickens's hero Martin Chuzzlewit meets in a hotel bar in America. Criticizing Dickens's work in his essay "Institutional America", Peter Conrad writes:

> The Americans Martin encounters are without exception listless, hollow-cheeked, tedious, and portentously verbose. The company in the hotel bar endlessly replicates the set of five or six types he has already met. When you've seen a thousand Americans, you've seen one. Their common worship of individualism has ended by effacing their individuality. They all value personality as a commodity, but because it is the same ideal personality which everyone wishes to acquire, the result is homogeneity. (57)

Dogville, not unlike Dickens's story – which may be thought to be less popular than his other masterpieces in English literature – is an artistic work that invents an imago of America that is meant to reflect a superficial and pretentious innocence, mixed with a religious hypocrisy that suppresses the erotic. Therefore, representing the sexual as always twisted, unnatural, and dominated by the economic seems to be targeting what is perceived by the inventor of *Dogville* as the innocent and religious nature of small-town America. In other words, one of the reasons why the sexual is suppressed, or, why America is desexualized, could be a particular view which sees the idea of sexuality to be incompatible with what is commonly perceived as America's Puritanism, pragmatism, and religious nature.

In spite of the fact that one of America's postures is that of being the home of commercialized sex, the religious spirit and the idea of innocence were always taken to be markers that distinguish America from Europe. America has always been thought to differentiate itself from Europe by a number of things, chief among them religiosity and references to God in national emblems. In *Democracy in America*, Tocqueville writes:

> America is still the place where the Christian religion has kept the greatest real power over men's souls; and nothing better demonstrates how useful and natural it is to man, since the country where it now has widest sway is both the most enlightened and the freest. (291)

Tocqueville's observation, even if debatable, does point to the uniqueness of America's character as a country whose quest for enlightenment, power, democracy and modernization, is paradoxically mixed with an avowedly religious spirit. Religious eschatology is therefore used by the creator of *Dogville* subtly to suggest that such eschatology must be firmly established in America's beliefs, and ought to be at its strongest in the American mind.

The film seems to make use of religious eschatology as well as to mock it. Its epitome, reached by Grace's transformation from the historical victim or the sacrificed son of God to the revengeful Christ of the Day of Judgment, can be interpreted in terms of the Freudian return of the repressed, but what establishes the film's satirical message is that it is made to look like a typical American stunt with guns blazing all around. The film seems to communicate to the viewer that the idea of the ultimate sacrifice, which is the core of Christianity and what constitutes its *Aufhebung*, or its (anti)thetical departure from Judaic thought, seems to be alien to itself due to its incompatibility with the eschatology. The final dialogue in the film between Grace and her father sums up the whole idea. He tells Grace: "Rapists and murderers may be the victims according to you, but I call them dogs, and if they are lapping up their own vomit the only way to stop them is with the lash". The final destruction of Dogville thus seems to symbolize the philosophical triumph of the Old Testament God, the father, over the New Testament merciful God, Grace.

The father's discourse suggests that God sacrificing himself, or part of himself, purposefully for alleviating the sin of humanity, i.e., to make humanity sinless or innocent, seems to be a sacrifice of himself for himself. "Arrogance" is the key word by which this position is described, and through which the idea is communicated to the viewer in one of the most engaging dialogues in the history of film making:

> - Grace: So I am arrogant, I am arrogant because I forgive people.
> - Father: My God, can't you see how condescending you are when you say that. You have this preconceived notion that nobody can possibly attain the same high ethical standards as you [...] I cannot think of anything more arrogant than that. You forgive others with excuses that you would never in the world permit for yourself.
> - Grace: Why shouldn't I be merciful?

- Father: You should be merciful when there is time to be merciful but, you must maintain your own standards, you owe them that. The penalty you deserve for your transgression they deserve for their transgressions.
- Grace: They are human beings.
- Father: And does every human being need to be accountable for their own actions? Of course they do. You don't even give them that chance, and that is extremely arrogant.

At the same time the eschatological idea of God returning to punish humanity for its sins completely destroys the core idea of sacrifice. Eschatology thus cannot but be human imagination inevitably reflecting human psychic turbulences; a limited imagination that seems to be unable to take off any farther than asserting – consciously or unconsciously – that the repressed has to return somehow, someday, in some form or another. What is supposed to be a divine scheme about where humanity originates from and where it is going seems to always fall back helplessly in what Lacan describes as "the realm of what is considered acceptable or, in other words, the realm of prejudices" (*Ethics of Psychoanalysis* 251). *Dogville* is a text that is aware of what it ridicules, though what is ridiculed in it is itself what is being used to communicate its final message of retribution.

The film's final message is certainly a violent one, not to mention that the idea of murder casts its shadow on it from its start to the very end. The figure of Grace, in spite of her victimization, seems to carry the air of the femme fatale. Her aura and her charm captivate, if not Dogville, then certainly the viewer. The idea that she ends up being the ultimate murderess, if carefully contemplated, actually carries no surprises. The conversion of the ultimate martyr to the ultimate murderer is in fact one of the most likely conversions. Grace seems to carry the germ of Sophocles's heroine, Antigone. There is no tyranny in her, and this means, precisely, no human weakness.

In his analysis of the tragedy of *Antigone*, Lacan writes about Creon: "We will see later what he is, that is, like all executioners and tyrants at bottom, a human character. Only the martyrs know neither pity nor fear" (*Ethics of Psychoanalysis* 267). He differentiates between Creon's and Antigone's antagonistic positions by pointing out that Creon's tyranny belongs to the "normal" barred subject, in other words, it belongs to the "sane" human being who is constituted by his symbolic network, while Antigone's martyrdom marks her total identification with her desire for death. At such a level of identification with one's own desire, there can be no difference between killing the self and killing the other. So, when Grace finally decides to kill everybody in the town, she also *literally* kills her own old forgiving self without which she cannot be "Grace" any more. But it is the style of the execution that evokes a countless number of similar scenes in Hollywood movies when guns start going off systematically and party-like. If the people of Dogville are made to represent the society of small town America, Grace herself is the ultimate representation of the familiar cinematic Hollywood image of the lonely

American cowboy, the vigilante killer, who saves the day by executing justice in his own way with his own gun.

America thus is represented in *Dogville* simultaneously and divergently as desexualized as well as murderous. The affinity between desexing and murder seems to have a certain implicit – sometimes explicit – legacy in literature and film. As for Hollywood productions, the examples range from classic cowboy films with the lonely American hero, who lives mainly in continuous transition between cities and townships, often away from what defines and confirms his sexuality, woman, up to the *Terminator* series. The difference between *A Fistful of Dollars* and *Terminator* is that in Sergio Leone's film, the hero is a man whose slow movements, slow speech and the unbelievable, mechanistic and superhuman speed by which he uses the gun resemble that of a machine, while in James Cameron's film, the hero is a machine that looks like a man. Both the desexualized machine-like man and the desexualized man-like machine, however, have the same cinematic cowboy ethics. As for literature, it can be argued that the establishment of such a theme of murderous desexualization goes back in the history of literary production at least to Shakespearean drama.

One of Shakespeare's most vivid images of the desexualized murderer is the Roman general Caius Martius, the male protagonist in *Coriolanus*, who is portrayed in most of the play as a desexualized war-machine. In act II, scene I, after capturing the city of Corioles and securing victory over the Volsces, Martius is given, as his mother Volumnia points out, "the whole name of the war", "Coriolanus". He gets his new identity out of what he destroys. From then on, Shakespeare's verses seem to give him a kind of mechanistic inhuman quality. Thus Volumnia's words: "Death, that dark spirit, in's nervy arm doth lie, which, being advanced, declines, and then men die" (533). But the most telling words come from Cominius in scene II, where he describes Martius's unrivalled systematic slaughter of the enemy in the battle of Corioles: "His sword, death's stamp, where it did mark, it took from face to foot. He was a thing of blood, whose every motion was timed with dying cries" (544). The resemblance between him and the cinematic terminator is striking.

Yet it seems that Shakespeare's most illuminating contribution to this discourse which marks the affinity between desexualization and murder is a female character. In her famous soliloquy in act I, scene V of *Macbeth*, Lady Macbeth prepares herself for murder by saying: "Come, you spirits that tend on mortal thoughts, unsex me here, and fill me from the crown to the toe, top-full of direst cruelty" (112–13). The somewhat scholastic notion of referring Lady Macbeth's actions to her love for her husband as a devoted wife has been rectified by the view that this is the very thing that she wants to disown: womanhood. But why "unsex"? And why "here"? Or more precisely, *where* is "here"? We are not helped by the fact that some of Shakespeare's many editors inserted a stage direction that says "touching her heart".[3] The use of the verb "unsex" followed

---

[3]   For example, Horace Howard Furness Jr., in the *New Variorum Edition of Shakespeare: Macbeth*, New York: Dover Publications, Inc., 1963, p. 78.

by an unidentified "here" puts this popular editorial stage direction in doubt. The prayer undoubtedly indicates a desire for a removal of something, but is it really just feminine qualities as compared to male ones that are meant to be removed? In other words, does Shakespeare really want to say that in order to become a killer you have to be masculine? And what does it mean to unsex oneself if the unsexing does not actually guarantee or secure gender inversion? Strictly speaking, rejecting womanhood still does not seem to either fulfill the wish of Lady Macbeth or to get us very far through the intricacies of Shakespeare's mind.

While John O'Connor interprets "unsex me here" typically as "remove all my feminine qualities" (26), Horace Howard Furness Jr states that "the very point here emphasized is that she abjured womanhood". He then includes the typical stage direction: "*me here* [Touching her Heart]" (78). Other possibly more skeptical editors, perhaps out of a sense of facing something that defies direct interpretations, chose not to comment on Lady Macbeth's line at all. Kenneth Muir in the 1992 Arden Shakespeare edition of *Macbeth* simply skips it, one needs to add, quite unexpectedly, since that edition in fact gives extensive comments on "Come you spirits that tend on mortal thoughts". The elaborate interpretation of evoking the spirits of death and destruction is followed by an unexplained complete silence about the purpose of such evoking.

In her *Shakespeare's Division of Experience*, Marilyn French points to what she sees as an "ambiguity about gender roles in Macbeth" that makes Lady Macbeth in her soliloquy "resolve [...] to align herself with the male principle" in a play in which imagery, French notes, "is divided into masculine and feminine categories" and in which priority is given to the masculine "courage, prowess, the ability to kill" over the feminine "compassion, nurturance, and mercy" (241–51). French, thus, seeks to locate the Shakespearean tragedy in a violent masculine realm marked by an acute gender division, which is quite uncharacteristic of Shakespeare, who often plays with genders in his plays.

In the Oxford Shakespeare edition of *Macbeth*, Nicholas Brooke seems to take an opposite view. He first gives priority to the interpretation of "mortal thoughts" as "human thoughts" over "deadly thoughts". He then comments on "unsex me here" in the following manner:

> "Sex" governs all the range of human experience ("mortal thoughts") that follows: kindness, remorse, pity, fertility; it is, in short, her humanity and not simply her femininity that Lady Macbeth wishes away – the thoughts are very close to those which disturb Macbeth in I.7. (113)

Brooke's editorial comments break away from the gender differentiation discourse. It is significant that he mentions "fertility". Fertility relates directly to the body and to sexuality. His primary comment that "sex governs all the range of human experience" removes barriers between humanity and sexuality. But why would Lady Macbeth wish away her fertility? It is Freud who has the answer to this question even though he seems to mix the cause with the effect with regard to

Lady Macbeth's character analysis, nevertheless, reaches to the core of the issue – quite characteristically of him – by one word. "Barrenness" is the key word by which Freud unlocks the character of Lady Macbeth. In his essay "The Character of Lady Macbeth", Freud writes:

> It would be a perfect example of poetic justice [...] if the childlessness of Macbeth and the barrenness of his Lady were the punishment for their crimes against the sanctity of generation – if Macbeth could not become a father because he had robbed children of their father and a father of his children, and if Lady Macbeth suffered the unsexing she had demanded of the spirits of murder. I believe Lady Macbeth's illness, the transformation of her callousness into penitence, could be explained directly as a reaction to her childlessness, by which she is convinced of her impotence against the decrees of nature, and at the same time reminded that it is through her own fault if her crime has been robbed of the better part of its fruits. (42)

Yet, it is not clearly justified that Lady Macbeth's barrenness, as Freud seems to allude, comes as a result from her unusual prayer to the spirits, in a Shakespearean attempt at poetical justice. If she is a barren lady, there is no reason to discard the possibility that she would be in a position to know this long before the tragedy takes place. Her barrenness could in effect be the instigator of the murder and not the effect of it. The point in such a case would be: "unsex me here, as I am already barren and useless, as I will not be able to found a dynasty of kings, and not even of noblemen, as I have nothing to lose, why not have a shot at the throne". In such a case, it would not be Lady Macbeth's intention to be a killer that is punished by barrenness as Freud seems to suggest. It would be her barrenness that made her a killer by wishing to give up the only thing that she still possesses: her sexuality, since she is already, de facto, not a woman. In her case, abjuring womanhood is meaningless.

In a memorable performance of the play, performed by an English cast on the stage of the Egyptian Opera House in Cairo in 1989, this writer witnessed a Lady Macbeth who violently, unequivocally, and with a loud sound that gave the audience a pain in the stomach rather than a hard-on, slapped her female organ instead of touching her heart. Although this came as a surprise that took the audience off guard, somehow it didn't seem or sound vulgar. It didn't seem out of context either. Her unusually deepened voice, her direct look into the eyes of the audience in the front rows – and not for instance up in the air as she is supposed to be talking to the spirits – and her violent gesture seemed desperate to communicate a very articulate message, a message that was obviously meant to be corrective of a long-standing tradition of interpretation. A message that says: It could as well be desperation, and not ambition, that dictates Lady Macbeth's actions in the first third of the drama.

Therefore, in view of such a message, Lady Macbeth's words would point to a radical desire for castration so as to constitute a certain lack. But the lack is supposed to be already there in the female. The lack in this case is not of an organ whether it is the heart or the genitals. It is a lack that does not differentiate between genders. It is a lack of sexuality itself that she desires, or, the removal of that which makes her aware of her human body. And sexuality, though it exceeds by far representation by single or particular human organs, has been orthodoxly associated with the genitals more than any other parts of the body.

It doesn't seem just a coincidence that the greatest dramatist of all time makes his hero in *Coriolanus* address his wife in a direct manner only twice, in two moments which stand out in an astounding contrast to each other. At the height of his victory and his newly war-acquired identity and self-confidence in act II, scene 1, Martius addresses Virgilia as "my gracious silence" (535), while in act V, scene 3, at his lowest moments, with no identity, and knowing that he will not be able to keep the promise he made to the Volsces and will probably be killed by them, he calls her "best of my flesh" (633). Yet, it is at this latter moment when he refers to the materialist and the body instead of the ideological that he is truly at his best, when he could abandon the idea of taking revenge on his own people.

It seems that what Shakespeare really wanted to say in *Macbeth* as well as in *Coriolanus* is that conscience, or that which works against the killing instinct, comes out of an awareness of the body, while the death of conscience is, *always*, a marker of cutting off the life of the body. What makes Martius an exceptional tragic hero, however, is Shakespeare's ambiguous presentation of him – a presentation that seems to make *Coriolanus* as a play at one and the same time a tragedy and a satire, with a hero who seems to derive both sympathy and laughter. His epic figure as the awesome Roman general is mixed with a sort of a boyish attitude which makes him his mother's boy. His unrivalled accomplishments as a highly experienced warrior are only matched by a kind of immaturity and innocence that make him a social and political failure.

It is not strange thus that *Dogville* seems to subtly associate these ideas of desexualization and murder with its main attack target: what it perceives as American innocence. American innocence is in fact a theme that has been handled by many writers in various ways. Michael Wood, for example, argues that America talks itself into being innocent via cinema with a discourse that suggests that:

> The innocence of victims stems from the principle that says that victims must be innocent, that unless you are innocent, you are not a victim. If you are guilty, even only slightly, the whole question changes, since merely getting more than your just deserves is plainly a matter of moral accounting rather than a miscarriage of justice.

He then argues that "at the back of all this lurks the American weakness for the idea of purity, for the notion of an entirely unflecked innocence" (140). While Wood investigates the effect of Hollywood's representations of American innocence on American society, Edward Said examines America's political motives behind that image of innocence which, for him, is already established in the collective

American psyche. In an essay entitled "The Other America", Said questions the American "collective we", which he perceives as:

> A national identity represented without apparent demurral by our president, our secretary of state at the UN, our armed forces in the desert, and our interests, which are routinely seen as self-defensive, without ulterior motive, and in an overall way, innocent in the way that a traditional woman is supposed to be innocent, pure, free of sin. (*Al-Ahram Weekly*)

Though this seems to be a human image of America as woman, it is not so far away from Hadaly who, as a machine, cannot but be innocent, pure and free of sin. Ihab Hassan, to take another example, creates one of the most sublime versions of American innocence in which it is seen as a form of positive neurosis that constitutes a "regressive force that prevents the self from participating fully in the world [...] As a result, the greatest values affirmed by the American conscience have often been affirmed against the ruling spirit of the land" (*Radical Innocence* 40).

What can be drawn from all of these accounts of American innocence is that America is always expected to go beyond just the country and its national interests. Everybody overloads the symbol with their own romantic images. Some (mis)recognize in it an un-worldly spiritual detachment, an epic quality, and an unrivalled conscience. Some question its isolationism. Some read violence underneath its image of innocence. And, some mutilate it, as it will be argued in what follows, out of love – a love, however, not for America, but for something that does not exist; yet. With regard to *Dogville*, the conclusion that is to be drawn here is that in spite of its totally negative imago of America – or precisely because of that – the film seems to belong to those works that mutilate America out of disappointed love. As one of numerous phantasmal representations of America, it overloads its invented imago of it with its own romantic, or traumatic, fantasies.

Like Villiers de l'Isle-Adam's *Tomorrow's Eve*, *Dogville* presents us with one of the principal heroes of the modern age, the Odysseus of enlightenment, who lives in an America that is made to sacrifice the sexual for a mixture of the scientific, the economic, the religious, and, in *Dogville*, the killing instinct. No human civilization has been more mythologized or dehumanized in the history of man. The myth seems to have gone even beyond Hollywood's wildest dreams. The fundamental difference between *Tomorrow's Eve* and *Dogville*, however, as texts created by European subjects, is that the European subject himself is represented in Villiers' novel by the second major character in it, Lord Ewald, while in *Dogville*, the European subject seems to shut himself outside the story, looking upon America without looking upon the self – a kind of repression that does not fail to point to the fact that this subject, just as Lord Ewald loves Hadaly, the mechanical android which represents the perfect romantic love, is himself in love with what America is supposed to represent.

Love, in Lacanian thought, is a coin that always carries aggressivity on its other side. Because love is of a "fundamentally narcissistic structure" (*Four*

Fundamental Concepts 186), the object of love is both a confirmation of the lover's ego and a destabilization of that ego at once. Because the lover always (mis)recognizes what he loves in the object of love, he tends to overload it with more than it can afford. Lacan sums this up by the following words: "I love you, but, because inexplicably I love in you something more than you – the *objet petit a* – I mutilate you" (268). Similarly, what the critique of America by the European subject seems to unconsciously say is: "I love you, but, because inexplicably I love in you something more than you – the myth, the dream, the universal home, the unattainable, that which goes beyond the country, or, that which never reified/will never reify – I mutilate you".

In other words, love is a letter which "*always arrives at its destination*" because the addressee, as Žižek puts it, is "from the very beginning the sender himself" (*Enjoy Your Symptom* 13), and the content of the message is his own being. It emanates from the subject and is reflected back on the subject, precisely because it is the field where the ego most practices its favorite ritual, self-alienation, or, that first erotic relation with the self which establishes itself in the mirror stage. Lacan states that:

> There is a sort of structural crossroads here to which we must accommodate our thinking if we are to understand the nature of aggressivity in man and its relation with the formalism of his ego and his objects. It is in this erotic relation, in which the human individual fixes upon himself an image that alienates him from himself, that are to be found the energy and the form on which this organization of the passions that he will call his ego is based. (*Écrits: A Selection* 21)

It comes as no surprise that this love/hate relationship often produces indicative texts around objects of love that are never complete, and thus, they always leave the subject hanging perpetually from an illusion that Lacan names as the *objet petit a*. The mutilation is thus largely caused by the disappointment that the subject suffers from first or repeated paranoiac (mis)encounters with the real, namely in this case, that his imagined object of love is in fact devoid of romantic or sublime traits. It may be arguable that *Dogville* can be interpreted simply as a work of bad conscience, yet, it seems that at its unconscious core, it is a paranoiac work which *produces* this mis(encounter) by taking the agency of creating an imago of America and attaining a kind of mastery over the creation to compensate for the unattainable imagined beloved.

Chapter 8
Said's America: America's Said

To live in New York, the epitome of America's capital and power, with the notion that one has been born in Jerusalem, the ancient holy land and the most disputed city on earth, in Edward Said's words, "centre of the world, *locus classicus* of Palestine, Israel, and Paradise" (*After the Last Sky* 36) must have carried a special sort of feeling. At the age of 53, and after 37 years of his residence in New York, Said writes: "The sheer gravity of my coming to the United States in 1951 amazes me even today […] to this day I still feel that I am away from home" (*Out of Place* 222). And this is in spite of the fact that the statement "I'm an American citizen" (6) seems to have been imposed on his being since his early childhood by his parents – a Palestinian-American father and a Palestinian mother who obviously wanted to secure their only son an American future, away from the Arab world and the Palestinian nightmare.

There seems to be no doubt that Edward Said's position as an Arab-American writer was a particularly problematic one. Almost all of Said's writings are marked by his self-consciousness as someone who carries within himself the two incompatible figures of an Arab and an American. Believing that the majority of Americans plainly think of Arabs to all intents and purposes as a virtually insignificant people, and that the majority of Arabs never study either America or its ally Israel seriously, even though their lives are most affected by both, this "hostility-and-ignorance" (*Culture and Imperialism* 294) relationship does not seem to be just an external political and cultural issue that is out there in a world registered by Said. As far as he himself lives in "between worlds" (Said, *Reflections on Exile* 554–68), it has, as it will be shown, some of the most revealing unconscious reflections. It might have been less complicated to live in America as just another Arab-American than to live in it as the celebrated American writer and professor whose country of origin just ceased to exist at a certain historical moment, and who had to live where he thinks the Palestinian cannot be represented except as "either a faceless refugee or a terrorist" (*Power, Politics, and Culture* 317).

In an interview entitled "The Road Less Traveled", Said mentions that he has been actually dubbed by a "very respectable magazine" as "the professor of terror" (*Power, Politics, and Culture* 414). Given his own view of the intellectual, however, this might have been something that he equally deplored and enjoyed. In another interview entitled "American Intellectuals and Middle East Politics", Said comments on the hidden "affinity between the two terms": Intellectual and terrorist (*Power, Politics, and Culture* 332). He is an intellectual who is particularly concerned with the role of the intellectual. To him, this role is summarized in the phrase "speaking truth to power" which entitles his core discussion in the 1993

BBC Reith Lectures. In this series of lectures, Said shows that he believes in the intellectual as a sort of prophet whose task in life is the advancement of freedom and justice.

Like most prophets, the intellectual, according to Said, no matter where he lives, should be "[an] exile and marginal, as amateur, and as the author of a language that tries to speak the truth to power" (*Representations of the Intellectual* xvi). Hence, he states that the intellectual "belongs on the same side with the weak and unrepresented" (22). In fact he goes further than that by suggesting that the intellectual who claims to be apolitical is some kind of an ersatz thinker: "The intellectual who claims to write only for him or herself, or for the sake of pure learning, or abstract science is not to be, and *must not* be, believed" (110).

His political writings thus come out of a firm belief that both writing and reading of texts are never done from an apolitical self-referential position. They must involve ideological conflicts, different political interests, and confrontations with an other. This other, according to Said, "willy-nilly turns interpretation into a social activity, albeit with unforeseen consequences, audiences, constituencies, and so on" ("Opponents" 3). In other words, just as history is included in or made by the text, the text itself must be a product of a historical moment, intrinsically situated in its own specific context. Said's works, accordingly, reflect what Shelley Walia describes as his "unabashed commitment to an ideology of historical reconstruction by critical and political involvement" (7).

The intellectual to Said is a highly charged and restless being. The "affinity" between the intellectual and the terrorist to him seems to allude to the fact that the intellectual's resistance to power, his exposure of its ideological coerciveness, his habit of disturbing accepted givens, and his belonging on the side of the weak and unrepresented seem to resemble the radical or rebellious nature of the terrorist. That is why in his comments on Yevgeny Bazarov, the intellectual nihilist hero of the Russian writer Ivan Turgenev's best known novel *Fathers and Sons*, Said touches on that idea: "When he falls in love with Anna Sergeyevna she is attracted to him, but also terrified: to her, his untrammeled, often anarchical intellectual energy suggests chaos. Being with him, she says at one point, is like teetering at the edge of an abyss" (*Representations of the Intellectual* 15). To Said, there seems to be something explosive about both figures. Perceived by many as a distinctive example of this, Said, in the words of one of his most sensitive critics, Mustapha Marrouchi, is the "intellectual figure as a vigilant *saboteur*" (7). In his essay "The Will to Authority and Transgression", Marrouchi writes:

> [Said] has been so spendthrift with himself, and so loud in praise of folly, that he has laid himself open to many charges […] For many in the West, he is still a slightly embarrassing presence, the unruly *enfant terrible* who makes a display of himself at the dinner table. (205–6)

If one is allowed to draw a radical equivalent, there is no human being who perceives himself to be materially more "spendthrift with himself" than the

Palestinian suicide bomber who, first and foremost, kills himself or herself so wastefully – an act which *loudly* praises what seems to be the folly of all follies. In spite of all the difficulties of exile, the fact that Said was a Palestinian admittedly had its own peculiar pleasures. In a video-recorded discussion with Salman Rushdie about his book *After the Last Sky*, Said says that being Palestinian "teaches one to feel one's own sort of particularity, not so much only as a problem, but as a kind of gift in a way [...] we are sort of set apart, and it gives us a kind of an aura if you like, of specialness" ("Ideas of Our Time"). This sounds particularly subversive in a discussion of a work in which the fundamental issues of the Palestinian community are taken down to their most basic existential crux by posing the enormous questions: "Do we exist? What proof do we have? [...] When did we become 'a people'? When did we stop being one?" (*After the Last Sky* 34).

Although America represented itself to him at an early stage of his life as liberation from British colonialism and the grim British education he received in Egypt, he seems to have gradually realized that what seems to be America's matriarchal absorption of the Orient is no less traumatic than Europe's patriarchal penetration of it. The difference between European Orientalism and American Orientalism to Said is of crucial importance. For while the former derives its strength from actual historical presence in the East, actual rule, cultural and philological study of nations, and controversial representations of Oriental cultures, the latter is mainly based on abstractions and is staged – most of the time cinematically – for specific political purposes.

In the case of Arabs and Muslims, for example, Said claims that America's Orientalism is just tritely connected to the indecorous idea of the creation of a Western democratic ally in the heart of the Islamic world and, in his own words, "is politicized by the presence of Israel" (*Media Education Foundation*). Apart from this staged and politicized kind of Orientalism, America remains that great conglomeration of world cultures as the immigrant society par excellence. Thus, "attempts made recently to declare that America is one thing and not another [...] the quarrel over what is the American tradition, and what is the canon, and what are the unifying aspects of America" was a disturbing phenomenon which Said witnessed in the last few years of his life. He believed that such discussions over American identity "can turn into a kind of imported [un-American] sense of nationalism" (Barenboim and Said, *Parallels and Paradoxes* 13).

It is revealing to note here though that what American cinema – and oddly enough some of the Third World cinematic productions as well – does to the theory of Orientalism goes far beyond just the American Orientalist politically-based staged spectacle. In his interview entitled "Orientalism, Arab intellectuals, Marxism, and Myth in Palestinian History", Said stated:

> *Orientalism* was basically used by Arab readers as a means for conflict and not for developing an analytical thought based on ideas. This factor made the term "Orientalism" an insult. If you want to insult someone, you call him

"Orientalist". This is one of the negative consequences of the caricatural reading of my book, because I do not say or imply anything like this. (*Power, Politics, and Culture* 438)

One has to say that this is *partly* true. If Said had used the word "some" – or even "most" for that matter – before "Arab readers" he would have avoided falling into Orientalist generalizations himself. The number of Arab readers and writers who did develop, analyze, utilize, expand, and in many cases evaluate and pass judgment on Said's ideas in *Orientalism*, in his own life, could not have been something that was virtually unknown to him. Besides, there are many reasons to believe that "Orientalist" does not seem to be any more insulting than the term *Oriental* itself, which also became a sort of an insult, especially in Eastern societies, and particularly since the writing of *Orientalism*.

It is true that Said rejected both terms at a later stage in "Orientalism Reconsidered" in which he argues that "there could be no Orientalism without, on the one hand, the Orientalists, and on the other, the Orientals" (*Reflections on Exile* 199). Yet, the fact remains that in the theory of Orientalism, as Walia puts it:

The totalizing force of Western discourse is rejected as "inauthentic", with the implicit assumption that there is a representation which is real. Yet, attempts at representing indigenous cultures invariably turn out to be orientalisms in reverse. (47)

This means that Said's uncovering of Western misconceptions of the Orient could only ever have possibly produced more misconceptions. Moreover, it can be argued that archiving everything related to Orientalism in a comprehensive clearly defined theoretical work tremendously helps in establishing what the work precisely seeks to eliminate. In fact, *Orientalism* can be effectively used by Orientalists themselves as a rich reference from which to get data on how to be deliberately an Orientalist, which might, in some pathological cases, be even a source of power and a way of exercising a kind of scientific, philological or cultural mastery. This is how a critique, in spite of the noble intentions of its writer, can be turned against itself.

On the other hand, it is the term "Oriental" which seems to have been completely wrenched from its previous geographical, historical, and cultural connotations. It can be argued that it is mainly because of Said's *Orientalism* that "Oriental" today can no more simply describe someone or something from the geographical Orient, be it Japan, China, India, or the Middle East. "Oriental" has been remarkably reduced so as to precisely designate *only* what is supine, negative, incompetent and useless as created by Western misrepresentations and put in sharp relief by Said himself.

Perhaps this also explains what seems to be a kind of awkwardness that is associated with discussing Said's theory of Orientalism. The conservatism by which some scholars talk about it is strangely often coupled with too much uncalled-for praise for the theorist himself, arguably to avoid and at the same time compensate for the embarrassment of discussing his work. Some of the clichéd statements that one often hears are: "The writer who revolutionized Western thought" or "the professor who completely changed Western thoughts about Oriental cultures", and so on, even though Said himself expressed his astonishment in 1998 that more than 20 years since writing *Orientalism*, the Western Orientalist discourse has actually gained much more strength (*Media Education Foundation*). It is thus not an exaggeration to say that the self negation of it all can actually create paranoiac positions. A "paranoiac stance", Žižek writes, can be "itself the threat, the destructive plot, against which it is fighting" (*For they know not* xxxvii).

This book does not intend to add to what Abdirahman A. Hussein describes as the "contentious response" to Said's *Orientalism* which, Hussein believes, "has helped cast a distorting – not to say inhibiting – sort of light on Said's work as a whole" (13). The argument is rather that, even while taking into consideration the fictional nature of both the Oriental and the Orientalist, it is the Orientalist that assumes any kind of presence in almost all discussions of and debates over Said's *Orientalism*. Consequently, talking from the position of criticizing Orientalism seems to be always already dominated by the odd omnipotence of an *over-critiqued* fiction that derives its strength primarily from being the subject of that critique. It is only the Oriental, whatever that is, that seems to remain largely irrelevant to the discussion. There is no question, however, about Said's criticism if seen solely from the point of the writer's intention as an intellectual who believes that he has a certain role in promoting social justice. In such a view, Said's criticism would not be seen as callously or arbitrarily aiming at establishing a general idea about how the West arrogantly gave itself the right to articulate what is known as the "Orient". As Hussein puts it: "Said's criticism as a whole involves an attempt to describe (and pass judgment on) the intellectual's variable positionality vis-à-vis the powerful ideologies which have shaped the modern world" (14).

It is only in America, and oddly enough in some of its incorporated "Third World" societies, that the Orientalist discourse is in fact seriously challenged by what Žižek refers to in a number of his essays as the literal identification with ideology. According to Žižek, "*the stepping out of (what we experience as) ideology is the very form of our enslavement to it*" (*Žižek Reader* 60).[1] The same ideological power applies to the Orientalist discourse. In his essay "*Orientalism and its Problems*", Dennis Porter states that "Orientalism in one form or another is not only what we have but all we can ever have" (180). In other words, there is no stepping out of it. While what can produce a kind of disheartenment of an

---

[1] This idea is also elaborated by Žižek in: "Fantasy as a Political Category", *The Žižek Reader*, p. 97, "How Did Marx Invent the Symptom?", *The Sublime Object of Ideology*, p. 30, and, "Are Cultural Studies Really Totalitarian?", *Did Somebody Say Totalitarianism?* p. 226.

ideological discourse is the "playful identification"[2] with it, subverting ideology, in Žižekan thought, can be achieved by nothing but a total and literal identification with its mandates or "the procedure of the ultra-orthodox subversion of the law through the very overidentification with it".[3]

It can thus be argued that in the case of Orientalism, whereas European Orientalism historically abstracted the Orient, America abstracted the abstraction itself. Hollywood does not revise or critique Orientalism, it takes it as it is and pushes it even further to the very limits of the completely unbelievable. Somehow this does not seem so much an affirmation of Orientalism as the only effective way of its destabilization. Whereas in Europe – and in European-affected societies – Orientalism is critiqued awkwardly, implying the uneasy postcolonial position of the critique, in America, as well as in some Third World societies, there is what can be described as a preposterous identification with the Orientalist discourse itself, but which at the same time seriously undermines it by being unexpectedly "too Oriental". In the American context, what results from this is not a utopian equality or a dialogue-based democracy: It is something which Baudrillard calls a "de facto freedom expressed in rivalry and competition" which "gives a singular vivacity and an air of openness to the confrontation between the races" (*America* 83).

What is at stake in such a context is neither the Orient – if it exists – nor non-Western cultures in general. In the realm of the American hyper-real, Orientalism is not so much the (mis)representation of indigenous cultures, but rather what is referred to as the Oriental has become the very representation of what is Orientalist. The figure of the terrorist could be the extreme contemporary example of this. The terrorist in American films as a distorted cinematic representation of the Muslim or the Arab cannot easily pass as the believable generalization about a whole religion or a whole culture, as Said pointed out on many occasions. Opposed to that, Osama Bin Laden, the figure of the present-day terrorist par excellence, is the very ipso facto illustration of the cinematic terrorist which America produced countless times in action films. He is the image of the image, the reality-product bouncing right out of American cinema rather than either the misrepresented Muslim fundamentalist or the actual horrid product of Islam itself as a religion which is now seen by many to have gone astray.

---

[2]   Žižek's example on this is how the Bosnian rock group *Top lista nadrealista* consolidated Bosnian solidarity during the war in Bosnia against Serbian racism through playful identification with the racist obscenities themselves. "Passions of the Real, Passions of Semblance", *Welcome to the Desert of the Real! Five Essays on September 11 and Related Dates*, London and New York: Verso, 2002, p. 18.

[3]   Žižek gives the example of Heinrich von Kleist's hero in the novella *Michael Kohlhaas: From an Old Chronicle* in which the hero identifies himself completely with law and justice to the very limits of overthrowing both in the process. "The Myth and Its Vicissitudes", *Did Somebody Say Totalitarianism? Five Interventions in the (Mis)use of a Notion*, London and New York: Verso, 2001, pp. 32–4.

One example of how the total identification with an Orientalist view can in effect subvert the whole Orientalist discourse is Tunisian critic and filmmaker Ferid Boughedir's film *Halfaouine: Child of the Terraces*. From what seems to be an acutely Orientalist point of view, the film tells the story of a thirteen-year-old Tunisian boy's sexual awakening through his regular visits to the local Turkish bathhouse with his mother, where he gets an uninhibited chance to gaze upon a spectacular assortment of nude female bodies, protected by his age and his ability to act as if he has no sexual awareness. At the same time, he displays "manhood" by recounting what he sees in the bathhouse to two older boy friends who do not treat him as an equal. His father beats him frequently while trying to teach him two golden rules in the course of becoming a "man": "Men should never cry" and "men should stay away from the society of women". One day, when his peeping adventures in the bathhouse get discovered, the women harshly kick him out for good. He finds himself utterly isolated from both worlds of men and women. He experiences the scene of the circumcision of his baby brother by the bearded Sheikh of the town as the traumatic threat of castration. He finally gets out of this dark circle of guilt and inhibition when a young maid gives him full access to her naked body. The film ends with a scene in which he briskly avoids his father's slapping hand, runs away and climbs a wall to the roof of the house, from which he smilingly mocks his father's curses.

In accordance with Said's theory, a standard anti-Orientalist critical approach to this film would be to show that it distorts the reality of a modern Franco-Arab society which is not actually as patriarchal as the film portrays. Another accusation would be that it is obviously tailored as an exotic account of Oriental Arab sensuality, strict gender division, and the difficulty of coming of age under the puritanical conventions of Islam, for the consumption of Western gaze. Such readings, however, miss the film's major point: That it is precisely because of the hypocritical ways by which sexual desire is dealt with in this extremely Oriental society of Turkish baths, same gender bonding, sacred matrimonial oaths, and authoritarian divisions that the highest sexual experiences can be achieved, through the law-infringing beguilement of illicit relationships.

Transgressions of the ethical codes regulating the lives of grown-ups, which occur abundantly in the film, seem to communicate the fundamental Lacanian message that "without a transgression there is no access to *jouissance*". The boy's broad smile in the final scene indicates that he has finally learned why there is a law of prohibition and why there is a father. He has finally learned that he has been kicked out of the women's bathhouse neither because "men should stay away from the society of women" nor because of the fact that most men actually *want* to be in that society, but because it is this staged prohibition itself that defines the Lacanian "tight bond between desire and the Law" (*Ethics of Psychoanalysis* 177).

Halfaouine is thus less of an Orientalist view of a non-Western *type* of inhibited "Oriental" sensuality than a compelling statement that the enjoyment of sensuality as such is based on the very hypocritical ethical codes which happen to reach their extreme limits in "Oriental" societies. While an anti-Orientalist reading works against the grain, revealing the Orientalist tendencies of the film, it does not seem to the present writer to be an effective way to combat the misconceptions of Orientalism or the persistence of Orientalist stigmatizations. Thus, an anti-Orientalist reading, in such a case, seems to be neither the best of choices nor does it seem to constitute any resistance to the supposed "Orientalist" mandate of the text. A Lacanian reading seems to be certainly more effective; it does not resist the text, on the contrary, it pushes it violently to its very limits and, in doing so, it completely subverts the text. The difference thus between a symptomatic anti-Orientalist reading and a Lacanian reading is itself the difference between resisting power ineffectively by creating that Foucaultian/Saidian academically-assured yet practically always-already aborted stance of resistance to power and ideology, and, the Baudrillardian "challenge to power to be power, power of the sort that is total, irreversible, without scruple, and with no limit to its violence". Baudrillard states that "it is in facing this unanswerable challenge that power starts to break up" (*Forget Foucault* 60–1).

The paradox in Said's "hostility-and-ignorance" relationship between America and the Arab world is that it also allows a strange sort of mutual attraction. There seems to be an implicit point of identification between what can be referred to as the ultimate West and what is called the Third World. In his essay "The Smell of Love", Žižek proposes that "the true opposition today is not the one between the First World and the Third World, but the one between the whole of the First and Third World (the American global Empire and its colonies) and the Remaining Second World (Europe)". Using Adorno's idea that the "administered world" is marked by a "direct pact between the Superego (social authority) and the Id (illicit aggressive drives) at the expense of the Ego", Žižek raises this question: "Is not something structurally similar going on today at the political level, the weird pact between the postmodern global capitalism and the premodern societies at the expense of modernity proper?". His answer to that question leans towards the positive because "it is easy for the American multiculturalist global Empire to integrate premodern local traditions – the foreign body which it effectively cannot assimilate is the European modernity" (*Welcome to the Desert of the Real* 146).

What seems to be missing, however, in Žižek's view is not only the schism between the peoples living in Third World societies and their authoritarian governments (starkly revealed recently by the public protests in many North African and Middle Eastern countries), but the intricacies of the unconscious vestiges of the colonial experience as well. For it can be alternatively argued that in the collective unconscious of the colonized, the history of what can be figuratively portrayed as the sexual relationship between the colonizing West and the previously colonized East moves from pre-colonial Orientalist exotic discourse (a hidden Western desire for penetration), to modern colonial imperialist discourse (the actual trial of penetration), to what is called the postmodern and postcolonial discourse (mainly repellence and insulting through cinematic representations – on both "Orientalist" as well as "Occidentalist" sides now). That is to say, while historical colonialism was an actual trial of penetration with Europe as the penetrating powerful patriarch, post-colonialism seems to be marked by a kind of sexual harassment with America as the powerful harassing – culturally, economically and militarily – non-penetrating and in fact decidedly penetrated female. Conveniently, being in the female position presumes innocence and egalitarianism, and this is precisely how America in certain imaginations became an Empire. Its consuming feminine power can be experienced as being much scarier, more subtle, and much more traumatic than the masculine penetrating one.

Scattered along the huge corpus of his works, Said's representations of America seem to be highly diverse and carnivalistic. He wrote many things about America, and yet it seems to have been intrinsically problematic for him to come up with a definite idea about the country where he lived for 52 years. America seems to be a nameless thing that has represented itself to him in various faces since his early childhood. It is the escapist world of cinema. It represents liberation from European colonialism. It is a protection against danger. It is the prime danger. It is multicultural, isolationist, free, authoritarian, sentimental, rational, and Zionist all at once. Said kept struggling with that nameless thing until the end of his life. He never really was able to read America or frame it and secure it as "knowledge". Being fond of interpretation and its cultural politics, the only text that seems to have defied his interpretations was America.

In his book *Culture and Imperialism*, Said shows how Europe's narrating of the Orient went hand in hand with narratives in European works of art, like Conrad's *Heart of Darkness*, Austen's *Mansfield Park* and Verdi's opera *Aida*. In Said's view, as Shelley Walia puts it, "the novel and the empire, it can be argued, were born at a stroke" (9). The point which is to be observed here is that one common trait between America and the Orient seems to be that both were historically narrated, though differently, by the old empire. Symbolic America, like the exotic East, is largely a European narrative. One of the effects of that is that the imago of America as the new imperialist, even though meticulously constructed and thoroughly analyzed by Said so as to justify the idea, does not go without its own major problems.

As an empire, the difficulty that America poses is that in spite of its hegemonic policies and imperial posture, somehow it does not quite fit into the category of the imperialist. In his essay "Freedom from Domination in the Future", Said draws a similarity between America's present-day interventionism and its "nineteenth-century doctrine of Manifest Destiny" which was an ideology to promote the process of "the territorial expansion of the United States", justifying it by a whole corpus of literature on self-righteous ideas such as "historical mission, moral regeneration, the expansion of freedom" (*Culture and Imperialism* 288). But he observes, in his introduction to *Culture and Imperialism*, that "narratives of emancipation and enlightenment in their strongest form were also narratives of *integration* not separation" (xxvi).

Based on this idea, it can be argued that whereas European colonialism, which was part and parcel of the Enlightenment, could be easily critiqued as a problematic narrative of inclusion, of containing the other, however, in a patronizing way, of an ability to (mis)represent the other or, ultimately, of a certain desire to articulate the other, American multiculturalism and inclusion of different races and nationalities is paradoxically interlinked with its isolationism and separatism. Somehow, America does not seem to patronize. One of its perceived images is that of the naïve superpower which confronts directly and either dominates or destroys. Yet it is precisely this American paradox that gives America the aura of a utopia that is about to be realized and yet never comes true.

Detecting a unitary vision encompassing all that has been written by Said, Abdirahman A. Hussein argues that there is a "radical vision of *sensus communis*" [underlying] all of Said's writings", a dream of an "interrelated plurality of cultures", "to fuse together (and transvaluate) two important themes in modern thought which are normally dissociated from, and sometimes even opposed to, each other: plurality and universality" (17). All of this can be argued to be Said's dream of a better *America*, of wishing to give America a role other than the one it is playing in the world. If Said thought that there is any place on earth that came anywhere close to combining the two contradictory themes of plurality and universality, this place cannot be other than America. The fact that it is seen as the creator of a "false universality that conceals ideological investments" (18) – which is implied by Hussein – must have been particularly agonizing for Said, since it is also perceived as being in a position to make *sensus communis* possible.

Whereas one of America's most frequent representations in Said's writing is that of the chillingly pragmatic imperialist, there seems to be an ever present implicit suggestion that its real malady is its politics of domination and interventionism. He elaborates, for example, how the Gulf War was "partly launched so as to lay the ghost of the 'Vietnam Syndrome', to assert that the United States could win a war, and win it quickly" (*Culture and Imperialism* 131), fully aware that such an assertion and the quickness of victory would almost certainly have undesirable consequences for the victors themselves. Involvement in Iraq, even up to this moment, seems to have managed only to awaken the ghost of the "Vietnam Syndrome". Said observes that:

> American domination is insular. The foreign-policy elite has no long-standing
> tradition of direct rule overseas, as was the case with the British or the French, so
> American attention works in spurts; great masses of rhetoric and huge resources
> are lavished somewhere (Vietnam, Libya, Iraq, Panama), followed by virtual
> silence. (289)

The masturbatory effect seems to be intentionally devised by Said here, yet used in the strict sense of getting rid of excremental excess. It is clearly accentuated by "insular domination", "works in spurts", "great masses of", and "followed by virtual silence". What Said hints at is what he sees as America's narcissistic, self-reflexive and masturbatory war behavior. To him, America's wars can no longer be plainly categorized as wars, as homoerotic engagement with the other, nor does victory seem to be necessarily a signification of winning anything.

Said's words can be further elaborated. While European colonialism involved physical contact, direct rule, wars and resistances, the major dominant figure in America's present-day wars is the pilot in front of what resembles TV screens in his hi-tech cockpit, at a safe distance from the "enemy", engaging in what seems to be an entirely virtual combat. The seduction of the digitalized visual resembles the seduction of pornographic films, of which usual effect on their lonely viewer is what Said would describe, in his father Wadie's ethical sense, as "self-abuse" (*Out of Place* 70–3). This masturbatory effect, in the particular sense of getting rid of an excess, seems to be linked to Žižek's skeptical question about America fighting enemies (as in the cases of Iraq and Afghanistan for example) that were originally supported and given strength as "allies": "Is not the USA fighting its own excess in all these cases?" (*Welcome to the Desert of the Real* 27). America's *jouissance*, in this specific sense, would be one that it derives mainly from harassment of, rather than any form of reciprocal engagement with, what it sees as its lesser others. The simple point is that America, being rich, powerful and domineeringly in control of the world, can *afford* it. *Jouissance* in the form of the opportunistic domination of the other is discussed by Lacan in his analysis of Freud's *Civilization and its Discontents* in the seminar on the ethics of psychoanalysis, where he argues that:

> [Freud] doesn't disguise his view of the fact that those *jouissances* which are forbidden by conventional morality are nevertheless perfectly accessible and accepted by certain people, who live under a given set of conditions and whom he points to, namely, those whom we call the rich – and it is doubtless the case that, in spite of obstacles that are familiar to us, they sometimes make the most of their opportunities. (*Ethics of Psychoanalysis* 200)

In spite of its various representations in his works, there seems to be a clear allusion that Said's main feeling about America was that he was being devoured, consumed, and made utterly exhausted every day, by an insatiable, sadistic, highly authoritative and powerful feminine figure – a feminine figure which acted, in his imagination, as a tyrannical lover, as a rival, as an evil counterpart, and as a replacement for the mother all at once. The great influence his mother has had upon his life and thought is something which Said discusses extensively in his memoir *Out of Place*. What is most revealing in his account of the figure of the mother is how she seems to be situated in an anatomical intersection in which she, America, and Palestine form a fusion of signifiers that, in a very paradoxical sense, refer to each other. Said points out that, from his early years, he was made to perceive America, just as he perceived the mother, as a source of protection, which oddly enough did not protect the mother: "My father and we children were all protected from the politics of Palestine by our talismanic U.S. passports [...] my mother, however, did not have a U.S. passport" (117).

As Mustapha Marrouchi writes in his essay "The Site of Memory", Said's mother, without an American passport, was "like a soul in limbo, forced to wait for a passage across the Styx" (150). America represented itself to him as both protection and exile even before experiencing it. On the other hand, the fact that his completely Palestinian mother in particular was not protected seems to have had a lasting effect on him, for it is precisely the dangerous "politics of Palestine" which he, at a later stage and for the rest of his life in America, unequivocally and repeatedly hurled himself into, like a child hurling himself into his mother's arms.

His virgin encounter with New York seems to have been profoundly and permanently marked by that strange triad of mother-America-Palestine: "When we first arrived in New York the question of my mother's status as a nonperson after the fall of Palestine once again became urgent" (*Out of Place* 132). The fall of Palestine, America's immediate welcoming, and his mother's insistence not to reside in America even though she was the one member of the family who ultimately needed American citizenship, seem to have formed Said's initial anxieties about that all too passionate embrace of immigrants America traditionally and ideologically lives out.

Whereas the mother's impressions about America could be explained in multifarious ways, Said seems to have perceived himself as a bone of conflict, an object of rivalry between two "females". His last days in the company of his mother in Cairo, before his departure to America in 1951, had "the effect of creating an image of an inviolate union between us, which would have, on the whole, shattering results for my later life as a man trying to establish a relationship of developing, growing, maturing love with other women". Chief among those "other women" was symbolic America itself from which the mother, in Said's own words, was trying to "win me back from America before I went" (221). Yet America's embrace was such a powerful one that the mother herself "ended up dying and ultimately being buried in the America she had always tried to avoid, had always basically disliked" (133).

It can be argued that Said's subtle insinuations about America's "feminine power" seem to be interconnected with a tendency to act as a love object of an overpowering female, something which he implicitly – and sometimes explicitly – suggests through recounting various episodes of his life where he seems to have *enjoyed* this role. There is the mother, Hilda. Said perceives himself as having been "her instrument for self-expression and self-elaboration" (222) in his youth, in other words, specifically in Lacanian terminology, "the instrument of [his] Other's *jouissance*" (*Écrits: A Selection* 354). There is "Eva Emad", one of the women he mentioned caring for besides his mother in his memoir, who was seven years older than he, and whom his parents obviously thought was manipulating him (*Out of Place* 250–5). There is "aunt Salimeh", one of the female personalities who fascinated him tremendously, and who was "an unmistakably lusty woman in her forties [...] elemental and irrepressible" with a certain "volubility and irreverence" (239–40). There is even a feminine figure who literally symbolized an "ideal America" for him, and to whom he admits enjoying the masochistic state of being at the mercy of:

> It is difficult to describe the tremendous power of her attraction, the romance
> of her body, which was for a time just beyond sexual reach, the overwhelming

pleasure of intimacy with her, the utter unpredictability of her wanting and rejecting me [...] At times, she represented that aspect of an ideal America that I could never gain admission to, but which held me enthralled at the gate. She had a moralistic "don't-say-bad-things" side to her, which sometimes made me feel even more alien, and put me resentfully on my best behavior. (282–3)

While being "beyond sexual reach" represents a stage of trying to understand his lover, as well as America, giving in to her "utter unpredictability" marks Said's transcendence beyond interpretations to the level of enjoyment. Acknowledging the inaccessibility of the "ideal America" is a moment in which he goes beyond Adorno's elaborations of the love-hate relationship between the European intellectual and America[4] to Baudrillard's non-interpretive acceptance of America's "originality, which comes precisely from its defying judgment and pulling off a prodigious confusion of effects" (*America* 67). Baudrillard's idea is precisely to enjoy what Said describes as the state of being "enthralled at the gate" of America. Being put on his "best behavior", "resentfully", seems to connote more of the enjoyment of the act of being "disciplined" by the lover than real resentment, knowing well enough that the lover's "moralistic" reproaches are themselves, most probably, an act. Being on the "best behavior" in this case is ultimately about trying to be a "complete American" which, for Said, involved acting. To him, being American is not something that comes naturally to any immigrant, it has to be acted and re-acted until mastered as an act. In other words, being American was always being American from a distance, watching the self's ideal ego.[5]

Where Said attempts to understand America, to have access to it, or to judge it, seems to signify an almost imperceptible line of demarcation between his submission to the capriciousness of a tyrannical lover and his "lifelong struggle and attempt to demystify the capriciousness and hypocrisy of a power whose authority depended absolutely on its ideological self-image as a moral agent, acting in good faith and with unimpeachable intentions" (*Out of Place* 230). His reference thus to America's occasional political representation of itself as a "traditional woman" who is supposed to be "innocent, pure, free of sin" in his essay "The Other America" (*Al-Ahram Weekly*) is meant to ironically suggest that America to him was precisely the opposite: a tyrannical, indulgently sinful, and promiscuously guilty woman. It is precisely the authoritative capriciousness of an ideological big Other that Said endows on that feminine figure which symbolizes America, the lover, and the mother, a feminine figure which aggrandizes his mother's "fabulous capacity for letting you trust and believe in her, even though you knew that a

---

[4] See the discussion of Adorno's critique of Aldous Huxley's *Brave New World* in Chapter 5.

[5] One of Said's examples on this is Edmund Alexander, one of two Cairo connections at Mount Hermon School, whose Arabic-affected American tongue seemed to undermine his efforts at "being as American as could be". *Out of Place: A Memoir*, New York: Vintage Books, 2000, pp. 228–9.

moment later she could either turn on you with incomprehensible anger and scorn or draw you in with her radiant charm" (*Out of Place* 60).

It is significant enough that out of the diversity of famous Egyptian artists of the first half of the twentieth century, Said is especially fascinated by Tahia Carioca, an Egyptian actress and belly-dancer whose cinematic persona precisely matches the authoritative, insatiable and manipulating feminine figure. Said describes Carioca as the "finest belly-dancer ever", a "political militant", and a "*femme fatale*" who is "so talented and so sexy [that] she has to be portrayed as a dangerous woman – the *almeh* who is too learned, too smart, too sexually advanced, for any man in contemporary Egypt" (*Reflections on Exile* 347 and 351). In the case of Carioca as an exceptional belly-dancer, the traditional *takhta* belly-dance scene which Said describes in his essay "Homage to a Belly-Dancer" seems to be less about the female as a sexual object than about the female with a "suggestive" voracious sexuality, overpowering the mesmerized audience as well as the seated male singer on whom she seems to exercise total control. "She would glide up behind him, as he droned on, appear as if to fall into his arms, mimic and mock him – all without ever touching him or eliciting any response" (348).

Excluding the evil aspect in the many cinematic characters she played, reflecting the "woman-as-devil figure" (351), Carioca's artistic persona as a man-consuming female is only slightly different from her real person. In real life, she married an assortment of different men – 14 of them are admitted, amongst which are several prominent figures – whom she considered to be a "shabby lot of bastards" (354). Said's Carioca, like his unnamed American woman who symbolized an "ideal America that [he] could never gain admission to" (*Out of Place* 282–3), is "so immediately sensual and yet so remote, unapproachable, unobtainable" (*Reflections on Exile* 349). She is the most sexually attractive belly-dancer the world will ever know, yet, with an unusual "entirely composed look about her" (348), connoting the same "moralistic 'don't-say-bad-things'" (*Out of Place* 283) attitude with which she reigns over her castrated men with absolute control.

It can be argued that behind that Saidian perilous feminine figure lies the legendary figure of Zulaikha, Joseph's beautiful Egyptian seducer (Potiphar's wife in the bible, and in the Qur'aan[6] the wife of the Aziz – a man who is believed to be a priestly eunuch). In the biblical text, while what Zulaikha says is the law, Joseph's voice disappears completely after the episode of her sexual harassment of him, just as Said's solitary voice as an intellectual who "speaks the truth to power" disappears while he, in Marrouchi's words, "[cries] in the Manhattan wilderness" (129). In her Qur'aanic version, Zulaikha is a completely unblushing sexual harasser who not only tries to seduce Joseph but publicly threatens to imprison him if he does not obey her orders. What seems to be particularly significant about

---

[6]   The story of Joseph and Zulaikha constitutes chapter 39 of "Genesis", *The Bible: Authorized King James Version with Apocrypha*, Oxford and New York: Oxford University Press, 1998, pp. 48–9, and verses 21–35 of Sura XII, *The Holy Qur'aan*, Brentwood, MD: Amana Corp, 1983, pp. 556–62.

the Qur'aanic version of the story is that it clearly reveals a Joseph who is not too sure of himself. His own sexuality comes into play:

> And with passion did she desire him, and he would have desired her, but that he saw the evidence of his Lord: thus did We order that We might turn away from him all evil and shameful deeds: For he was one of Our servants, sincere and purified. (A. Yusuf Ali, 558–9)

In fact, this Qur'aanic verse is often (intentionally?) badly translated from the original classical Arabic text. A more accurate translation would remove "would have" from the sentence. There is an affirmative "did" in the Arabic text which grammatically and semantically applies to her "desiring him" as well as to his "desiring her". Not to mention that the entire use of the verb "to desire" is totally inaccurate due to the fact that the Arabic verb used has no one-worded equivalent in English. It can, however, be translated as "to be ready to make love", which clearly describes an emotional as well as a physical state that can hardly be expressed adequately by the verb "to desire". The conclusion to be drawn here is that the text seems to simultaneously construct Zulaikha as a figure of male anxiety and Joseph as an object of masochistic fantasy – a fantasy in which most men, unlike the chaste prophet, would probably be either too scared or only too pleased to submit to the tyrannical woman's desire. It can be thus argued that Zulaikha herself, as a castrating figure, comes out of a dual uneasiness marking the masculine position by a deep sense of anxiety towards, and at the same time a craving for playing the victim of, the phallic insatiable female.

Said's imago of America seems to be structurally similar, a Zulaikha whose symbolic spouse is such a powerful yet seen as institutionalized – hence contested – European Anglo-Protestant culture that she always found other cultures, though regarded as periphery from an Anglo-Protestant point of view, irresistibly attractive. Yet, America's beloveds are no victims in the usual sense. Said, for one, sees himself as a "true follower of Adorno" (*Power, Politics, and Culture* 458), whom he considers to be the "dominating intellectual conscience of the middle twentieth century" (*Representations of the Intellectual* 54). Unlike Adorno, however, he acknowledges certain pleasures associated with the state of being in exile. This is something that Adorno most likely never acknowledged, at least while living in exile in America. While Adorno took the first chance to leave America and go back to Germany, Said never had the option to return to his Palestinian home, nevertheless, he claimed that "the intellectual as exile tends to be happy with the idea of unhappiness" (53).

In his essay "Edward Said and the Writing of History", Shelley Walia writes: "Said feels a deep affinity with Joseph Conrad, whose homelessness finds a parallel with his own experience of being in the "third space", almost outside in the establishment" (5). Whether Said feels an affinity with Conrad or constructs this affinity is a point that can actually be debated. The point that seems to be indisputable, however, is that both writers share an exceptional success in transforming the hardships of the state of being exiled into the richest source of their creative writing, where memories of forgotten or lost homes, as well as narratives and fantasies of an alien present existence, amalgamate with cultural politics and different discourses of power. This particular point of semblance between the two creative minds is best illuminated, as well as astutely problematized in an indirect way, by Abdirahman A. Hussein in his essay "Reflexivity and Self-creation in Said and Conrad", where the writer offers an insightful critique of Said's *Joseph Conrad and the Fiction of Autobiography*, of which a specific part will be referred to later in this chapter (19–52).

Yet figuratively speaking, there seems to be an affinity between Said and that much older, biblical Joseph, the son of Jacob, with whom he seems to share a set of other similarities. Both come from the same ancient land of prophets, a land which even today seems to have left an unmistakable mark on those who have even the slightest connection to it. Said himself is an example since he never really stayed in Jerusalem, or anywhere in Palestine, any longer than a few of his early formative years. Both lived most of their lives away from what they considered to be home, and were famous and of high status in their newly adopted homeland. Joseph is known to have been a prophet who used his intellect to save Egypt from the ravages of famine. Said is an intellectual who believed that the true intellectual has a prophetic mission. In the history of religious beliefs, the prophet, like Said's intellectual, has always been a figure who "speaks truth to power".

The story of Said and his imago of America, however, is an unbiblical story of a Joseph who had no way out, who had to commit himself to Zulaikha's demand. Not before her final sexual crescendo, which is his total capitulation by the act of writing, by submitting himself to her as the Other, does he realize that his unconscious has been entirely overwhelmed by her long before embarking on the task of "understanding" her. Not before imagining her intensive and impossible phallic *jouissance*, of which he is the instrument, thus experienced as his own, and which is paradoxically perceived as conditioned by his very castration, does he realize that his subjectivity is put in question – and hence must be continuously held on to by writing – the moment he committed himself to the act of love.

"For Said, writing is an act of remembering", writes Marrouchi, "a faculty of 'memory for forgetfulness', in Mahmoud Darwish's celebrated phrase, for retaining mental and physical impressions in, and for recalling them to, the mind" (169). But writing, in a fundamental sense, is also creation par excellence. As Žižek puts it, whereas the creation of man is an act of "supreme egoism" by which God "expels – discharges, casts out, rejects out of himself – his real side, the vortex of drives, and thus constitutes himself in his Ideality, as a free subject", the creation of the Word is an act by which He "articulates outside himself – that is, he discloses, (sur)renders – this very ideal-spiritual essence of his being". Writing thus is a "paradigmatic case of *creation*" in which the writer 'hands over to the Other the innermost essence of his being'" (*Žižek Reader*

262). Thus, writing stands as a supreme paradoxical act of a vital confirmation of subjectivity as well as the ultimate destabilization of it. It is with this contradictory perception of writing that Kafka, for example, writes:

> writing means revealing oneself to excess; that utmost of self-revelation and surrender, in which a human being, when involved with others, would feel he was losing himself, and from which, therefore, he will always shrink as long as he is in his right mind. (*Letters to Felice* 156)

"At the level of *Jouissance*", Žižek writes, "truth is simply *inoperative*, something which ultimately doesn't matter" (*For they know not* lxvii). It can be argued that the act of writing shares this peculiarity with *jouissance*. When Marrouchi doubtingly questions Said's account of being scolded by his father for not having wet dreams – the father was implying that his son was copiously masturbating – he actually touches upon Said's secret *jouissance* as a creative writer, presumably without paying enough attention to name it as such. Instead, Marrouchi shifts his focus to the contradictory effect Said's story has on its reader:

> Can Wadie really have commanded, in English, Arabic, or any other language, "Have a wet dream!" as the author claims? In trying to find an answer to the question posed here, one comes away with a dizzying sense of contradiction. On the one hand, [Said's] father "never spoke of making love [...] and certainly not of fucking", and on the other, his mother gets impregnated because she, with the help of her husband, "wrote a letter to Jesus and he sent [them] a baby!". (153–4)

Marrouchi correctly identifies the contradiction, seems to implicitly suggest that it pales in the shadow of Said's creative writing and the domination he exercises over his material – which is evidently true – but does not quite articulate the direct connection between the writing and the writer's secret *jouissance*. The point is that such a Saidian story is not just about the contradiction between discussing the secret habit of young Said and his authoritative and religious parents. It is more about Said, the creative writer who creates his subjectivity out of the very masochistic imago he draws for himself. In his account, the father appears to be overpowering and authoritative, the son the masturbating law-breaker and self-abuser who is embarrassingly cornered into confession. Yet it is the son/writer's creative powers and his position of being in control of the narrative that invent such a father figure with such an impossible command. It is the writer's secret *jouissance*, far more than the son's masturbatory one, that corresponds with what Lacan describes as desire's "secret collusion with which it envelops the pleasure of knowing and of dominating" (*Écrits: A Selection* 184). In the case of an autobiographical account, it is the secret knowledge of what has really happened that creates the *jouissance* of total domination over what is being constructed in writing. If writing in this particular case can be thought of as a transgressive practice, it clearly demonstrates, again, the Lacanian idea that "without a transgression there is no access to *jouissance*" (*Ethics of Psychoanalysis* 177).

Even though his parents subjected him to a thorough process of depoliticization from his early childhood right through his first years of being a literature professor, in his memoir *Out of Place* Said writes about the fall of Palestine and the imposition of Israel in place of it as an imposition upon his very being. Consequently, one of the aspects which particularly embittered him about America is its unconditional support for Israel. Asked by an interviewer once about what pushed him into political activity and whether it was something in his childhood, Said answers: "No. Because my family is completely apolitical [...] I think it was the experience of living in America, where you can become radicalized very quickly" (*Power, Politics, and Culture* 412). It is noteworthy that to Said, America, where acculturation takes its strongest form, where the philosophical discourse is cancelled out in the pursuit of happiness, and where the political is supposed to be flattened out by the very process of acculturation, is precisely where one can become radicalized, and "very quickly".

There can be no doubt that the Palestinian problem backgrounded Said's political fervor, but it was not the sole issue. Another was criticizing the "present cultural moment" in which he lived in America, a moment "in which the social and historical setting of critical activity is a totality felt to be benign [...] uncharacterizable as a whole [...] and somehow outside history" (Said, "Opponents" 2). Arguably, his major aim was to contaminate society and its everyday life, popular cultural venues and mass media with the politics of interpretation of literary texts. To him, the confinement of the practice of criticism inside academia is "depoliticization with a vengeance", and the American way of life sustains it. In the early 1980s, Said saw such confinement "as an integral part of the historical moment presided over by Reaganism" (20). As a result, however, the image Said made out of himself as a media figure, a public intellectual with a remarkable ability to take his critique across different fields inside and outside the academy, does seem quite often to carry an air of *professionalism* which opposes his own idea of the intellectual's amateurism.

America's Zionism at times was strangely more evident and more incomprehensible to Said than Israel's. America was where "anti-Semitism is really made the umbrella for any form of criticism of Israel" (Said, *Writers Talk*). He wondered why his interview entitled "My Right of Return" was published in an Israeli daily but "*certainly not in a U.S. equivalent*" (*Power, Politics, and Culture* 443). But was that just felt as American Zionism to Said? Was it strictly perceived as America's politically-charged negative reply about the return of a Palestinian to his homeland? Said wrote about the Palestinian problem directly and extensively, and he published primarily in America. His passion about the Palestinian right of return is irrefutable, thus, his desire to be given the right of his own return would be unquestionable. Marrouchi writes: "If Said could pass one law, it would certainly be one that gives the Palestinian people the right to return" (129). But why was "My Right of Return", in particular, denied publication in an American daily? It has been published in America as a part of a book entitled *Power, Politics, and Culture: Interviews with Edward W. Said*, where its readership would be less than in the case of a daily. But "why not a daily?" was Said's question. The question in his mind could be formulated in this way: "Why does America feel uncomfortable with the idea of having my discussion about my right of return in between the hands of most ordinary Americans reading a regular daily"?

It seems that the answer to such a question goes beyond America's Zionism and the whole of the Israeli-Palestinian political debate. For what really matters to *Said's* America is the unsaid implication of "my right of return". It is a title which sounds too personal. Things might have stood differently if the piece of writing had been entitled in more general terms, for example: "The Palestinian Right of Return", which describes one of the major political problems already known to the whole world. By being in a daily, a part of everyday American life, and not a part of what would be read mostly by academics and intellectuals, the state of de jure behind the phrase "my right of return" might, by some implausible probability, become a state of de facto. What guarantees that the right of return, if supported by public opinion and somehow granted, would not have been used? And what if this actually happened? What if Professor Edward Said, as an individual, had been granted his right to return to Palestine or Israel (the difference between the two at this point becomes utterly unimportant)? And what if he actually used it in order to *permanently* return?

There can be no return without a certain *departure*, and this is precisely the unsaid of "My Right of Return". Returning home does not simply mean returning home. And, it does not only mean finally giving up his chosen state of exile as "an Arab living and writing from *within* the safety of the West" (Marrouchi 129), where Said had "*chosen* to remain the misunderstood stranger" (153) mainly in order to "prolong [the] deep *oppositional* thought" of the "irreducible tension between colonial domination and native resistance" (199). It also means, beyond both ideology and politics, departing from America, from Zulaikha, from the beloved tyrannical lover – a departure to which Said's imagined America would characteristically respond: "Return! What return? Do you think you can just walk out on me? Besides, can't you see we are so perfect for each other"?

In "Reflexivity and Self-creation in Said and Conrad", Hussein writes:

> What Said detects in [the] slow, fissured development of Conrad's self-reflection is a strange marriage of irony and heroism, of egoism and self-transcendence: in the torsions of an "either/or" dialectic, the artist experiences intense self-abnegation in order to win authenticity, a dialectic that for Conrad attains its final synthesis through a complete identification with European humanity and civilization in the last stage of his career. In the end also ratifying, if only implicitly, European imperialism, this self-transformation is, according to Said, realized at an exorbitant moral and aesthetic price. (28)

It is this total identification with Western civilization that marks what is taken to be a major difference between Said and Conrad as writers of and about exile. Conrad's final total identification with the dominant culture is seen as something which has never been either achieved or indeed desired by Said. A fundamental problem remains, however. It can be argued that it is precisely the exile's self-transformation at this "exorbitant moral and aesthetic price" that further reinforces his or her state of being an outsider. Conrad's "deep strain of pessimism" and the "grim stoicism" which results from it seem to be markers of an elemental oddity: a fundamental incompatibility at the heart of his very identification. Contrasted to that, Said's maintained distance, his deliberate and studied intellectual non-identification with Western culture, or indeed America, seems to mark his symbolic identification with the gaze of America itself. In "The Site of Memory", Marrouchi writes:

> "Said is American" is a lie or a legal fiction; and yet for him, to say, "I am not American", is a breach of courtesy and shows a lack of gratitude due to hospitality, the stormy, intermittent hospitality of the state and of the nation in the first instance but also infinite hospitality of the language, the medium he uses to write back to the West. (161)

This could be indeed true. Yet, even if it is, the issue of Said's American self, over and above propriety and gratitude, seems to go far deeper than that. It is the difference between Lacan's i(o) (ideal ego) and his I(O) (ego-ideal) that is of crucial importance here. Lacan states: "It is in the Other that the subject is constituted as ideal, that he has to regulate the completion of what comes as ego, or ideal ego – which is not the ego ideal – that is to say, to constitute himself in his imaginary reality" (*Four Fundamental Concepts* 144). This *constituted* identity, which happens at the level of the Lacanian mirror stage, expresses an identification which reflects the image of the other back on the ego. Symbolic identification, on the other hand, results in an ego-ideal, which marks an end to the detour of the barred subject along the whole loop of the Lacanian graph of desire with the "Che vuoi?" question as the fundamental instigator of fantasy. As Žižek puts it:

> Imaginary identification is identification with the image in which we appear likeable to ourselves, with the image representing "what we would like to be", and symbolic identification [is] identification with the very place *from where* we are being observed, *from where* we look at ourselves so that we appear to ourselves likeable, worthy of love. (*Sublime Object* 105)

It can be argued thus that Conrad's perceived final total identification with the dominant culture marks at the same time a "constituted" identity which can be in effect, away from any moral or aesthetic issues, the cause of his "grim stoicism". On the other hand, Said's theoretical non-identification, which is fundamental to his idea of the intellectual, marks a "constitutive" identity which, from a psychoanalytic point of view, cannot be acquired except through the symbolic identification with the gaze of the big Other, the "place *from where*" he is being observed. This place, in Said's case, cannot but be America. Said's hybrid self, which he scrutinizes in details in many of his basic writings, testifies to the fact that his identification with the Palestinian cause was purely based on principle, on the responsibility of the writer, the proper role of the intellectual, which he firmly believed to be unconditionally supportive to the "weak and unrepresented" (*Representations of the Intellectual* 22), but not out of total identification with the Palestinians themselves.

In "My Homeland, the Text", Marrouchi designates *After the Last Sky* as Said's "most personal work", yet recognizes Arif Dirlik's subtle point that it also marks Said's "distance from the immediacy of Palestine", his "self-identification as a Palestinian" as "an imagined if not a willed self-identification" (120) which is indicated by Said himself when he writes: "I am perhaps an extreme case of an urban Palestinian whose relationship to the land is basically metaphorical, I view the Palestinian community at a very great remove" (quoted in Marrouchi 121). It can be argued thus that Said's identification with the Palestinian people reigns in so far as it is merged with the intellectual's power to represent – that double-edged sword of the power to articulate the other. Palestinians, like Israelis, are others to Said. The difference between them is that the Palestinians are the oppressed group on the side of which he indeed belonged as an "intellectual with a mandate" (Marrouchi 31–72). It is the power to gaze at and articulate the other's lack which also marks an inevitable distance of non-identification. In his American exile, Palestine, more or less like America, slips from reality to the imagination. Marrouchi shrewdly observes that "*After the Last Sky* slides from fact into fiction [...] It will not and cannot settle its materials, mainly because it is the most jeweled of Said's works on *his* Palestine" (124).

It can be argued that Said's ultimate identification, however, in spite of his ideological stance with the Palestinians, and which seems to be fundamentally against America as Israel's biggest benefactor, is his symbolic identification with the gazing power of America itself and its symbolic role as the high-handed broker trying to process peace from afar, however unsuccessfully, in the Middle East. His identification with one of the modern world's most oppressed minorities, oddly enough like Conrad's perceived identification with the world's dominant culture, cannot but be an imaginary one, in other words, taking place at the level of the Lacanian mirror stage.[7] The highest point of that identification came in the year 2000, when a worldwide debate was inaugurated by Said's symbolic act of throwing a rock in the direction of an Israeli guard post on the Lebanese border. It is obvious enough that in the view of those whom Said would describe as power-serving intellectuals, this "act of violence" only reifies Said's perceived imago as the "professor of terror" (Said, *Power, Politics, and Culture* 414). For

---

[7]   The mirror stage is explained by Lacan in chapter 1 of *Écrits*, pp. 1–8, and its illustration appears in the lower half of Lacan's graph II of desire in chapter 9, *Écrits: A Selection*, translated by Alan Sheridan, London and New York: Routledge, 1989, p. 339.

others, there can be no doubt that it was a symbolic act of solidarity with the oppressed, of belonging "on the same side with the weak and unrepresented" (Said, *Representations of the Intellectual* 22) against Israel, which is represented by the United States and other rich European countries as well as supported unconditionally by advanced arms and huge funds.

Away from the political debate, however, there is another much more real and far more enlightening controversy that Said's – maybe carefully calculated – symbolic act creates. Photographed red-handed, his image throwing a rock – which was immediately reproduced in various newspapers and websites – captures a rare paradoxical moment in which the Lacanian subject's imaginary identification is almost indistinguishably mixed with his symbolic identification. While it is a moment in which Said seems to be a true Palestinian, it is also a moment in which this imaginary identification itself is taking place "*on behalf of a certain gaze in the Other*" (Žižek, *Sublime Object* 106). This gaze is precisely the gaze of America, which is also *his own*, with which he is symbolically identified and, most importantly, *to which* an unmistakable Saidian message is being delivered: "Here I am, at this particular moment, Palestinian to the bone, Jerusalemite to the bone, and not American". Yet, it is exactly this moment in which he is completely American. Like the Lacanian letter, Said's stoning message, definitely "arrived at its destination".

Chapter 9
Hassan's Radical Identification with America

The move from Edward Said to Ihab Hassan within the context of analyzing America's heterogeneous imagos seems to be both idiosyncratic and radical at once. There are many reasons for comparing the two thinkers – the subject is clearly well worth writing a whole book different from the one at hand, therefore it cannot possibly be given justice here. However, a few points in this regard should be pointed out as they seem to be useful in the present context. Both writers, coming from an underdeveloped part of the world, made it to the ultimate West and were able to firmly establish their names in the registers of Western thought – in different circumstances and with different intellectual positions. Both were educated in Egypt in their youth, went to America to continue their education within the same decade and made literature, criticism and the study of culture their lives' axis. Both of their names became synonymous with two major theories in the field of cultural studies – Orientalism and Postmodernism. Yet, while Said's and Hassan's biographical similarities are remarkable, the differences between them as writers and critics are deep-seated to the point of an acute non-reconciliation, even antagonism.

In fact, Said's highly aggressive review of Hassan's *The Dismemberment of Orpheus*, published in *Diacritics* in the Spring of 1972 under the title "Eclecticism and Orthodoxy in Criticism", and Hassan's unflustered and equally severe "Polemic" in the Fall of the same year, seem to defy even comparing them together in the first place, as the two thinkers almost claim that each appears nonsensical to the other. While Hassan's "type of criticism" seems to Said to be "the ultimate corruption of thematics, that hot-house adjunct to intellectual history" (5), Said's real concern, in Hassan's opinion, is "more than his sense of the dignity or sufficiency of criticism; it is his model of being" ("Polemic" 56), a model of being that may be seen as completely incompatible with Hassan's view of the critic's responsibility within the context of what he sees as a "re-visioning" of the "human form", "including human desire and all its external representations" (*Right Promethean Fire* 201). While Hassan's work seems to Said to be "all wrestling and no particular opponent" ("Eclecticism" 6) – hence thought to be senseless since it does not seem to confront an Other or assume an ideological stand either from an attacking position or a defending one – Said's accusations seem beside the point to Hassan, since "the best defense may be neither attack nor yet defenselessness, as Rilke thought, but self-transcendence" ("Polemic" 60). To Said, "everything is equally apocalyptic" in Hassan's writing, and this is precisely why "everything [Hassan] says sounds ungainly" ("Eclecticism" 6). To Hassan, this is not surprising since his works "affront [Said] not so much because they move out of the known realm of critical discourse [...] but because they make direct assertions about reality, what we call the human condition" ("Polemic" 58). To Said, "[Hassan] cannot commit himself to a tradition, in the traditional sense of the word, and so he falls back upon what he calls 'silence', which is nothing less than a disjunctive category holding together his interests" ("Eclecticism" 6). To Hassan:

> The critical game is not to choose or judge sides. It is rather to increase the possibilities of discernment even in the most shadowy of realms" by paying attention to the "new gnosticism", the "new languages of silence" which "are no longer confined to a subversive literary imagination, intent on protesting itself. ("Polemic" 60)

Said's ultimate statement on what Hassan makes out of literature and criticism makes the worst possible case of both. Since "literature for [Hassan] amounts to a biography plus a flood of slogans on subversion", his criticism seems to be nothing but "a wholly verbal ambience created out of disembodied phrases. These phrases are intended by Hassan to indicate the presence of a [postmodern] tradition" ("Eclecticism" 6). To Hassan, there does not seem to be much difference between literature and criticism, in both of which biography stands on a high ground and autobiography stands on an even higher one since it is "no less inquiry than brooding" ("Confessions" 131), in other words, criticism and literature in one. In fact he describes one of his most speculative theory-bound books, *The Right Promethean Fire: Imagination, Science, and Cultural Change*, as a "fragment of an autobiography" (*Right Promethean Fire* xxi). Thus, in criticism, critics seek "the full resonance of their voices, the scope of their languages and lives" ("Confessions" 123). The intellectual, to Said, is "the author of a language that tries to speak the truth to power" (*Representations of the Intellectual* xvi). In Hassan's view of the world, "Said invokes large ideas of reason, truth, and justice", such as "looking for and trying to uphold a single standard for human behavior when it comes to such matters as foreign and social policy", yet his response to Said's point is: "I find this genuinely admirable and heroically naïve – that is, how I wish it were true" ("Negative Capability" 316). In short, if one is allowed the nonchalance of putting it geographically, Said in America seems to have grown to resemble crammed, excited, compact, Atlantic-connected, racially confrontational and restless New York; Hassan increasingly became the vast, comparatively tranquil, remote, esoteric, more relaxed and self-indulgent American mid-West.

Yet, writing now about Hassan and his work, "self-indulgent" is being used with reluctance. For it seems that Hassan's greatest paradox lies in what can be considered an Archimedean point in his thought where the very definition of self empowerment consists in precisely opening the self to the invasion of the other. In his essay "Parabiography: The Varieties of Critical Experience", Hassan writes: "The strongest self is least self-absorbed; it opens and imperils itself continually. Its best achievement, both mystics and nonmystics say, may consist in self-overcoming" (*Postmodern Turn* 166). How, then, does Hassan see his own self empowerment – another Hassanian name of this is "negative capability" ("Negative Capability" 305–24) – defined as being "least self-absorbed" when his own autobiography admittedly dictates his theoretical and critical writing? In order to explore the depths of Hassan's thought one must first shed a considerable light on where autobiography stands in it.

"In desiring, in reading, in making", writes Hassan, "the critic acts out his autobiography, compounded of many selves" (*Postmodern Turn* 158). If the act of writing, as Žižek asserts, is a "paradigmatic case of *creation*" in which the writer 'hand[s] over to the Other, the innermost essence of [his] being'" (*Žižek Reader* 262), Hassan seems to take it down to its pragmatic base by directly putting autobiography in the forefront of any writerly message. In his analysis of Hassan's corpus of work in "Ihab Hassan: Re-visioning Man", Jerome Klinkowitz writes: "He is drawn to Henry Miller's disposition that 'writing is autobiography, and autobiography is therapy, which is a form of action' […] there is no theory that is not in fact a carefully concealed part of the theorist's own life story" (118). To Hassan, then, the best way towards the exegesis of a theory is by making clear its autobiographical origin or background however "acrid, like a schizophrenic's mouth" autobiographical "reflective awareness" may taste ("Confessions" 131).

This pragmatic approach may seem to evade the problems of autobiographical writing so clearly identified by Paul de Man in his seminal essay "Autobiography as De-Facement", yet it does so with such a radical directness that it seems to seek to highlight those problems rather than to suppress them. It is as if de Man's unanswerable question whether "life *produces* the autobiography" or "the autobiographical project may itself produce and determine the life" (*Rhetoric of Romanticism* 69) is at once markedly stressed by the critic's "many selves" – corresponding to "prosopopeia" or the "giving and taking away of faces" (76) – as well as completely marginalized by pragmatically submitting to the fact that this continual bracketing of "who the author is" is categorically unavoidable, hence altogether practically inconsequential – especially in conveying theory or criticism.

In other words, since in autobiographical writing, as de Man asserts, "the transcendental authority had first to be decided […] between the author *of* the text and the author *in* the text who bears his name" (72), Hassan consciously establishes that authority as well as destabilizes it by all too purposefully putting autobiography to work in critical writing and at the same time playfully detaching himself from it – as for example in the "Parabiography" of which the main point is to show how living the critical experience itself to him cannot be separated from living the life of which he talks about as someone else's. An autobiography, therefore, cannot be written. Yet, it is equally true to say that *all* writing is autobiographical. It is significant enough that de Man's very essay which questions autobiography can, in effect, be considered the most autobiographical of all of his writings. Throughout the 35 years of his life in America, Paul de Man repressed his early anti-Semitic writings for the Nazi-controlled Belgian newspaper *Le Soir* in the early 1940s. "Autobiography as De-Facement" can thus be considered the most self-reflexive/ autobiographical work by de Man, and in the most fundamental sense of *de-*

facing his own biography. It is as if the discovery of his collaborationist past is autobiography's most violent comeback to the writer who destabilized the notion of autobiography.

Besides the problems of self-indulgence, Hassan's direct autobiographical approach to the question of theoretical and critical writing may also sound over-confident in its "direct assertions about reality" and in his growing insistence to "speak more and more in my own voice" ("Polemic" 58). However, he also explains that it was actually the "critical *reluctance*" (emphasis mine) of the postmodern moment – the propitious signs of which he notes in the late 1960s – which steered his thoughts towards autobiography:

> In the late 1960s and 1970s, the clues to a new cultural vision were evident everywhere. I did not look for them always, as others did, in continental philosophy. I looked for them closer to home, in American pragmatism, and even closer, I looked in autobiography, time's rubble, for a way out of critical reluctance. ("Confessions" 124)

Thus, Hassan's theory of postmodernism, his recognition of a postmodern tradition, or what Klinkowitz calls his "postmodern habit of thought"[1] cannot be solely an "acting out of his autobiography", it is also a detection of a certain cultural moment in the history of Western thought calling for the articulation of the self in light of the exhaustion of philosophical discourses, metanarratives and modern art.

So, according to Hassan, if postmodernism remains somehow elusive to definitions, this is because it "more than equivocal autobiography [...] defines itself, if at all, as a continual exercise in self-definition" ("Privations of Postmodernism" 2). The summary of all this may be that, in Hassan's view, writing is inevitably contaminated by autobiography; autobiography is affected by perceived cultural phenomena; what is perceived, read, or defined, reads back or defines in turn *the reader*. Therefore, Hassan often reminds his readers of this vicious circle out of which there can be no effective escape. So, the collection of essays in *The Postmodern Turn* "turn in time, reflecting their author's biography" (*Postmodern Turn* xi) just as *The Right Promethean Fire* is a "fragment of an autobiography". It is also why *Between the Eagle and the Sun*, on one level, detects "traces of Japan"; at another provides insights about America; and still at a deeper stratum about Egypt. Yet at their innermost core, Hassan knows and admits, "the insights may curve back on themselves, revealing more of the perceiver than the perceived" (*Between the Eagle*

---

[1]   Klinkowitz argues that in order to make sense of a period of aesthetics, it is perhaps profitable to study the thinking habits of its thinkers. He chooses Harold Rosenberg, Roland Barthes, and Ihab Hassan as examples to study from the fields of art, semiotics, and literature respectively in order to show their revolutionary critical interests which belong to what Klinkowitz calls a "postmodern habit of thought", *Rosenberg/Barthes/Hassan: The Postmodern Habit of Thought*, Athens, GA: University of Georgia Press, 1988, pp. 1–11.

and the Sun 76). This is also how Hassan dealt with America – an America of which he seems to be characteristically aware that it is only *his*.

In the epilogue of his first book, *Radical Innocence: Studies in the Contemporary American Novel*, Hassan writes the following about America: "Conceived as a dream, it has shown that dreamers may also awake in the cold sweat of a nightmare, and sleep to dream again […] The curse of Columbus is still with us: every one must rediscover America for himself – alone!" (336). More than two decades later, Hassan comments on this himself in the "Parabiography" revealing that the stuff which persisted in his own nightmare was actually rather the "curse [of] Eternal Egypt" (*Out of Egypt* 16): "*Foreign born, he still recalls that nothing terrified him more than the prospect of forced repatriation. He opened every letter from the Immigration and Naturalization Service with dry mouth, leaden hand*" (*Postmodern Turn* 161).

It seems that the role which Hassan's willful detachment from Egypt plays in his radical identification with America cannot be a minor one. It is a detachment which also represented itself to him as an ever-present anxiety of being threatened by a place that is so distant – physically and culturally – yet somehow frighteningly close – close enough to persist in dreams. The most dreadful nightmare to Hassan was the "bad dream" of returning to Egypt: "I dreamt that I was compelled to go back, complete some trivial task – close a door left ajar, feed a canary, whisper a message […] there was terror in that banal dream" (*Out of Egypt* 108). The terror seems to have been not only about leaving America, but about spending any period of time, even the shortest one, in Egypt where he seems to have the feeling that a whole lifetime can be wastefully spent in banal activities.

It is as if the nightmare of repatriation reveals how Hassan's identification with America was partly shaped by his abject position with regard to Egypt. Arguably like Julia Kristeva's "abject" who tries to establish his being out of tearing himself away from the mother yet lives under the constant threat of a traumatic fall back into the mother's domain, Hassan's radical break away from Egypt shows that his relation to it is no less adversarial. The difference may be that, in the case of Kristeva's abject, the "violent, clumsy breaking away [from the mother entails] the constant risk of falling back under the sway of a power as securing as it is stifling" (Kristeva 13). In Hassan's case, however, it seems that the threat of returning to Egypt represented to him the risk of falling back under the sway of a cultural power that is *only stifling*. While America was seen as a country that "manufactures dreams, nightmares, and profound critiques of both" (*Right Promethean Fire* 8), Egypt to Hassan was a country that stifled all dreams.

Because his identification lies in what could be perceived as the complete opposite of Egypt, this complete opposite of Egypt is what he likes to imagine America is. It can thus be argued that what Hassan makes out of the American Self is to a certain extent what he wishes it to be, or what he imagines it to be: that great entire opposite of a self that is so radically opposed to an Egyptian Self, the restrictions of whose self-indetermination curbed it across two thousand years of foreign rule and over half a century of oppressive military national rule. His own self-empowerment thus lies precisely with total identification with *his* imagined

American Self which mainly belongs to literature. So, if going to America is backed by Hassan's "desire to remake or recreate oneself" (Ihabhassan.com), it is precisely to remake oneself in an ideal ego that fundamentally opposes "what I foresaw of my life in Eternal Egypt" (*Out of Egypt* 107).

It can thus be argued that in his conception of an ideal version of himself as American, Hassan takes the Lacanian detour of the misrecognition and internalization of the specular image of the other as the essence of identity. The misrecognition, however, in Hassan's case, does not seem to be unsuspecting of the fact that it is part of a process of willful remaking. Similarly, Hassan must be aware of the paradoxical process that the creation of this ideal American ego launches: the irreversibility yet unsustainability of an American immigrant identity that is destined to fluctuate between the desire for individuality and the struggle of assimilation. Since both are in effect unattainable, Hassan tends to take this unattainability to its highest possible level by creating an imago out of the American Self that Americans themselves can only aspire to.

America thus comes to one of its most romanticized epical imagos in Hassan's writings. Almost like figures such as Ralph Waldo Emerson and Seymour Martin Lipset, sublimating the American Self seems to inspire most of them. *Radical Innocence* in fact seems to be his seminal work out of which all of his other works emerge, even though he states that he began to speak more and more his own voice starting from *The Dismemberment of Orpheus*. In *Radical Innocence*, Hassan draws one of the most sublime versions of American innocence. He argues that American innocence is a form of positive neurosis that constitutes a "regressive force that prevents the self from participating fully in the world […] As a result, the greatest values affirmed by the American conscience have often been affirmed against the ruling spirit of the land" (40). Hassan also believes that such "regressive force that prevents" is not an unconscious one, on the contrary, it is a force that is consciously controlled at will: "Yet if the contemporary self is in recoil, it is not, we hope and believe, cravenly on the run. Its *re-coil* is one of the resources of its awareness, a strategy of its *will*" (5).

Recoiling, as emphasized by Hassan, describes a very specific behavior that connotes vigilance, self-awareness, and controlled power. It is revealing how this "recoiling" strikes a resemblance with the famous classic representation of America that Benjamin Franklin described in his letter, "The Rattle-Snake as a Symbol of America", in which America is portrayed as innocent, wild and fatal at the same time, and which is worth quoting here in full:

> She never begins an attack, nor, when once engaged, ever surrenders: She is therefore an emblem of magnanimity and true courage. The weapons with which nature has furnished her she conceals in the roof of her mouth so that, to those who are unacquainted with her, she appears to be a most defenseless animal. And even when weapons are shown and extended for her defense, they appear weak and contemptible; but their wounds, however small, are decisive and fatal. Conscious of this, she never wounds 'till she has generously given notice, even to her enemy,

and cautioned him against the danger of treading on her. Was I wrong, […], in thinking this a strong picture of the temper and conduct of America? (Matthews 62)

The image is that of a place of its own type, a place detached from the rest of the world, where an American Self is created that is unwilling to participate fully in the world in a kind of self-awareness of controlled power. This non-participation also alludes to a sort of imagined self-sufficiency that *does not need the world*. So, participation takes place only when necessary and ideologically correct, but, the need is not there in any case. It can be argued that this sense of America as an entity that is self-sufficient in every respect creates an imago of an impossible completeness that is nevertheless perceived as absolute and real completeness. When Hassan talks about the "European attitude" towards America, which is rarely "wholly free of subliminal envy and resentment, admiration and detestation, toward the Lone Superpower" (Ihabhassan.com), he touches upon a fundamental issue which obviously exists although it is often misinterpreted. He who knows what envy is must also be aware of the image of completeness that causes it. The fundamental difference between envy and jealousy, as Lacan teaches, is that the former is much more than the need of something possessed by the other, much more than the desire for objects of the other's desire, and even much more than need as such:

> [Envy is what] makes the subject pale before the image of a completeness closed upon itself, before the idea that the *petit a*, the separated *a* from which he is hanging, may be for another the possession that gives satisfaction, *befriedigung*. (*Four Fundamental Concepts* 116)

To say that there is no doubt that the world – and not just Europe – envies America is not an original proposition. What is important, however, is that America seems to derive envy not as a democratic model, a story of economic success, an advanced military superpower, and so on, but as a country which evokes that image of a completeness that is closed upon itself if only by its detachment or what Hassan calls "re-coil" from the world. The "possession that gives satisfaction" is an impossible possession since the *petit a* is the very unattainable in Lacanian psychoanalysis. It seems that imagining that closed self-sufficient system is what creates the sense of envy on part of the world when it comes to America as a master signifier in language. The relationship between the (American) immigrant and America thus, no matter how it develops, must start from that notion on the immigrant's behalf that "I need America much more than it needs me", a stigma that positions the immigrant from the very beginning in some kind of discredit. Kipling's remark that "it must be an awful thing to live in a country where you have to explain that you really belong there" (quoted in P. Conrad 95) belongs to the same sense of America connoting an "image of completeness" that is bound to make the immigrant perceive himself or herself as an excess.

One of the first impressions that any reader of Hassan's work is bound to have is that he is determinately an apolitical thinker. In "Confessions of a Reluctant Critic", he recalls that "memories of the great, erratic student riots of my youth in Egypt [...] insinuated themselves, four decades later, in [a] passage from *The Postmodern Turn*" where he confesses his "ambivalence towards politics, which can overcrowd our responses to both art and life" (125). This apolitical position seems to be closely reasoned not just by favoring the aesthetic experience nor by solely adhering to the American tradition of the pursuit of happiness, but also by an acute hatred of Egyptian politics that started in Egypt and must have increased interminably in America. Yet, it is precisely because Hassan's determined disinterest in politics came as a radical reaction to his sense of being "born in Egypt to fustian and a tumult of impotent passions" (*Between the Eagle and the Sun* 197) that the present book will seek to trace the *political* element in his thought. By doing this it will eventually be revealed that the way Hassan dealt with his version of America may be startlingly political.

"I confess to some distaste for ideological rage [...] and for the hectoring of both religious and secular dogmatists", writes Hassan, "I admit to a certain ambivalence toward politics, which can overcrowd our responses to both art and life" ("Confessions" 125). But, is this to be taken as an apolitical position? In what way can criticizing certain political discourses be considered apolitical? In his essay "Making Sense: The Trials of Postmodern Discourse", Hassan criticizes Marxist thinkers, such as Edward Said and Fredric Jameson, in the following manner:

> I find phantasmic their tendency to privilege Marxism as the only discourse of dissent, indeed of independent thought, regardless of its theoretical difficulties, economic predicaments, political oppressions, and prophetic failures. (*Postmodern Turn* 203)

It seems that Hassan believes that other non-Marxist discourses of dissent exist. In fact, he seems to implicitly suggest that his position can be an effective discourse of dissent in its own way. His does not seem to comfortably fall into the category of "silent" or "passive" discourses of dissent. On the contrary, it is a discourse of dissent which seems to find its definition in the Žižekian "procedure of the ultra-orthodox subversion of the law through the very overidentification with it" (*Did Somebody Say Totalitarianism* 32). Theoretically, it is the overidentification with what may be seen as a coercive system that can create a situation of what Hassan calls political "ripeness". For according to Hassan, the question "what is politics?" has two radically oppositional answers. Politics can be either "the right action when ripeness calls" or "an excuse to bully or shout in public, vengeance vindicating itself as justice and might pretending to be right, a passion for self-avoidance, immanent mendacity, the rule of habit, the place where history rehearses its nightmares, the *dur désir de durer*, a deadly banality of being" ("Confessions" 125).

In other words, politics is either waiting for the right moment calling for practical action or a premature, untimely, and ineffective "show" of resistance that can never bring any real change. The second kind of politics inevitably evokes his grievances about Egyptian politics in particular, the banality of which has always been about rage without bringing about any effectual changes or development in any real sense "beyond some streets and squares renamed" (*Out of Egypt* 14). Its comparably much more benign equivalent in America is "Marxist theory without Marxist praxis" which is, to Hassan, "no Marxism at all". This deformation of Marxism, he believes, "allows neo-Marxist philosophy to persist in America – precisely where it has never been 'tried' – as a 'dialectical immaterialism', an omnibus of grievances, a theology of hope – and beyond that, as an intellectual exercise, conferring on its practitioners moral superiority with total immunity" (*Postmodern Turn* 203).

So, what does one do in waiting for the moment of "ripeness"? Hassan's theoretical position seems to suggest nothing but an overidentification with the staged ideological positivity of the existing system. As for the political discourse of Marxists, Hassan writes: "I find constricting their need to grant politics priority, not merely due significance but *priority*, in the justification of human existence" (203). Politics, then, is significant but has no priority, since giving it priority necessitates the full time occupation of resisting a dominant ideology and thus falling prey to it. That is why, to Hassan, traditional political resistance constricts itself.

Where Hassan comes from, where he lived for the first 20 years of his life, is where the oldest authoritarian culture on earth manifested itself, even on an individual level, from the ancient Egypt of Pharaonic times to the postcolonial Egypt of the disillusioned Nasser, the assassinated Sadat, and the recently deposed Hosni Mubarak. It is also a culture which seems to have an ineradicable stamp on those who are born to it – Hassan is no exception. It can be argued that it was what he saw as an ever increasing ugliness of modern Egyptian reality, which in a sense always tied itself to him if only by virtue of his proper name, that lurked behind his all too frequent attempts to give no weight to the fact that he was born in Egypt. Any reader of Hassan cannot miss his obsession with repeating statements like "I consider my birth in Egypt an accident, not a destiny", "I consider my own birth in Cairo hazard, not destiny" (Ihabhassan.com), or phrases about Egypt as a place "to which I have never returned" ("Confessions" 130), a country with "a culture [that] I never chose" (*Between the Eagle and the Sun* 159). Yet, this hazardous accident seems to have resulted in resentments that, in Hassan's case, never subsided even after getting old enough, distant enough, and secure enough in his American life away from Egypt.

To live abroad with a resolve to settle down is something, and to actually never return even for a short visit to one's own birthplace is something else. Hassan "never returned", and he kept dreaming his terrifying "banal dream" for many years in America. It is as if the fact of his Egyptian birth, which he asserts to have never been "decisive in my life" (*Out of Egypt* 2), *decided* his radical turn away from Egypt. This turn away itself was also supposed to be a turn away from politics as such, which seems to Hassan to often fall into its all too familiar frame of Egyptian politics as mainly fustian rhetoric and "impotent passions". His intellectual apolitical stance thus can be described as less "American" than anti-Egyptian. Yet, politics does not seem to be the whole point. Raised in Egypt, Hassan seems to be one of those extremely atypical individuals who could perceive at an early stage of life that democracy is not a system of government but a *culture*, a way of thinking, a behavior which manifests itself on an individual private level as much as – even more than – on a collective public one. His radical flight from Egypt was one from a culture whose marked historical love of dictators and authority penetrates all aspects of daily life to what he must have perceived as its extreme opposite. His subsequent detachment from "the New Egypt I ignore" (*Out of Egypt* 14) seems to be determined by a belief that Egypt is a particularly hopeless case as far as democratic culture is concerned.

And how is Hassan to be blamed when, in political discourse, the collective ideology of Egypt has always been contentedly named after its ruler? "Farouk's Egypt" ended by Nasserism; Nasserism replaced by Sadatism; Sadatism by Mubarakism – all the time a dictatorship covered in sentimental quasi-democratic, quasi-social and quasi-religious mantras. In spite of the so called 1952 revolution – which was in fact a planned military coup by army officers rather than a flame originating within the nation's civil ranks, but which was nevertheless popularized and romanticized as a national revolution that was expected to change the Egyptian nation's destiny and fortune – real revolutions actually have never taken place in Egypt since 1919 – until the the 25 January 2011 when the Egyptian youth finally decided to destroy the ridiculous idea of the 'President-as-the-loving-father-of-the-nation', which metamorphosed particularly in Mubarak's time into downright godfather gangsterism with the President and his family as the head racketeers backed by an army of "policemen" and "state security" thugs protecting them.

Hassan concurs with the Greek god Hermes Trismegistus's legendary prophecy that "this most holy land, the abode of shrines and temples, will be most full of graves and of dead men" (*Out of Egypt* 112). Hassan's view of modern Egyptian culture, in spite of its manifest pessimism, cannot be easily discarded. Before 25 January 2011, nothing could have seemed more difficult than to imagine a real democratic project taking place in Egypt. That is not to say, however, that democracy is now easy to achieve. For, as Chantal Mouffe maintains in her essay "Deconstruction, Pragmatism and the Politics of Democracy", "the creation of democratic forms of individuality is a question of *identification* with democratic values and this is a complex process that takes place through a diversity of practices, discourses and language games" (5).

The problem is not that regimes, like the overthrown regime of Mubarak, were always corruptly seeking more power while claiming to achieve slow procedural steps towards democracy by changing an item or two in the constitution, but that what was claimed to be sought in the first place is *not* democracy, since what was being "cured" is merely a system of government and has nothing to do with planting democratic culture in individuals in their formative years. In such conditions, even if a democratic system of government were introduced, the authoritarian culture would probably persist in a society in which many individuals seem to love playing the role of miniature dictators in their own limited social space. In other words, after 60 years of dictatorial rule, pompous empty slogans, "national" mantras and, to add insult to injury, radical Islamist tendencies, Egypt does not only need a change of regime and system of government, it needs above all to be re-educated through a whole new system of education.

Hassan's embrace of American pragmatism, whose greatest attribute according to him is that it "brackets Truth (capitalized), circumvents Metaphysics and Epistemology; [...] finds no universal "ground" for discourse" (*Postmodern Turn* 204) seems to correspond with the Derridean view that the only successful democratic project, as Mouffe asserts, is to "transform the pluralist democratic ideal into a 'self-refuting ideal' since the very moment of its realization would coincide with its destruction" (11).[2] It is this "bracketing of Truth" that has always been sorely missed in countries like Egypt and, at large, the Arab and Muslim worlds.

This is where Hassan's understanding of the American pragmatic tradition as a vacillation in which no single discourse has a monopoly on Truth, can be useful towards an *individual* democratic culture – a political project in its essence with its own revolutionary viewpoint. It is also where his pragmatism differs from that of figures such as Richard Rorty whose view of both "ethics and politics" muddles them up as "a matter of reaching accommodation between competing interests, and as something to be deliberated about in banal, familiar terms – terms which do not need philosophical dissection and do not have philosophical presuppositions" (17).

It comes as no surprise then that at a low moment, Hassan thought that "writing manuals for circuit-breakers and advertising copy for eggbeaters till I died in some decently modest house in Germantown [is] better than [being] a landlord in Egypt" ("Confessions" 120–1). When he writes that the American Self is "an aboriginal self the radical imperatives of whose freedom cannot be stifled" (*Radical Innocence* 6), he finds no disparity between this radical imperativeness which refuses to accept reality and the pragmatic self, since the pragmatic self, in its continual adaptation to different realities, never holds its ground in any, therefore, continually cancels them out.

There is a spiritual dimension in Hassan's pragmatism in which the senses of spirit "centre on something fundamental to human existence yet intangible, an activating principle, a cosmic curiosity, a deeper meaning, often religious or metaphysical in character" ("Privations of Postmodernism" 4). In the context of postmodern materialist ideologies, spirituality to him may not mean "adherence to orthodox religions – Christianity, Judaism, Hinduism, Islam – though it would not exclude them". The "spiritual attitude" should be:

> Compatible with emergent technologies; with geopolitical realities (population, pollution, the growing obsolescence of the nation state); with the needs of

---

[2]   Mouffe bases this argument on Derrida's notion that democracy always "remains to come" or remains "the theme of a non-presentable concept", Jacques Derrida, "For the First Time in the History of Humanity", *Politics of Friendship*, translated by George Collins, London: Verso, 1997, p. 306.

the wretched of the earth; with the interests of feminists and minorities and multicultural societies; with an ecological, planetary humanism; and perhaps even with millennial hopes. (5)

Jerome Klinkowitz takes this further in "Ihab Hassan: Revisioning Man" – perhaps further than Hassan himself intends. He argues that "a 'Gnostic desire' to see the human condition as pure spirit pervades both Hassan's analysis of the postmodern condition and his own activities as critic" (115). Even though this is argued in the context of universal consciousness of which one of the most manifest instigators is technological capability, it is remarkable how such an idea detaches itself so decidedly from the body – in what seems to be a gesture of emulation of the sublimated imago of the American Self which "recoils" from the world. It finds some resonance in Hassan's critique of political agitation in American universities by what he sees as "gauche political harassment of students" which is "as insistent as anything sexual" ("Confessions" 126).

The analogy may be justified, yet it also seems to implicitly point to some sort of debasement of "anything sexual". Hassan seems to sublimate with an awareness of the problems of his own sublimation and, the sublime par excellence to him seems to be his own version of America. Yet, a desire to "see the human condition as pure spirit" sounds too extremist – probably even to Hassan himself. Where the spirit is involved, Hassan seems to tie it with the tradition of American pragmatism. In other words, it is not that his desire is to elevate the human condition to the status of pure spirit; it seems to be rather the opposite: to employ the idea of spirituality pragmatically to serve the human condition through the agonies of its daily reality.

The spiritual in Hassan's thought, or that which is not confined within the boundaries of the body, is the force behind man's predominance in the universe known to him. When he uses Faulkner as an example on this particular thought, he indicates how Faulkner's language in non-fiction works like *Essays, Speeches, and Public Letters* reflects an attitude of "ultimate resolution" that is evident from the obdurate use of certain vocabulary. Hassan's argument is that "language creates meaning, by the very force of its commitment […] the 'tale told by an idiot, full of sound and fury', is *made* to signify something" ("Privations of Postmodernism" 6). The spiritual, then, may not be confined by the body, but it does not seem to escape the confinements of language. Hassan does not deny the Shakespearean point, but argues that man's prevalence is based on this "will to meaning" which "outlasts all denials" (7). It is needless to point out that if this is to be articulated in the full resonance of Hassanian thought, it would be erroneous to think that this *willed* or *made* signification has anything to do with any Truth (capitalized). One might actually rephrase the statement in the following manner and still refer it to Hassanian thought without consternation: The "tale told by an idiot, full of sound and fury" is *always* made to signify something at a certain time and place, within a certain context, according to a certain human desire, and even affected by a certain biography.

In "Travel as Metaphor: Unmargined Realities", Hassan makes the idea of employing spirituality pragmatically clearer by arguing that "the idea of divinity expresses not only our fears and needs but also a kind of radical poesis; and that, as James would beamingly agree, "religion is highly pragmatic" despite its otherworldliness, and 'it is far more important for a particular idea of God to *work* than for it to be logically or scientifically sound'". He sympathizes with Karen Armstrong's idea of "mystical agnosticism" and agrees with her that "when people 'try to find an ultimate meaning and value in human life, their minds seem to go [to travel?] in a certain direction'" (176). The idea thus seems to be a determinate attachment to an ideological big Other in order to empower the self. Such an idea, however, cannot go without its problems. Most obvious of these problems is that particular ideas of God do work in certain malignant ways and can be employed in order to commit the most outrageous crimes.

The belief in God in such context may fall too easily in the frame of Adorno's analysis of the idea of "belief" in a certain psyche as the "abstract belief in power" in the course of the "pragmatization of politics" (*Authoritarian Personality* 726, 734–8). At a deeper level, self empowerment by pragmatically employing the idea of God in Hassanian thought seems to create a certain paradox. It is both revolutionary and anti-revolutionary: revolutionary in the sense that the divine seems to be deprived of its essence as eternal truth in order to serve immediate human needs, or even nonconformist individual positions; anti-revolutionary because employing the idea of the divine, even when it is emptied out of its metaphysical sense, determinately posits the ideological big Other as such – superimposed in the name of the Father. It is significant enough that Žižek argues for just the opposite: that "depriving [individuals] of support in the 'big Other', in the institutional symbolic order" is how "a true 'cultural revolution' should be conducted" (*For they know not* lxxii).

Hassan identifies a "postmodern spiritual attitude [which] may become deeply acquainted with kenosis – self-emptying [...], but also the self-undoing of our knowledge" in writers as diverse as Kierkegaard, Kafka, Derrida and Samuel Beckett. It is remarkable that he manages to link between his pragmatic thought of "employing the spiritual" with the idea of "kenosis" or the "exigencies of spirit" which threaten the "extinction of the social, even the historical self".[3] To Hassan,

---

[3]　Hassan gives examples on "kenosis" or the "exigencies of spirit" using some of Faulkner's fictive works like "Spotted Horses", from *The Hamlet* (1940) where the work's "moral weight" is felt by its very "exhausted moral vacuity", "Old Man", from *The Wild Palms* (1939) where "raging impotence" describes the human condition of "affronting a destiny that declines to answer to man", and "The Bear", from *Go Down, Moses* (1942) where a "drive to dispossession" marks the novelette which is, to Hassan, less about the "tragic story of the South" than the "story of America, no, the human condition". "The Privations of Postmodernism: Faulkner as Exemplar (A Meditation in Ten Parts)", *Faulkner and Postmodernism: Faulkner and Yoknapatawpha, 1999*, edited by John N. Duvall and Ann J. Abadie, Jackson, MS: University Press of Mississippi, 2002, pp. 5, 12–15.

thus, positing the big Other pragmatically can also coincide with the "self-undoing of our knowledge". He seems to be aware that to some readers this may seem to be an anti-*jouissance* act. When Hassan writes: "There is always the possibility that my voice, something in the aggressivity of stance or style, puts Mr. Said off; for I know this to have been the response of some of my readers" ("Polemic" 59), he seems to be aware that this "putting off" may also be caused by the determinate act of positing the ideological big Other which may be perceived, justifiably enough, as an insistent anti-eroticism – the postmodern subject acting in strange discord with his own desire.

The reader may detect what seems to be a contradiction at this point. For it is written elsewhere (see chapter III) that Kafka's heroes may enjoy an erotic masochistic relationship with the Law as an ideological big Other. Yet the argument is that this is precisely because that big Other is *imposed on*, and not posed by, them. In other words, K, standing in complete apprehension in front of his incomprehensible symbolic mandate, may enjoy his own suffering masochistically, while his creator, Kafka, who creatively and masterfully *posits* the big Other with all its arbitrariness in his writing, seems somehow to set an example of tying sexual impotence with the act of writing. "When I didn't write", writes Kafka to his fiancée, "I was at once flat on the floor, fit for the dustbin" (*Letters to Felice* 20) – words which, according to Erich Heller, allude to *The Metamorphosis*: "Where at the end the charwoman applies the broom to the insect corpse of Gregor Samsa, and afterwards laughingly announces to his parents and sister that they need not worry any more about 'how to get rid of the thing next door'" (xvi–xvii). In another letter, Kafka writes to Felice:

> My worries about you and me are the worries of life, are part of the fabric of life, and for this reason would ultimately be compatible with my work at the office, but writing and office cannot be reconciled, since writing has its centre of gravity in depth, whereas the office is on the surface of life. (279)

It is remarkable that Kafka's relationship with the woman that he immensely loved could be described as both compatible with his working place which he totally hated and as being "on the surface of life". In his letter dated 10 July 1913, Kafka seems to reveal what really causes this great anxiety towards Felice which he describes as "my *dread of the union* even with the most beloved woman, above all with her" (289). So, even his love for Felice Bauer, who herself seems to be posed as a big Other by Kafka, expressed and confirmed by literally hundreds of letters – "always arriving at their destinations" – in the span of just four years, seems to have been so devoid of sexual fulfilment. To him, as a woman, she is compatible with the office, on the surface of life. As the elevated beloved, she belongs to the letters, to literature. The fear of the union thus seems to be the fear of the union with what he himself posited as the big Other. The sexually attractive woman is nowhere to be found. The feminine figure seems to oscillate between the dullness of the office and the non-figurative asexual beloved who belongs to the letters.

Yet, positing the ideological big Other in Hassanian thought is rather austerely determined by pragmatically staying within the limits of the notion of the "pursuit of happiness". Hassan reiterates V. S. Naipaul's statement about the "pursuit of happiness" as an idea that "explains the attractiveness of Western civilization to so many outside it". He writes: "Born in Egypt, to which I have never returned, I feel the statement – though its Christian precept has been honored more in the breach – feel it to the marrow bone" ("Confessions" 130). Again, his attachment to Western civilization, ultimately to America, seems to be articulated in terms of a conscious detachment from authoritarian Egypt. So, any musing about America's epitomic closure of philosophical or metaphysical discourses is ruled out immediately by Hassan's pragmatic beliefs which seem sometimes to consciously disallow second reflective thoughts. In *Between the Eagle and the Sun* he writes:

> I know personally what Naipaul means. I know, too, that happiness may be construed differently in Harare and Hollywood, Cairo and Kobe. But let us not quibble unduly: happiness is found in freedom from hunger, disease, bondage, pain. I do not hesitate to offer it as a genial principle of transcultural values. (136)

Although this sounds like an ideologically correct statement, there is no doubt that it makes it difficult for anyone to theoretically disagree with what Hassan is saying, especially when he adds: "Happiness, though, as we all know, demands more than freedom from pain and want; it demands dignity, self-realization, transcendence" (136). His view, however, seems to disregard – rather than miss – the fact that desire may take one beyond his own happiness. One is thus obliged to speculate that desire in Hassanian thought seems to be thought of as something that should be disciplined; therefore, the question whether Hassan's intellectual position is in accordance with his own desire or not can only remain unanswered in the present book.

Unlike both Adorno and Said, Hassan's writing seems to denote in an almost Kafkaesque way that he is constantly aware that America *is* his own version of America, even though he cautions himself against adopting an oppositional stance to something that does not really exist except as a trope in literature: "Locked into an oppositional stance, we may also find ourselves speaking, in reaction to some allegorical "Amerika", as quasi-apologists for Mao, Castro, or Galtieri, Gaddafi, Khomeini, or Saddam" ("Confessions" 127). He does not explain at this point why a reaction to an allegorical America has to be Maoist, Castroist, Saddamist, Gaddafist or Khomeinist. Again, one feels that Hassan is uncompromisingly against whatever idea that might approach "quasi-anything". He may be unconsciously rejecting emphatically anything that might remind him of the "quasiness" of Egyptian politics. For it is not really immediately possible to ascertain that Hassan's America, the one that he identifies himself with completely, is not itself an allegorical one. And, why does an allegorical America, as his statement seems to implicitly suggest, have to exist solely in the minds of oppositionists? In fact, it can be argued that Hassan's vigilant stance itself against an allegorical America speaks the power of America's existence as a symbol in the minds of advocators and oppositionists alike.

Reading his statement, one can argue that Hassan's awareness of his American self can be put in the following words: "symbolic America does not exist because we Americans know, obviously, that we exist outside literature". Yet a careful reader of Hassan's work in its totality will unmistakably recognize his secret knowing smile coming from the arcane depths of his thoughts, proclaiming paradoxically: "But we Americans, Egyptians, Japanese, Turkish or whoever we might be, are nothing but literature". In fact, one can only come closest to the kernel of his existence at that Kafkaesque moment when he can assert unhesitatingly: "[I] am made of literature, I am nothing else, and cannot be anything else" (*Letters to Felice* 304). Spontaneously, after positioning himself at variance with the "reaction to some allegorical 'Amerika'", Hassan questions: "How can we avoid detesting literature, which snaps wire and string, and sets us pitilessly adrift on reality? I, too, have my wires and strings; I hope they are not steel" ("Confessions" 127). In other words: "How to avoid detesting literature which seems to remind us constantly of the unreality of America and our American-ness, indeed the unreality of our being?"

Hassan's America, in particular, assumes an "image of completeness" the power of which seems to go beyond both politics and culture. It is a power of unmatched creative dimensions. America's perpetual recreation of itself derives from its power to change people, to give them new identities or deprive them of old ones. Yet, Hassan does not lose sight of the fact that he is "discovering America" on his own and according to his own "acting out of his autobiography". Being recreated by America is intrinsically conditioned by *creating* it. One feels that his belief in America, or rather his total identification with his own sublime imago of America, indeed seems to go beyond any cultural analysis of it. Wherever some sort of a critique is attempted, it seems to be submerged immediately by that belief. In *Between the Eagle and the Sun*, Hassan writes: "I can speak of America only in three – at least, three – voices". The first voice asserts that "America confuses desires with needs, rights with responsibilities, expectations with merits, a society superficial in depth" (124). The second speculates:

> America has suffered too long from disrepair in its human and physical infrastructures; perhaps, with the end of the cold war and the resurgence of nations defeated in the last war, America has become bemused, even bruised, in its identity. (125)

The third appears to be questioning yet unconditionally committed to the American Dream; a voice which does not attempt to interpret the phenomenon of "the staunchless flood of immigrants [...] who often risk their lives to start a new life in America", but only points to it, disregarding any political, social or economic conditions that may be thought of as the result of America's global economic hegemony. It also asserts that "however tarnished the Statue of Liberty may seem to disaffected Americans, it can still raise its torch in Beijing or Prague,

Tijuana or Dhaka". It acknowledges the fact that "the American Century is about to end", but it ends with the rhetorical question: "What other nation can better seize the twenty-first century?" (126) Hassan's implicit answer seems to be: "none other than the American nation".

It is as if the three critical voices are encompassed by a single, unalterable, silently assured – hence actually much louder – voice which, not so unlike the first statement of Francis Ford Coppola's famous trilogy, declares positively and unhesitatingly: "I believe in America" – as if Hassan somehow remains immersed in the immediacy of his own experience in front of his own sublimated American imago despite the critical tone. The result is that instead of any sense of contradictions between his "three voices", they seem to ally to envisage an America with a non-self-contradictory totality of meaning. Its "superficiality" and "bruised identity" are nothing but the dramatic and stoic affects of its "historic role": "to create (precariously, violently) a new order of diversity" that is "neither 'melting pot' nor 'rubbish heap', neither sociolect nor idiolect, but the One and the Many mediated dangerously, toward a uni-verse" (*Out of Egypt* 46).

It is because of this that Hassan may seem most unlike himself at moments when he poses questions like: "What can present America contribute to transcultural values [...]? Export McDonald's, Madonna, Disney World, and the Terminator? [...] It's hardly what the world needs" (*Between the Eagle and the Sun* 137). At such moments, Hassan seems to suggest that America should think about what the world needs. What remains unexplained, however, is how America can pursue its own happiness "pragmatically" without maintaining its economic hegemony of which exporting those American products to the world is an indispensable part. McDonald's, Madonna, Disney and Terminator may not be what the world needs – if one is going to believe in Hassan's moment of concern about what happens outside America – but they undoubtedly represent what America needs. Hassan sounds much more original when he writes that America "violently dreams the world into a better place" (*Out of Egypt* 113). For Hassan's radical America seems to be an America that does not and *cannot* "contribute" to anything; it is an America that makes everything anew. Its very originality is not that it "tries to make the world a better place" but that it perpetually dreams of a new world in its own image, a world that it perceives as better than the existing non-American world. Exporting American products to the world may be thought of as America's down-to-earth fulfillment of that dreamy violence however unromantic this may sound.

In *Out of Egypt*, Hassan recalls how his first entrance into America was "from its secret, gloomy underside" – that is New Orleans instead of New York. He was not "greeted by the Statue of Liberty" upon his first arrival. Although this entrance seems less celebratory or less memorable, the fact that he immediately shifts to the present right after this scene of virginal initiation ("Forty years have passed") (103) seems to suggest that there is really nothing of significance between that historical moment and the present. Nothing in between seems to even slightly match the ever-present ecstatic feeling that he not only was lucky enough to escape the Kafkaesque sign of castration, but also could resurrect this moment of access to America through "its secret, gloomy underside" with all the secret *jouissance* associated with the memory. It comes as no surprise that "the song American literature sings", according to Hassan, is a song of the modern soul "eternally poised on the eve of Creation" (*Radical Innocence* 326); in other words, as Klinkowitz puts it, "initiation is endless, with only the Self existing" (95). This initiation of the American Self, which is endless, seems also to be Hassan's own initiation into America – *made* endless.

Yet as always when one is dealing with Hassan's work, one is not even sure that the word initiation can be used here. For if Adorno detachedly interpreted America, and if Said enjoyed his erotic relationship with it, Hassan's unwavering radical identification with it seems to paradoxically suggest that it was always already sealed to him. Even though he is the one who completely identifies himself with America, his sense of it seems to be paradoxically Kafkaesque. America, like the castle or the door to the Law, seems to be made into more than just an object of desire to Hassan. It can be argued that his ever-determined sublimation of it makes it an object of desire that is elevated to the vacant place of the Lacanian "das Ding".[4] In the case of Hassan, America does not seem to be only an unattainable dream, it is made to be the "*manufacturer of dreams*"; not only the Law but *that which makes it*; not only the impossible but also the *prohibited*; not only the "*objet petit a*" but the completely inarticulable *creator of desire as law*.

If it is sublimated to the level of the "Sovereign Good" then it must be *inaccessible* since both culture and psychoanalysis agree that "at the level of the pleasure principle [...] there is no Sovereign Good". Lacan's point, which he refers to Freud, is that "the Sovereign Good, which is *das Ding*, which is the mother, is also the object of incest, is a forbidden good, and that there is no other good".[5] Hassan is naturally aware that America is *not* the Good, but he believes that this is precisely what people seek in it; "they seek, beyond 'struggling afflictions', Blake's prophecy of America: 'another portion of the infinite'". He is aware that this "is not a place: there is an informing power of the mind that neither 'Atlantis' nor 'America' circumscribes" (*Paracriticisms* 176). Hassan's America thus seems to correspond with Žižek's "sublime object of ideology" which is "no longer an (empirical) object indicating through its very inadequacy the dimension of a transcendent Thing-in-itself (Idea) but an object which occupies the place,

---

[4]   Lacan gives two successive lectures about "das Ding" or "the Thing" in his 1959–60 seminar on the subject of the ethics of psychoanalysis, "*Das Ding*" and "*Das Ding* (II)", *The Ethics of Psychoanalysis 1959–1960*, edited by Jacques-Alain Miller, translated by Dennis Porter, London: Routledge, 1999, pp. 43–70.

[5]   Its place is *vacant* because the Lacanian "Sovereign Good", "*das Ding*", "the mother", "the object of incest", or the "forbidden good" belongs to the Real, or, that which cannot be talked about. In other words, the presence of "das Ding" can be articulated only in terms of its prohibition by the law of desire. "*Das Ding* (II)", *The Ethics of Psychoanalysis 1959–1960*, edited by Jacques-Alain Miller, translated by Dennis Porter, London: Routledge, 1999, p. 70.

replaces, fills out the empty place of the Thing as the void, as the pure Nothing of absolute negativity" (*Sublime Object* 206).

Just as the sublime object of ideology is not the Real but, as Žižek puts it, "a miserable 'little piece of the Real'", Hassan's America is not the infinite but a portion of it which is perceived as the embodiment of the infinite. Just as "the State as the rational organization of social life *is* the idiotic body of the Monarch", or as "God who created the world *is* Jesus, this miserable individual crucified together with two robbers" (207), Atlantis, the American Dream, the Promised Land, Democracy, or Freedom *is*, by the same token, America. The point to be highlighted here, however, is that Hassan is aware of his own act of sublimation as such. It is as if he is accepting America's ideological discourse radically in order to actually materialize it; as if saying to America: "you *are* actually sublime, you *are* the dream of humanity, you *are* emancipation, you *are* the Thing, and therefore, *you are asked to live up to what you are*". It is precisely because of this that it is hard to believe that Hassan truly believes that his apolitical stance is really outside politics, escapes politics or, as he asserts, constitutes a "resistance to politics" ("Confessions" 127). For if his radical act of sublimating America and the American Self is not in its essence a political act then nothing is.

Another Žižekan moment in Hassan acknowledges that "the pre-emptive nature of ideological discourse reduces any challenge to the terms of the ideology itself – no 'exteriority' (Levinas), no otherness, is possible. The end is power, indeed self-empowerment, the means a pretence of the higher moral ground" (126). This is precisely what seems to constitute the political factor in Hassan's radical identification with America. The "pretence" seems to be another name for Žižek's "literal identification".[6] It can be argued that Hassan's own pretence of the higher moral ground is precisely an assumption that he did not *become American*, he was *always American*, and in the full *ideological* sense of being an American in which the adjective "American" belongs to a most sublime version of America. This seems to be Hassan's tactic in dealing with America's excessiveness. He dealt with America by literally identifying with its own hyper-reality. He seems to know that this must be a pretence, but his originality lies in the fact that he does not deny it, he just asserts throughout all of his writings that it is the right thing to do. This literal identification with American ideology thus seems to constitute a major part of Hassan's own "negative capability" or "self-empowerment" which may be

---

[6] Literal or radical identification as a way of resistance to an ideological mandate is an idea which recurs in many of Slavoj Žižek's works. It can be found in: "Are Cultural Studies Really Totalitarian?", *Did Somebody Say Totalitarianism? Five Interventions in the (Mis)use of a Notion*, London and New York: Verso, 2001, p. 226, "Fantasy as a Political Category: A Lacanian Approach", *The Žižek Reader*, p. 97, "The Spectre of Ideology", *The Žižek Reader*, edited by Elizabeth Wright and Edmond Wright, USA, UK and Australia: Blackwell Publishing, 1999, p. 60, and "How Did Marx Invent the Symptom?", *The Sublime Object of Ideology*, London and New York: Verso, 1989, p. 30.

thought of as his way of dealing with the unavoidable presence of the fiction of America's castrating power.

Adorno could not become an American. Said became an American who claims that this "is a lie" as Marrouchi puts it (161). Hassan's radical identification with America pronounces no less than what he knows to be an impossibility: that he has never been anything but American. And, to him, this is *not* a lie, precisely because it is this lie itself that makes one truly American. In its essence, this is cultural politics par excellence. To think about it in terms of the notion of losing one's roots and its contingent results between what can be thought of as a work of mourning and a melancholic identification with a lost object of love one will be only perplexed by Hassan's position. It seems that there can be no question about any conscious identification with anything preceding his American experience. Mourning thus does not constitute any part of it. Does melancholy then? Adorno's clash with America as a European intellectual may be considered a case of acute melancholy – a melancholy marked by his conflicting disappointment in, and attachment to, Europe. Said's controversial relation to it may be seen as reflecting a certain understanding of, and a politically correct position with regard to, melancholy itself; that which considers the importance of the image of holding to one's lost roots as a lost object of love.

In his essay "Melancholy and the Act", Žižek argues that melancholy is "an exquisitely *postmodern* stance, the stance that allows us to survive in a global society by maintaining the appearance of fidelity to our lost 'roots'" (*Did Somebody Say Totalitarianism* 142). It is remarkable that Hassan, who is frequently dubbed as "the father of postmodernism" (uwm.edu), never seemed to take that "*postmodern* stance". As far as his Egyptian roots are concerned, his declared apolitical "American" stance thus seems to be *politically incorrect* in the highest sense. The political factor in it, the nonconformist voice, consists in what may be understood in terms of the Lacanian *act* which, according to Žižek, "is nothing but this withdrawal by means of which we *renounce renunciation itself*, becoming aware of the fact that we have nothing to lose in a loss" (*Enjoy Your Symptom* 43). In other words, it consists in what can indeed be considered as a revolutionary declaration: That nothing is lost, precisely because nothing was ever acquired in the first place, and thus assumes a position which seems to be beyond both mourning and melancholia.

Coda: America as an Unrealized Idea

In his introductory essay to *Love and Death in the American Novel*, Leslie Fiedler writes:

> The European mind had dreamed for centuries before the Enlightenment of an absolute West: Atlantis, Ultima Thule, the Western Isles – a place of refuge beyond the seas, to which the hero retreats to await rebirth, a source of new life in the direction of the setting sun which seems to stand for death. (xxxii)

Yet, it does not seem to be just the European mind that dreamed of an absolute West. It can be argued that the idea of a legendary absolute West which signifies both death and rebirth lived in the dreams of humanity since the very dawn of civilization. Nor was it a dream of centuries but of millennia. Ancient Egyptians called death "Ma'at" which also meant "truth", "justice" and "cosmic harmony". It was symbolized by a legendary powerful winged goddess of justice who carried its name. It was believed that in the underworld, Ma'at weighed the heart of the dead against one of her feathers. Balancing the scales was the only way to attain eternal life after death, which the ancients, for reasons supposedly known yet which remain highly debatable, called "Ankh Imnt" or "life in the West"; while "failure to balance the scales resulted in the most feared second death, and the loss of the possibility of the afterlife" (Forty 34).

Being the precondition of that blissful life after death, death itself became something of an excessive and extreme concern for ancient Egyptians. The giant pyramids of Giza gracefully stand as an ultimate witness to that. Given the logic and the philosophy of the ancients, serving as prestigious graves for Pharaohs remains the most realistic reason for building them, in spite of the numerous speculative hypotheses by Egyptologists who are still baffled until this moment by the impracticality of going through such an ordeal to build gigantic buildings with primitive methods and which seem to exceed by far their functional use. What mattered, however, was not their functional use but what they symbolized.

In the world of ancient Egypt, the only thing that mattered in worldly life was its end, a fact that reduced the purpose of life to the meticulous preparation for "life in the West". Theologically, associating death and eternal life with the West was significant in ancient Egypt. The sun, "Ré", the source of life, who "was said to have created mankind from his tears" (Forty 38), disappeared every day in the west. The east symbolized the birth of worldly life while the west the end of it. Historically, the geographical east, south, and eventually the north were known, fought or traded with. While in the west, desert lands, with primitive and scattered populations, were cut off suddenly by that great impassable ocean. The west ultimately stood for the unknown to ancient Egypt and, though least written about in terms of civilizational clashes, it was certainly the direction towards which the fascinated look of the ancients was transfixed.

Today, the look of humanity still seems to be transfixed towards the symbolic ultimate West, towards America, where death "found its ideal home" according to Baudrillard who, in 1986, posed the question which seemed to frame the whole story of man's dream about the ultimate West in what seems to be a highly reductive view:

> In the very heartland of wealth and liberation, you always hear the same question: "What are you doing after the orgy?" What do you do when everything is available – sex, flowers, the stereotypes of life and death? This is America's problem and, through America, it has become the whole world's problem. (*America* 30–1)

Baudrillard's question seems to suggest that America, being the ultimate West, is indeed the home of cultural death by its fictional character, utopian or dystopian space, ahistoricism and uncompromising capitalism, the principle of the good reduced to the free market exchange of goods, including sex, religion, love, nationalism, and so on, in many forms, amongst which the cinematic is the most popular one.

There is no sense in denying that there is a truthful side to such a view, but, somehow it does not seem to capture the whole sense of America in the consciousness of the world. Somehow America remains both an ultimate destination as well as an unrealized – even undefined – idea. Attempts at defining what America is, what it really stands for, or what it means to different people may differ, yet, that they mainly oscillate between idealized and deformed imagos of America seems to be beyond doubt. The fiction of the castrating power of America comes out of that oscillation. On the one hand it is made to be an idealized model and on the other a criticized source of fear; admired and denigrated at the same time; a dream of freedom and an imperial threat. How it is perceived, however, seems to reflect more on its perceivers. On the other side of its various constructed imagos lie other imagos of its inventors themselves.

What is notable about this idea is that it seems to be inherent in the ideological discourse of America as a making or a re-making of the self. In discussing what he sees as the most original idea in "The Autobiography of Benjamin Franklin", William Andrews writes:

> The real American, the true student of schoolmaster Ben, remakes himself not in spite of, or in opposition to, what America is but *because* he is an American. America is the land of inventors, and the greatest of Americans is the self-inventor – and the self-reinventor. (10)

This seems to be symbolic of America's biggest fantasy. That it continues to exert such a fascination on the world – even on itself – is not just due to perceiving it as a democratic model, a story of economic success, an unmatched political and military monolith, or even an imperial power. At their core, imagos of America seem to represent a romantic dream for writers on America: the impossible dream of being the "self-inventor" – like Shakespeare's Roman general, Coriolanus, who once dreamt the same dream when he wanted to "stand as if a man were author of himself" (*Three Roman Plays* 633) only to come to the disappointing final realization that nobody can really be the author of himself.

Symbolic America's biggest fantasy is not just creating a society which "allowed itself to imagine it could create an ideal world from nothing" as Baudrillard says (*America* 77) but, much more than that, creating that romantic discourse of individual self-invention while in fact *it remains the author even of its very authors*. While defining it in terms of self-invention makes the act of creating the self or recreating the self the precondition of its very existence as idealized imago, it is that idealized imago that, paradoxically, makes Andrews precede the aforementioned statement by:

> Franklin's retailing of his public successes along with his homely advice on how to make it in the world are not what is most original in the *Autobiography*. What is fundamentally new is that nowhere in his story does Franklin imply that the act of remaking oneself, the perpetual reinvention of one's role and image in the social order, is in any way revolutionary or even abnormal – *certainly not for an American.* (emphasis mine) (10)

It is as if "an American" names a defined identity that *precedes* the act of "remaking oneself". On the one hand, there seems to be an implication that "what America is" cannot be talked about in the first place as something that is there before this act of self-invention. Yet, while being American is defined as being mostly a self-inventor, inventing America itself is an invention of the self.

Perhaps some readers will conclude that America as a country has nothing to do with the main thrust of this study. Such an idea can be met with neither concurrence nor objection from the viewpoint of this book. It cannot either totally agree or disagree with it. Yes, America has nothing to do with the focus of this study. However, saying that America has everything to do with the focus of this study is equally true. In fact, this seems to be the main reason why there is a whole corpus of literature about America. The very existence of that corpus of literature seems to indicate that, as far as America is concerned, something always remains unsaid. The concluding lines of the introduction of this book state that the temptation of articulating the inarticulable – America – has proved itself irresistible to this writer, too. Trying to conclude now the work of a few years of his life, this writer realizes and admits that a sense of doubt never left him while working on it: 'Am I really writing anything at all about America?

There is no doubt that this book said much more about the writers who wrote about America than about America itself. But this is typical of the discourse of symbolic America, since imagos of America are intrinsically tied with the imagos of America's inventors. In light of this, it cannot be safely claimed that this book completely escapes the problems that it raises. Its own perceptions, representations, and the problems of the ideal ego of its writer are destined to remain inherent in it. Nevertheless, it partly escapes one of its main revealed pitfalls: that texts which particularly focus on demonstrating how other texts about America communicate an unreliable message themselves communicate an unreliable message. "Partly" is used here in order to indicate that this is not done by claiming to have said something reliable or absolute about America but rather by showing that this *cannot* be possibly achieved.

Endeavoring to articulate what America is, what it has been, or what it should be, is an ongoing process. In recent years, particularly since the terrorist attacks of 11 September 2001, attempts to redefine America and its role in the world became more pressing. Samuel Huntington, for example, seems to provide "choices" such as: "America becomes the world. The world becomes America. America remains America. Cosmopolitan? Imperial? National? The choices Americans make will shape their future as a nation and the future of the world" (366), while in fact tending to promote a kind of Anglo-Protestant nationalism that seeks to acknowledge the precedence of what he calls "settlers" over "immigrants" in the history of America (38–46) – forgetting, needless to say, the precedence of aboriginal inhabitants over European settlers. Others, like Niall Ferguson, maintain that America should be imperial in the full sense of the word:

> Far from retreating like some giant snail behind an electronic shell, the U.S. should be devoting a larger percentage of its vast resources to making the world safe for capitalism and democracy [...] The proper role of an imperial America is to establish these institutions where they are lacking, if necessary – as in Germany and Japan in 1945 – by military force. There is no economic argument against such a policy, since it would not be prohibitively costly. (140–1)

This seems to plainly pose the question: 'Since America can afford it, why not go on an imperial military rampage?' Unfortunately, this indeed seems to have been the choice of America's leaders in the past few years. For if one defines America's "war on terror" away from its emblematic banners, i.e., in light of Ferguson's crude view of an imperial America, it becomes clear that it is more than just a sort of post-modern repetition of the modern "White man's burden" discourse turning into "enlightened colonialism". The mantras that accompanied waging the war a few years ago were that global capitalism, Western civilization, the American way of life and even the values of freedom and democracy might be facing a dire threat because of terrorism.

Yet instead of resiliently seeking those who are behind the terrorists themselves who took innocent lives on 11 September, a group of what seems to be sundry countries and regimes were picked up as political enemies of the US. In its xenophobia, the "war on terror" seems to have been nothing but a candid answer to capitalism's wildest dreams. In view of its total political absurdity and its direct or indirect *fuelling* of Islamic fundamentalism, it cannot be defined in any sensible way except in terms of surplus ability as well as some projected financial, ideological and promotional revenues. In other words, in accordance with Ferguson's view, the US seems to have spent abundantly on such a war simply because "it could".

That global image of a crudely imperial US which seems to have been jointly created by the Bin Ladens and the Bushes of the world, however, does not summarize America. It cannot possibly reflect the story of America or the American dream or America's history. For America is not a maker of *a* past, as Hassan once wrote, in comparison to Europe, which possesses one (*Out of Egypt* 45). America is an *inheritor* of *the* past, not just of European past, but the past of humanity in its totality. It is a continent where, in Lacan's words:

> It would be untrue to say that history loses its meaning since it is there that it finds its limit – it would even be wrong to think that history was absent there, since, having been already formed over several centuries, it weighs all the more heavily there by virtue of the gulf that represents its all too limited horizon – but it is denied with a categorical will that gives the industrial corporations their style, a cultural ahistoricism peculiar to the United States of America. (*Écrits: A Selection* 127)

In other words, history lives in America's unconscious, willfully repressed so as to maintain an image of departure from it. This departure, however, does not seem to be adequately explained solely by America's capitalistic drive; for it is this departure itself which makes America an imagined and unrealized *idea*.

Even though its founding fathers of the Age of Reason saw their country as an "actualization of an idea" (P. Conrad 3), and in spite of the exultant or melancholic views of "utopia", "dystopia", the "end of history", or the place "where the road came to its definitive end", the *idea* of America is far from actualized. It is as if its very resistance to articulation reflects its radical intolerance of any form of legal contract or mandate committing it to "existence", *and therefore to a kind of death*. As if it views its very realization as an injustice, a prejudice, or an act of tyranny. In its radical, uncompromising and eternal predisposition against this act of tyranny, it appears to be most tyrannical, reiterating after one of its greatest founders, Thomas Jefferson: "I have sworn upon the altar of God, eternal hostility against every form of tyranny over the mind of man" (511). As long as articulating America – even in the most American of terms – can in itself be viewed as an act of tyranny, it is this kind of sworn "eternal hostility" that will keep it alive as an unrealized *dream* – beyond its many imagos.

Works Cited

Adorno, Gretel. *Theodor W. Adorno and Walter Benjamin: The Complete Correspondence 1928–1940*. Edited by Henri Lonitz. Translated by Nicholas Walker. Cambridge, MA: Harvard University Press, 2000.

Adorno, Theodor W. *The Authoritarian Personality*. Edited by Max Horkheimer and Samuel H. Flowerman. New York: Norton, 1969.

——. *Prisms*. Translated by Samuel and Shierry Weber. Cambridge, MA: The MIT Press, 1988.

——. *Minima Moralia: Reflections from Damaged Life*. Translated by E.F.N. Jephcott. London and New York: Verso, 2000.

——. *The Culture Industry*. Edited by J.M. Bernstein. London and New York: Routledge, 2001.

——. *The Stars Down to Earth*. Edited by Stephen Crook. London and New York: Routledge, 2002.

——. *In Search of Wagner*. Translated by Rodney Livingstone. London and New York: Verso, 2005.

Adorno, Theodor W. and Benjamin, Walter. *Theodor W. Adorno and Walter Benjamin: The Complete Correspondence 1928–1940*. Edited by Henri Lonitz. Translated by Nicholas Walker. Cambridge, MA: Harvard University Press, 2000.

Ali, A. Yusuf. [Translation of] *The Holy Qur'aan*. Translated by A. Yusuf Ali. Brentwood, MD: Amana Corp., 1983.

Andrews, William L. *Classic American Autobiographies*. New York: Mentor, 1992.

Barenboim, Daniel and Said, Edward W. *Parallels and Paradoxes: Explorations in Music and Society*. Edited by Ara Guzelimian. New York: Pantheon Books, 2002.

Baudrillard, Jean. *America*. Translated by Chris Turner. London and New York: Verso, 1988.

——. *Forget Foucault*. Translated by Nicole Dufrense. Los Angeles, CA: Semiotext(e), 2007.

Beauvoir, Simone de. *America Day by Day*. Translated by Carol Cosman. Berkeley, Los Angeles, CA London: University of California Press, 2000.

Benjamin, Walter. *Reflections: Essays, Aphorisms, Autobiographical Writings*. Edited by Peter Demetz. Translated by Edmund Jephcott. New York: Schocken Books, 1986.

——. *Illuminations*. Edited by Hannah Arendt. Translated by Harry Zorn. London: Pimlico, 1999.

———. *Theodor W. Adorno and Walter Benjamin: The Complete Correspondence 1928–1940*. Edited by Henri Lonitz. Translated by Nicholas Walker. Cambridge, MA: Harvard University Press, 2000.

———. *The Arcades Project*. German volume edited by Rolf Tiedemann. Translated by Howard Eiland and Kevin McLaughlin. Cambridge, MA, and London: The Belknap Press of Harvard University Press, 2002.

Borges, Jorge Luis. *Labyrinths: Selected Stories and Other Writings*. Edited by Donald A. Yates and James E. Irby. New York and London: Penguin, 2000.

Brecht, Bertolt. *The Good Person of Szechwan*. Translated by John Willett. London: Eyre Methuen, 1974.

———. *The Resistible Rise of Arturo Ui*. Translated by Ralph Manheim. London: Eyre Methuen, 1976.

Brod, Max. "Afterword". *Amerika*. Translated by Edwin Muir. New York: New Directions Books, 1946.

———. "Nachwort zur ersten Ausgabe". *Amerika: Roman Herausgegeben von Max Brod*. Frankfurt am Main: Fischer Taschenbuch Verlag, 1979.

Brooke, Nicholas. *The Tragedy of Macbeth – The Oxford Shakespeare*. Edited by Nicholas Brooke. Oxford and New York: Oxford University Press, 1990.

Brooks, Charles W. *America in France's Hopes and Fears, 1890–1920, Volume I*. New York and London: Garland Publishing, Inc., 1987.

Buck-Morss, Susan. *The Dialectics of Seeing: Walter Benjamin and the Arcades Project*. Cambridge, MA and London: The MIT Press, 1999.

Ceaser, James W. "Reconstructing America: The Symbol of America in Modern Thought". *American Social and Political Thought*. Edited by Andreas Hess. Edinburgh: Edinburgh University Press, 2002.

Claussen, Detlev. "Intellectual Transfer: Theodor W. Adorno's American Experience". *New German Critique*. 97 (Winter, 2006). Durham, NC: Duke University Press, 2006.

Conrad, Joseph. *Heart of Darkness – with the Congo Diary*. Edited by Robert Hampson. London and New York: Penguin Books, 1995.

Conrad, Peter. *Imagining America*. London and Henley: Routledge & Kegan Paul, 1980.

Crook, Stephen. "Adorno and Authoritarian Irrationalism". *The Stars Down to Earth*. Edited by Stephen Crook. London and New York: Routledge, 2002.

Derrida, Jacques. *Acts of Literature*. Edited by Derek Attridge. New York and London: Routledge, 1992.

———. *Of Grammatology*. Translated by Gayatri Chakravorty Spivak. Baltimore, MD, and London: The Johns Hopkins University Press, 1997.

———. *Politics of Friendship*. Translated by George Collins. London: Verso, 1997.

———. *Acts of Religion*. Edited by Gil Anidjar. New York and London: Routledge, 2002.

Emerson, Ralph Waldo. "Two Essays: The American Scholar and The Young American". *American Social and Political Thought*. Edited by Andreas Hess. Edinburgh: Edinburgh University Press, 2002.

Ferguson, Niall. "Clashing Civilizations or Mad Mullahs: The United States between Informal and Formal Empire". *The Age of Terror: America and the World after September 11*. Edited by Strobe Talbott and Nayan Chanda. New York: Basic Books, 2001.

Fiedler, Leslie. *Love and Death in the American Novel*. Cleveland, OH, and New York: Meridian Books, 1962.

Forty, Jo. *Ancient Egyptian Mythology*. Edison, NJ: Chartwell Books, 1996.

French, Marilyn. *Shakespeare's Division of Experience*. New York: Summit Books, 1981.

Freud, Sigmund. *Civilization, Society and Religion*. Edited by Albert Dickson. Translated by James Strachey. London and New York: Penguin Books, 1991.

———. "The Character of Lady Macbeth". *Macbeth*. Edited by Alan Sinfield. Basingstoke and London: Macmillan, 1992.

Fukuyama, Francis. *The End of History and the Last Man*. London and New York: Penguin Books, 1992.

Furness, Horace Howard, Jr. *A New Variorum Edition of Shakespeare: Macbeth*. New York: Dover Publications, Inc, 1963.

Gardiner, Michael. "Bakhtin's Carnival: Utopia As Critique". *Critical Studies. Vol. 3 No. 2 – Vol. 4 No. 1/2*. Edited by Myriam Diaz-Diocaretz. Amsterdam and Atlanta, GA: Rodopi, 1993.

Hassan, Ihab. *Radical Innocence: Studies in the Contemporary American Novel*. Princeton, NJ: Princeton University Press, 1961.

———. "Polemic". *Diacritics*. (Fall 1972, Volume II, Number 3). Ithaca, NY: Cornell University, 1972.

———. *The Right Promethean Fire: Imagination, Science, and Cultural Change*. Chicago, IL: University of Illinois Press, 1980.

———. *Paracriticisms: Seven Speculations of the Times*. Urbana and Chicago, IL: University of Illinois Press, 1984.

———. *Out of Egypt: Scenes and Arguments of an Autobiography*. Carbondale and Edwardsville, IL: Southern Illinois University Press, 1986.

———. *The Postmodern Turn: Essays in Postmodern Theory and Culture*. Columbus, OH: Ohio State University Press, 1987.

———. "Confessions of a Reluctant Critic; or, The Resistance to Literature". *The Emperor Redressed: Critiquing Critical Theory*. Edited by Dwight Eddins. Tuscaloosa, AL: The University of Alabama Press, 1995.

———. *Between the Eagle and the Sun: Traces of Japan*. Tuscaloosa, AL: The University of Alabama Press, 1996.

———. "Negative Capability Reclaimed: Literature and Philosophy Contra Politics". *Philosophy and Literature*. (1996, 20.2). Baltimore, MD: The Johns Hopkins University Press, 1996.

———. "Travel as Metaphor: Unmargined Realities". *Dissent and Marginality: Essays on the Borders of Literature and Religion*. Edited by Kiyoshi Tsuchiya. London and New York: Macmillan Press and St. Martin's Press, 1997.

——. "The Privations of Postmodernism: Faulkner as Exemplar (A Meditation in Ten Parts)". *Faulkner and Postmodernism: Faulkner and Yoknapatawpha, 1999.* Edited by John N. Duvall and Ann J. Abadie. Jackson, MS: University Press of Mississippi, 2002.

——. "Globalism and Its Discontents: Notes of a Wandering Scholar". Retrieved December 19, 2004, from http: // www. Ihabhassan.com / globalism _ its _ discontents. htm.

——. "Ihab Hassan Honored: Uppsala Confers Honorary Degree". Retrieved December 19, 2004, from http://www. uwm.edu/ News/ report/ old/ feb96/ 4390.html.

——. "Ihab Hassan in Focus: An Interview with Ihab Hassan". Retrieved December 19, 2004, from http: // www. Ihabhassan.com / durczak _ interview _ ihab _ hassan. htm.

Heller, Erich. "Kafka's True Will: An Introductory Essay". *Letters to Felice.* Edited by Erich Heller and Jürgen Born. Translated by James Stern and Elisabeth Duckworth. London: Secker and Warburg, 1974.

Horkheimer, Max and Adorno, Theodor W. *Dialectic of Enlightenment: Philosophical Fragments.* Edited by Gunzelin Schmid Noerr. Translated by Edmund Jephcott. Palo Alto, CA: Stanford University Press, 2002.

Horkheimer, Max and Flowerman, Samuel H. "Foreword to Studies in Prejudice". *The Authoritarian Personality.* Edited by Max Horkheimer and Samuel H. Flowerman. New York: Norton, 1969.

Huntington, Samuel P. *Who Are We?: America's Great Debate.* London: Free Press, 2004.

Hussein, Abdirahman A. *Edward Said: Criticism and Society.* London and New York: Verso, 2002.

Jay, Martin. "Adorno in America". *New German Critique.* 31 (Winter, 1984). Durham, NC: Duke University Press, 1984.

——. "Taking On the Stigma of Inauthenticity: Adorno's Critique of Genuineness". *New German Critique.* 97 (Winter, 2006). Durham, NC: Duke University Press, 2006.

Jefferson, Thomas. *The Life and Selected Writings of Thomas Jefferson.* Edited by Adrienne Koch and William Peden. New York: The Modern Library, 2004.

Kafka, Franz. *Amerika.* New York: New Directions Books, 1946

——. *Briefe an Felice, und andere Korrespondenz aus der Verlobungszeit.* Germany: S. Fischer Verlag, 1967.

——. *Letters to Felice.* Edited by Erich Heller and Jürgen Born. Translated by James Stern and Elisabeth Duckworth. London: Secker & Warburg, 1974.

——. *Amerika: Roman Herausgegeben von Max Brod.* Frankfurt am Main: Fischer Taschenbuch Verlag, 1979.

——. *The Complete Novels.* New York: Vintage, 1999.

Klinkowitz, Jerome. *Rosenberg/Barthes/Hassan: The Postmodern Habit of Thought.* Athens, GA: The University of Georgia Press, 1988.

Klossowski, Pierre. *Sade My Neighbour*. Translated by Alphonso Lingis. London: Quartet Books, 1992.

Kristeva, Julia. *Powers of Horror*. Translated by Leon S. Roudiez. New York: Columbia University, 1982.

Lacan, Jacques. *Écrits: A Selection*. Translated by Alan Sheridan. London and New York: Routledge, 1989.

——. *The Four Fundamental Concepts of Psycho-Analysis*. Edited by Jacques-Alain Miller. Translated by Alan Sheridan. Harmondsworth: Penguin Books, 1994.

——. *The Psychoses 1955–1956*. Edited by Jacques-Alain Miller. Translated by Russell Grigg. New York and London: W.W. Norton and Company, 1997.

——. *On Feminine Sexuality, The Limits of Love and Knowledge: Encore, 1972–1973*. Translated with notes by Bruce Fink. New York and London: W.W. Norton and Company, 1998.

——. *The Ethics of Psychoanalysis 1959–1960*. Edited by Jacques-Alain Miller. Translated by Dennis Porter. London: Routledge, 1999.

——. *Écrits: The First Complete Edition in English*. Translated by Bruce Fink. New York and London: W.W. Norton and Company, 2006.

Lawrence, D.H. *Studies in Classic American Literature*. Harmondsworth: Penguin Books, 1977.

Lipset, Seymour Martin. "American Exceptionalism – A Double-Edged Sword". *American Social and Political Thought*. Edited by Andreas Hess. Edinburgh: Edinburgh University Press, 2002.

Lunev, Stanislav. "America's Strange Financial Ties to China". *Newsmax.com*. 17 November 2000. Retrieved 24 November 2007, from http:// archive. newsmax. com/ archives/articles/ 2000/11/17/141838. shtml

Lyon, James K. *Bertolt Brecht in America*. Princeton, NJ: Princeton University Press, 1980.

Man, Paul de. *The Rhetoric of Romanticism*. New York: Columbia University Press, 1984.

——. "Dialogue and Dialogism". *Rethinking Bakhtin*. Edited by Gary Saul Morson and Caryl Emerson. Evanston, IL: Northwestern University Press, 1989.

Mann, Klaus. "Preface". *Amerika*. Translated by Edwin Muir. New York: New Directions Books, 1946.

Marrouchi, Mustapha. *Edward Said at the Limits*. New York: State University of New York Press, 2004.

Mathy, Jean-Philippe. *Extrême Occident: French Intellectuals and America*. Chicago and London: The University of Chicago Press, 1993.

Matthews, Chris. *American: Beyond Our Grandest Notions*. New York: Free Press, 2003.

Mouffe, Chantal. "Deconstruction, Pragmatism and the Politics of Democracy". *Deconstruction and Pragmatism*. Edited by Chantal Mouffe. London and New York: Routledge, 1996.

Murrin, John M. "A Roof without Walls: The Dilemma of American National Identity". *Beyond Confederation*. Edited by Richard Beeman, Stephen Botein and Edward C. Carter II. Chapel Hill, NC, and London: University of North Carolina Press, 1987.

Naipaul, V.S. "Our Universal Civilization". *City Journal*. Issued by The Manhattan Institute for Policy Research, Summer 1991. Retrieved 21 March 2007, from http://www.city-journal.org/article02.php?aid=1597.

O'Connor, John. *Macbeth – William Shakespeare*. Harlow: Pearson Education Limited, 2003.

Porter, Dennis. "*Orientalism* and its Problems". *The Politics of Theory*. Edited by Francis Barker, Peter Hulme, Margaret Iversen and Diana Loxley. Colchester: University of Essex, 1983.

Rorty, Richard. "Remarks on Deconstruction and Pragmatism". *Deconstruction and Pragmatism*. Edited by Chantal Mouffe. London and New York: Routledge, 1996.

Said, Edward W. "Eclecticism and Orthodoxy in Criticism". *Diacritics*. (Spring 1972, Volume 2, Number 1). Ithaca, NY: Cornell University Press, 1972.

——. "Opponents, Audiences, Constituencies, and Community". *Critical Inquiry*. 9 (September 1982). Chicago, IL: The University of Chicago Press, 1982, 1983.

——. *Writers Talk – Ideas of Our Time: Edward Said with Salman Rushdie*. The Roland Collection of Films on Art: Northbrook, IL, 1989.

——. *Culture and Imperialism*. New York: Vintage Books, 1994.

——. *Orientalism*. London and New York: Penguin Books, 1995.

——. *Representations of the Intellectual: The 1993 Reith Lectures*. New York: Vintage Books, 1996.

——. *Edward Said on Orientalism*. The Media Education Foundation. Race & Diversity Series: Northampton, MA, 1998.

——. *After the Last Sky: Palestinian Lives*. Photographs by Jean Mohr. New York: Columbia University Press, 1999.

——. *Out of Place: A Memoir*. New York: Vintage, 2000.

——. *Power, Politics, and Culture: Interviews with Edward W. Said*. Edited by Gauri Viswanathan. New York: Vintage Books, 2002.

——. "The Other America". *Al-Ahram Weekly Online*. Issue No. 630. 20–26 March 2003. Retrieved 2 October 2005, from http: // weekly. ahram. org. eg / 2003 / 630 / focus. htm.

——. *Reflections on Exile and Other Essays*. Cambridge, MA: Harvard University Press, 2003.

Shakespeare, William. *The Tragedy of Macbeth – The Oxford Shakespeare*. Edited by Nicholas Brooke. Oxford and New York: Oxford University Press, 1990.

——. *Three Roman Plays*. Edited by Norman Sanders, Emrys Jones and G.R. Hibbard. London and New York: Penguin Books, 1994.

Shambaugh, David. *Beautiful Imperialist: China Perceives America, 1972–1990*. Princeton, NJ: Princeton University Press, 1991.

Sloterdijk, Peter. *Critique of Cynical Reason*. Translated by Michael Eldred. New York and London: Verso, 1988.

Sontag, Susan. *In America: A Novel*. London: Jonathan Cape, 2000.

———. "Writer Susan Sontag". *The Connection*. 5 April 2000. Retrieved 22 September 2007, from http:// www. The connection. org:80/shows/2000/04/20000405_b_main.asp.

———. "Conversation with Susan Sontag". 2 February 2001. *Online NewsHour*. Retrieved 22 September 2007, from http://www.pbs.org/newshour/ conversation/ jan-june01/ sontag _02-02.html.

———. *Regarding the Pain of Others*. New York: Picador, Farrar, Straus and Giroux, 2003.

Stannard, David E. *American Holocaust: The Conquest of the New World*. Oxford and New York: Oxford University Press, 1992.

Tambling, Jeremy. *Lost in the American City: Dickens, James and Kafka*. New York: Palgrave, 2001.

Tocqueville, Alexis de. *Democracy in America*. Edited by J.P. Mayer. Translated by George Lawrence. New York: HarperPerennial, 1988.

Villiers de l'Isle-Adam, Auguste, comte de. *Tomorrow's Eve*. Translated by Robert Martin Adams. Champaigne, IL: University of Illinois Press, 2001.

Walia, Shelley. *Edward Said and the Writing of History*. London: Icon/Totem Books, 2001.

Walsh, Martin. *The Brechtian Aspect of Radical Cinema: Essays by Martin Walsh*. Edited by Keith M. Griffiths. London: British Film Institute Publishing, 1981.

Wood, Michael. *America in the Movies, or, "Santa Maria, it had slipped my mind"*. New York: Columbia University Press, 1989.

Žižek, Slavoj. *The Sublime Object of Ideology*. London New York: Verso, 1989.

———. *The Plague of Fantasies*. London and New York: Verso, 1997.

———. *The Žižek Reader*. Edited by Elizabeth Wright and Edmond Wright. Oxford and Malden, MA: Blackwell Publishing, 1999.

———. *Did Somebody Say Totalitarianism? Five Interventions in the (Mis)use of a Notion*. London and New York: Verso, 2001.

———. *Enjoy Your Symptom! Jacques Lacan in Hollywood and out*. New York and London: Routledge, 2001.

———. *For they know not what they do: Enjoyment as a Political Factor*. London and New York: Verso, 2002.

———. *Welcome to the Desert of the Real! Five Essays on September 11 and Related Dates*. London and New York: Verso, 2002.

Filmography

An Autumn's Tale. Directed by Mabel Cheung. Screenplay by Alex Law. Hong Kong, 1987.

The Birth of a Nation. Directed by D. W. Griffith. Written by Thomas F. Dixon, Jr., D.W. Griffith and Frank E. Woods. Los Angeles, CA: Epoch Film, 1915.

Die Hard. Directed by John McTiernan. Screenplay by Jeb Stuart and Steven E. de Souza. Los Angeles, CA: 20th Century Fox, 1988.

Die Hard 2: Die Harder. Directed by Renny Harlin. Screenplay by Steven E. de Souza and Doug Richardson. Los Angeles, CA: 20th Century Fox, 1990.

Die Hard with a Vengeance. Directed by John McTiernan. Written by Roderick Thorp and Jonathan Hensleigh. Los Angeles, CA: 20th Century Fox, 1995.

Dogville. Directed and written by Lars von Trier. Lions Gate Home Entertainment, 2003.

Empire of the Sun. Directed by Steven Spielberg. Screenplay by Tom Stoppard and Menno Meyjes. Burbank, CA: Warner Bros., 1987.

Farewell China. Directed by Clara Law. Written by Eddie Fong. Hong Kong, 1990.

A Fistful of Dollars. Directed by Sergio Leone. Written by A. Bonzzoni, Victor Andrés Catena, Sergio Leone and Jaime Comas Gil. Los Angeles, CA: United Artists, 1964.

The Godfather. Directed by Francis Ford Coppola. Screenplay by Mario Puzo and Francis Ford Coppola. Los Angeles, CA: Paramount Pictures, 1972.

Halfaouine: Child of the Terraces. Directed and written by Ferid Boughedir. New York: Kino Video, 1997.

La vita è bella. Directed by Roberto Benigni. Written by Vincenzo Cerami and Roberto Benigni. Italy: Cecchi Gori Group Tiger Cinematografica, 1997.

The Prince of Egypt. Directed by Brenda Chapman, Simon Wells and Steve Hickner. Los Angeles, CA: DreamWorks, 1998.

Pulp Fiction. Directed and written by Quentin Tarantino. Burbank, CA: Miramax Home Entertainment, 1994.

Schindler's List. Directed by Steven Spielberg. Written by Steven Zaillian and Thomas Keneally. Los Angeles, CA: Universal Pictures, 1993.

Snow White and the Seven Dwarfs. Directed by David Hand, William Cottrell, Wilfred Jackson, Larry Morey, Perce Pearce and Ben Sharpsteen. Story adaptation by Ted Sears, Richard Creedon, Otto Englander, Dick Rickard, Earl Hurd, Merill De Maris, Dorothy Ann Blank and Webb Smith. Los Angeles, CA: Walt Disney, Distributed by RKO Radio Pictures, 1937.

The Terminator. Directed by James Cameron. Written by James Cameron and Gale Anne Hurd. Los Angeles, CA: Orion Pictures, 1984.

Terminator 2: Judgment Day. Directed by James Cameron. Written by James Cameron and William Wisher, Jr. United States: Tri-Star Pictures, United Kingdom: Guild Film Distribution, 1991.

Terminator 3: Rise of the Machines. Directed by Jonathan Mostow. Written by John D. Brancato and Michael Ferris. Los Angeles, CA: Warner Bros., 2003.

Index